Introductions to
the Wissenschaftslehre
and Other Writings
(1797–1800)

J. G. Fichte

Introductions to
the Wissenschaftslehre
and Other Writings
(1797–1800)

Edited and Translated,
with an Introduction and Notes,
by

Daniel Breazeale

Hackett Publishing Company, Inc.
Indianapolis/Cambridge
1994

Johann Gottlieb Fichte: 1762–1814

Printed in the United States of America

10 09 08 07   3 4 5 6

Text design by Dan Kirklin

Cover by Listenberger Design & Associates

For further information, please address

Hackett Publishing Company, Inc.
P.O. Box 44937
Indianapolis, Indiana 46244-0937

www.hackettpublishing.com

Library of Congress Cataloging-in-Publication Data

Fichte, Johann Gottlieb, 1762–1814.
    [Selections. English. 1994]
    Introductions to the Wissenschaftslehre and other writings, 1797–1800/
Johann Gottlieb Fichte: translated, with introduction and notes, by Daniel
Breazeale.
        p.   cm.
    Includes bibliographical references and index.
    ISBN 0-87220-240-2 (cloth: alk. paper).
    ISBN 0-87220-239-9 (pbk.: alk. paper).
    Contents: An attempt at a new presentation of the Wissenschaftslehre —
Review of the Journal for truth — Note to "Fichte and Kant, or an at-
tempted comparison . . ." — Postscript to the preceding article and preface
to the following one — On the basis of our belief in a divine governance of
the world — From a private letter — Concluding remark by the editor, 1800
— Public announcement of a new presentation of the Wissenschaftslehre.
    1. Philosophy.   I. Breazeale, Daniel.   II. Title.
B2808 1994
193—dc20   93–50569
                                                      CIP

ISBN-13: 978-0-87220-240-5 (cloth)
ISBN-13: 978-0-87220-239-9 (pbk.)

The paper used in this publication meets the minimum requirements of American
National Standard for Information Sciences—Permanence of Paper for Printed
Library Materials, ANSI Z39.48-1984.

Contents

Editor's Introduction

J. G. Fichte (1762–1814) prided himself on having provided the transcendental philosophy inaugurated by Immanuel Kant in his three *Critiques* with a systematic unity it had previously lacked. More specifically, he believed that his own "system of freedom"[1] had succeeded in clearly displaying the underlying unity of theoretical and practical reason and that it was able to accomplish this precisely because it took seriously the Kantian insistence upon "the primacy of practical reason," not just within the realm of willing, but also within the entire domain of human cognition and experience.

Admitting that some of his own philosophical claims concerning such matters as "intellectual intuition" and the incoherence of the concept of a thing in itself appear to conflict with the letter of Kant's philosophy, he nevertheless maintained that they were true to the spirit of the same. Few of Fichte's readers, however, have been convinced by this claim, and his critics and admirers alike have usually concurred in interpreting his own system of transcendental idealism, the so-called *Wissenschaftslehre* ("Theory of Scientific Knowledge" or "Doctrine of Science"), as a genuinely original philosophical contribution in its own right and hence as one of the first and most fateful steps in the development of what is sometimes called "post-Kantian idealism." Indeed, many historians of the history of philosophy, beginning with Hegel, have tended to treat Fichte's

---

1. "Mine is the first system of freedom. Just as France has freed man from external shackles, so my system frees him from the fetters of things in themselves, which is to say, from those external influences with which all previous systems — including the Kantian — have more or less fettered man. Indeed, the first principle of my system presents man as an independent being" (Draft of a letter from Fichte to Jens Baggessen, April/May 1795). "My system is from beginning to end nothing but an analysis of the concept of freedom, and freedom cannot be contradicted within this system, since no other ingredient is added" (Letter to K. L. Reinhold, January 8, 1800). A critical edition of Fichte's correspondence is contained in Part III of the still incomplete critical edition of Fichte's works, *J. G. Fichte: Gesamtausgabe der Bayerischen Akademie der Wissenschaften*, ed. Reinhard Lauth, Hans Jacob, and Hans Gliwitzky (Stuttgart–Bad Cannstatt: Frommann, 1964 ff.) [henceforth = GA, and cited by part, volume, and page numbers].

Wissenschaftslehre as if its entire significance lay in its alleged historical role as a rung on the ladder "from Kant to Hegel" — an interpretation first put forward by none other than Hegel himself, who, despite his own considerable indebtedness to Fichte's thought, dismissed the *Wissenschaftslehre* as an illustration of the limits of any "philosophy of reflection" and as an historically superseded form of "subjective idealism."

It is only in recent decades that scholars have finally succeeded in removing Fichte's system from the shadows cast by the philosophies of Kant and Hegel and, for the first time in almost two centuries, allowing Fichte to speak for himself. As a result, there has been a growing and widespread appreciation of the genuine originality and intrinsic importance of Fichte's thought and of its relevance to a variety of contemporary debates and problems. Many have found this resurgence of interest in Fichte to be somewhat surprising, since Fichte is a prime example of a philosophical system-builder, an uncompromising philosophical foundationalist, and a tireless proponent of what might be called a "subject-centered" view of reality. Such a philosophy would thus appear to be spectacularly out of step with an age whose best-known philosophers and theorists celebrate the "death of the subject" and call for the creation of a new, "edifying," post-modern, and non-foundationalist approach to traditional philosophical questions. Nevertheless, Fichte's distinctive voice is beginning to be heard with increasing frequency in contemporary exchanges concerning the proper task, method, and starting point of philosophy; in debates over the limits of certainty and the relationship between knowledge and belief; and in discussions of topics of broader concern, such as the character and limits of human freedom, the nature and basis of human rights, and the relationship between persons and society.

The present volume is intended as a contribution to the dual and ongoing task of obtaining a more accurate historical understanding of Fichte's philosophy and facilitating the contemporary appropriation of some of the central insights of the same. It attempts to do this by providing fresh translations of several of his most accessible, important, and influential writings — including the celebrated first and second "Introductions to the *Wissenschaftslehre*" of 1797, and the notorious essay "On the Basis of Our Belief in a Divine Governance of the World," which was the original provocation for the so-called Atheism Controversy that swept German philosophy at the end of the eighteenth century and eventually led to Fichte's dismissal from his position at the University of Jena. In addition, this volume also includes several other less familiar and previously untranslated writings from the same period (1797–1800), including Chapter One of *An Attempt at a New Presentation of the Wissenschaftslehre*, a text that has frequently been cited in recent debates concerning the structure and character of self-consciousness (and which contains Fichte's own unequivocal rejection of any purely reflective account of self-consciousness). Several of the other newly translated texts continue the project, begun in the two "Introductions," of directly addressing specific misunderstandings of Fichte's philosophy, many of which are as pervasive today as they were two centuries ago, while others offer Fichte's own response to the charge of atheism. Finally, the text with which this collection closes, Fichte's November 1800 announcement of a "New Presentation of the *Wissenschaftslehre*," contains his own account of the strengths and limitations, as well as the unfortunate reception, of his own earlier writings, in addition to his announcement of his plans for the future.

All of the texts included in this volume belong to what might be called the period of the "second presentation" or "first revised version" of the Jena *Wissenschaftslehre* (which is the name conventionally bestowed on that version of his system which he first sketched in unpublished manuscripts while living in Zurich in the winter of 1793/94, subsequently articulated in his classroom lectures at the University of Jena from 1794 to 1799 and disseminated to the public in a number of treatises published during these same years, and finally abandoned for good in Berlin during the winter of 1800/01). Taken together, these texts provide an excellent introduction to Fichte's thought during the period of its greatest contemporary and historical influence, though anyone whose interest is piqued by this introduction will surely want to advance beyond these preliminaries and turn to a study of Fichte's own systematic (or, as he preferred to put it, "scientific") presentation of the leading principles of the *Wissenschaftslehre*. But to which presentation should one turn?

Over the course of his career Fichte produced no fewer than sixteen different expositions of the first principles of his system, many of which differ utterly in format, structure, and vocabulary from all of those that preceded and followed. One must therefore exercise caution when referring to "Fichte's *Wissenschaftslehre*." For the term "*Wissenschaftslehre*" does not refer to any particular stage or presentation of Fichte's philosophy, and still less to any particular book; it refers instead to Fichte's overall system, to the general orientation of his thinking in the broadest and most encompassing sense. The scope of this term is clearly signaled in the title of the first of Fichte's many publications to include this word in their titles:

Concerning the Concept of the Wissenschaftslehre or of So-Called Philosophy.[2]
As Fichte saw it, the *Wissenschaftslehre* is not simply one of many compet-
ing systems of philosophy; it is synonymous with philosophy itself. To be
sure, this single philosophy can be presented or expounded in any number
of more or less successful ways; and Fichte himself, with an appeal to the
same sort of distinction between the spirit and the letter he employed in
defense of his controversial claim concerning the harmony between the
spirit of Kant's philosophy and that of his own, viewed the series of
Wissenschaftslehren he himself produced between 1794 and 1814 as simply
so many different presentations of the same underlying philosophy — even
if, as he realized as early as 1795, "not a single letter of my system is yet
presented in the form in which it shall remain."[3] To be sure, not all scholars agree with this assessment, and many point to what they consider to be
fundamental differences between the earlier and later versions of the
Wissenschaftslehre. Fichte's point, nevertheless, remains well taken: One
must always distinguish between his overall system and *any* of the particular presentations of the latter.

The first version of the Jena *Wissenschaftslehre* was announced in the spring
of 1794 in the above-mentioned *Concerning the Concept of the Wissenschaftslehre*, a prospectus written by Fichte in order to attract students
to the lectures he delivered during his first two semesters at Jena. It was in
these lectures that he provided the first public presentation of his new
system, or rather his first presentation of the "rudiments" or "foundations" (*Grundlage*) of the same. First printed only for classroom distribu-
tion, the text of these lectures was soon published under the title
Foundations of the Entire Wissenschaftslehre[4] (1794/95). Since, of all of
Fichte's many attempts to provide a systematic presentation of the foundations of his system, this remained the only version to be published during his lifetime, it is hardly surprising that the 1794/95 *Foundations* was
and is widely, albeit quite inaccurately, treated as if it were identical to

2. *Ueber den Begriff der Wissenschaftslehre oder der sogenannten Philosophie.* English
translation in *Fichte: Early Philosophical Writings*, ed. and trans. Daniel Breazeale
(Ithaca, N.Y. and London: Cornell University Press, 1988) [henceforth = EPW].

3. Letter to Johanna Rahn Fichte, September 27, 1795.

4. *Grundlage der gesamten Wissenschaftslehre.* Translated into English by Peter
Heath as *Foundations of the Entire Science of Knowledge*, in Fichte, *Science of Knowledge*, trans. and ed. Peter Heath and John Lachs (Cambridge: Cambridge University Press, 1982).

"Fichte's *Wissenschaftslehre*." This, however, is doubly misleading.

First of all, as the very title of the work indicates, the *Foundations* was never intended to be a presentation of the "entire *Wissenschaftslehre*," but only of the first principles or "foundations" of the same. The *entire Wissenschaftslehre* is the larger system that is to be erected on this foundation, a system that includes an application or extension of these first principles: first of all, into the realm of nature, or, rather, into the domain of natural science (the domain of what Fichte called "theoretical philosophy"); and secondly, into the much larger and, in Fichte's eyes, much more important, domain of "practical philosophy" — a domain that includes not just the purely "practical" discipline of ethical theory, but also the more "mixed" (albeit still autonomous) disciplines of political philosophy and philosophy of religion.[5] The 1794/95 *Foundations* is thus no more than a presentation of the first part of a much larger systematic whole; and in fact most of Fichte's "scientific" publications during his Jena years were devoted to the task of articulating and developing this larger system, first in *The Foundations of Natural Right According to the Principles of the Wissenschaftslehre* (1796/97) and then in *The Theory of Ethics According to the Principles of the Wissenschaftslehre* (1798).[6]

Second, the 1794/95 *Foundations* is a less than adequate or definitive presentation even of the bare "foundations" of Fichte's system. The purely tentative or preliminary character of this work was clearly signaled by the author himself in the subtitle he insisted on adding to the published version: "a manuscript for the use of my students." Indeed, the decision to issue a public edition of the printed text of his lectures on the *Foundations of the Entire Wissenschaftslehre* is one that Fichte soon came to regret, as he encountered, both in conversation and in print, the most egregious misunderstandings and misinterpretations of the aim and content of that work.

---

5. Fichte's own clearest statement of the overall structure of his Jena system occurs in the concluding section of his lectures on the *Wissenschaftslehre nova methodo* (see below, note 8). See too Reinhard Lauth, "J. G. Fichtes Gesamtidee der Philosophie," in Lauth, *Zur Idee der Transzendentalphilosophie* (Munich and Salzburg: Anton Pustet, 1965), pp. 73–123.

6. *Grundlage des Naturrechts nach den Prinzipien der Wissenschaftslehre* and *Das System der Sittenlehre nach den Prinzipien der Wissenschaftslehre*. Both of these works were translated — albeit very inadequately — into English during the nineteenth century by A. E. Kroeger, the first as *The Science of Rights* (Philadelphia: J. B. Lippincott, 1869); the second as *The Science of Ethics as Based on the Science of Knowledge* (London: Kegan Paul, Trench, Trübner, 1897).

Attributing such misunderstandings, at least in part, to the defective form of his 1794/95 presentation, Fichte resolved to undertake a completely revised presentation of the rudiments of his system. Accordingly, when he next had the opportunity to lecture on this subject — i.e., during the winter semester of 1796/97, in a course announced under the title "Foundations of Transcendental Philosophy *(Wissenschaftslehre) nova methodo*" — he completely recast and rewrote his presentation of the first principles of his system, "as if I had never worked it out at all, and as if I knew nothing about the old presentation."[7] Fichte twice repeated his lectures on the foundations of transcendental philosophy during his career at Jena, and it is the written text of these lectures — usually referred to simply as "the *Wissenschaftslehre nova methodo*" — that constitutes what was referred to above as the second presentation of the foundations of the Jena *Wissenschaftslehre*.[8]

Almost all of Fichte's published books were actually revised versions of his lectures, and he intended from the first to revise his lectures on *Wissenschaftslehre nova methodo* for publication. In 1796 Fichte became co-editor of the *Philosophisches Journal einer Gesellschaft Teutscher Gelehrter*, a journal founded only a few years earlier by his colleague at Jena, F. I. Niethammer, and to which Fichte had already been a frequent contributor. Accordingly, when he finally resolved to publish the text of his lectures on *Wissenschaftslehre nova methodo*, he elected to do so in a series of installments in the *Philosophisches Journal*, under the general title *An Attempt at a New Presentation of the Wissenschaftslehre*.[9] The preface and first introduction to this *New Presentation* appeared early in 1797 in the *Philosophisches Journal*, where over the course of the following year three

7. Letter to K. L. Reinhold, March 1797.

8. In fact, Fichte's original manuscript of the *Wissenschaftslehre nova methodo* has not survived, and the work referred to by this name exists only in the form of two student transcriptions: (1) the "Krause transcript," in *Wissenschaftslehre nova methodo. Kollegnachschrift Chr. Fr. Krause 1798/99*, ed. Erich Fuchs (Hamburg: Meiner, 1982); and (2) the "Halle transcript," in GA, IV,2: 17–267. English translation, *Foundations of Transcendental Philosophy (Wissenschaftslehre) nova methodo*, ed. and trans. Daniel Breazeale (Ithaca, N.Y. and London: Cornell University Press, 1992). For a detailed discussion of the evolution of the Jena *Wissenschaftslehre* and of the relationship between the *Foundations* and the *Wissenschaftslehre nova methodo*, see the Editor's Introduction to the English translation of the latter.

9. *Versuch einer neuen Darstellung der Wissenschaftslehre*. Like the *Foundations*, this *New Presentation* was never intended to be a presentation of the *entire* system of the *Wissenschaftslehre*, but only of the first principles or foundations of the same. This

more installments of the same also appeared: the lengthy second introduction (published in two separate installments) and Chapter One.

A comparison between the opening sections of the transcripts of the *Wissenschaftslehre nova methodo* and the published portions of the *New Presentation* leaves no doubt that the latter is a revised version of the former. However, Fichte did more than simply revise his lectures for publication; he greatly expanded the published installments (especially the "Second Introduction") in order to respond to certain public challenges and criticisms.

First of all, and very probably at the direct instigation of his colleague Friedrich Schlegel,[10] Fichte added a long section (§ 6 of the "Second Introduction") in which he undertook a detailed public defense of his frequently reiterated — and disputed — claim that the spirit of Kant's philosophy was embodied in his own *Wissenschaftslehre*. Secondly, as Fichte noted in his preface to the *New Presentation*, "In order to facilitate an examination of the basis of this system, I intend, in this new presentation, to indicate every point at which this system must be attacked." With this aim in mind he devoted much of the second installment (§§ 1–6 of the "Second Introduction") and virtually all of the third installment (§§ 7–12 of the "Second Introduction") to a detailed rebuttal of a number of specific objections to various aspects of his philosophy, many of which prove to be rooted in one or another misunderstanding of the quite unique character of Fichte's "absolute I."

Though many of the objections in question had circulated for some time (and, indeed, continue to circulate to this very day), Fichte specifically addressed them in the aggressive form in which they had been formu-

---

is made explicit by Fichte himself at the conclusion of his 1798 preface to the second edition of *Concerning the Concept*, where he refers to the *New Presentation* as "a new attempt at a purely and strictly systematic presentation of the foundations of the *Wissenschaftslehre*" (GA, I,2: 163; EPW, p. 100).

10. In a review of the *Philosophisches Journal* published in the March 21 and March 22, 1797 issues of the *Allgemeine Literatur-Zeitung* Schlegel called attention to the controversy surrounding Fichte's claim that the *Wissenschaftslehre* deals with the same questions as Kant's philosophy and answers them in the same way as Kant. After remarking that it would take an entire book to examine this claim, Schlegel then proceeded to express his hope that Fichte himself "will very soon find the leisure and the inclination to provide a *complete proof* of this claim." Fichte's first and only detailed account of the relationship between his philosophy and Kant's was published only a few months later and included an allusion to Schlegel's review (see below, p. 52).

lated by one particular author, F. K. Forberg, another of his colleagues at
the University of Jena. Though Forberg had never made any secret of his
misgivings concerning various aspects of the *Wissenschaftslehre*, Fichte's
project of publishing a *New Presentation* of the same appears to have provoked him to gather his objections and to formulate them in an article titled
"Letters on the Most Recent Philosophy." The amusing circumstances
that led to the publication of Forberg's "Letters," as well as Fichte's reply
to the same in his "Second Introduction," are described as follows by an
anonymous contemporary witness:

> For some time Forberg had been providing Fichte with hints that he
> definitely intended to settle accounts with him once again and in
> earnest — hints that finally turned into a declaration of war. [. . . .]
> Suddenly the small man appeared in Fichte's study, where he took
> the philosopher by surprise and declared at once, "You know that I
> come to declare war on you, and I will attack your system vigorously
> and roughly." "Good," replied Fichte. "And I will do so in your own
> *Journal*, where you must publish my attack." "Fine," responded
> Fichte. "In addition," declared Forberg, "you must pay me a high
> honorarium." "I will do this as well," agreed Fichte. "Finally," con-
> tinued Forberg, "you must promise me that you will respond to my
> refutation." After he had obtained Fichte's promise to do so, he pro-
> duced his manuscript and said, "Look, you must respond to this
> point and to this point. Here I have got you, and you will not be able
> to extricate yourself so easily from my clutches."[11]

As promised, Fichte did indeed publish Forberg's "Letters" (in two
installments) in the *Philosophisches Journal*, along with his own "Second
Introduction" to the *Attempt at a New Presentation of the Wissenschaftslehre*, where he duly and patiently replied to each of Forberg's objections,
though without ever mentioning Forberg by name.[12]

11. *Vertraute unparteiische Briefe über Fichtes Aufenthalt in Jena, seinen Karakter als
Mensch, Lehrer und Schriftsteller betreffend* (1799). Quoted in *Fichte im Gespräch*,
ed. Erich Fuchs, vol. 1, p.475 (Stuttgart–Bad Cannstatt: Frommann-Holzboog,
1978).

12. Though the first installment of Forberg's letters appeared in the same issue
of the *Philosophisches Journal* as the second installment of Fichte's "Second Introduction," Fichte's response to Forberg actually began even earlier, in the first
installment of his "Second Introduction." As co-editor of the *Philosophisches*

Though Fichte once again lectured on the foundations of transcendental philosophy in the winter semester of 1798/99, no further installments of the *New Presentation* ever appeared in the *Philosophisches Journal* following the publication of Chapter One of the same, and this despite the fact that Fichte himself regarded this incomplete *New Presentation* as one of his clearest, most felicitous, and most successful literary productions.[13] Though he himself never offered any explanation of his decision to suspend publication of his *New Presentation* in 1798, there can be little doubt that the immediate reason for this interruption had to do primarily with the fact that his time and effort were increasingly absorbed by a quickly mushrooming controversy provoked by another essay he published in the *Philosophisches Journal* later that same year. Once again, the immediate catalyst for the latter essay was yet another contribution by Forberg, who by this time had left Jena to become co-rector of a secondary school in Saalfeld.

Sometime in the spring or summer of 1798 Forberg submitted for publication in the *Philosophisches Journal* a brief essay titled "Development of the Concept of Religion," in which he proposed an interpretation of the concept of God as a mere "regulative Idea of reason" and claimed that religious belief amounts to nothing more than a purely "practical faith" in a moral world order, a faith that in no way warrants any theoretical knowledge claims concerning the existence of a supreme being.[14] Somewhat alarmed by the rather skeptical tone of Forberg's essay (and no doubt concerned that readers might confuse Forberg's position with his own at least superficially similar one), but unwilling simply to reject it, Fichte at first asked Forberg to withdraw his contribution. When he refused, Fichte decided to attempt to redress what he took to be the excesses of Forberg's treatment by composing an essay of his own on the same topic and publishing it in the same issue of the *Philosophisches Journal* as Forberg's. The

---

Journal he was, of course, acquainted with the content of Forberg's "Letters" prior to their publication.

13. See, e.g., Fichte's letter to Reinhold, April 22, 1799; his letter to Friedrich Johanssen, January 31, 1801; and his preface to the second edition of *Concerning the Concept*, as well as the announcement of a new presentation of the *Wissenschaftslehre*, which is translated in this volume.

14. The most important passages from Forberg's essay are available in English in Hans Vaihinger's *The Philosophy of "As If*," trans. C. K. Ogden, 2nd ed., pp. 319–27 (London: Routledge & Kegan Paul, 1935).

issue in question duly appeared in the fall of 1798, with unanticipated and fateful consequences.

Shortly after the appearance of the issue of the *Philosophisches Journal* containing the essays by Fichte and Forberg, there began to circulate an anonymous tract with the title "A Father's Letter to His Son, Studying at the University, Concerning the Atheism of Fichte and Forberg," which not only attacked the essays of Fichte and Forberg as having the most deleterious consequences for both religion and morality, but went on to accuse both authors of disseminating in their classrooms an atheism of the most shameless sort.[15] These rumors and allegations soon reached Dresden and the ears of officials in the court of Friedrich-August, Prince-Elector of Saxony. On November 26, 1798 the administrative council, acting in the name of the Prince-Elector, officially declared both essays "atheistic" and issued a decree confiscating all copies of the offending issue of the *Philosophisches Journal*. In addition, the Saxon authorities threatened to bar any of their subjects from studying at the University of Jena (located in the neighboring Duchy of Saxe-Weimar) unless the accused authors and editors were appropriately reprimanded and punished.

As news of this surprising development began to spread, both opponents and defenders of Fichte entered the growing public fray with their own broadsides and pamphlets. The *Atheismusstreit* (or "Atheism Controversy") was under way. All too predictably, Fichte himself was by no means content to sit idly by and wait for events to unfold; instead, he leaped to his own defense in January of 1799 with the publication of a rather

15. *Schreiben eines Vaters an seinen studierenden Sohn über den Fichtischen und Forbergischen Atheismus.* Rpt. in *Die Schriften zu J. G. Fichtes Atheismus-Streit*, ed. Frank Böckelmann (Munich: Rogner & Bernhard, 1969), pp. 63–82. In fact, this was hardly the first public indictment of Fichte as an atheist. From the time of his arrival at Jena, where his appointment had been vigorously opposed by conservative elements in the Weimar administration, who particularly objected to his "Jacobin" defense of the principles of the French revolution in his *Beitrag zur Berichtigung der Urtheile des Publikums über die französiche Revolution* (*Contribution toward Rectifying the Public's Judgment of the French Revolution*) (1793/94), he had been under almost constant attack from various self-appointed defenders of "throne and altar." (See, e.g., his reference to the libelous assertions of the "Eudämonists" in his long, concluding footnote to the "Second Introduction" to the *New Presentation*, below, pp. 103–4.) Concerning Fichte's tumultuous career at Jena and the various controversies in which he was embroiled, see Breazeale, "Fichte in Jena," Editor's Introduction to EPW, pp. 2–49.

intemperate *Public Appeal Against the Charge of Atheism.*[16] Tensions and tempers continued to rise throughout the first half of 1799, with the appearance of a flurry of new pamphlets, decrees, and student petitions.

In the heat of this crisis, Fichte seriously miscalculated and badly overplayed his own hand. He and Niethammer, as requested, prepared and sent to the Weimar authorities a "Juridical Defense" of their behavior; and then, as a tactical move, Fichte wrote a letter to these same authorities in which he stubbornly declared himself unwilling to accept the slightest censure and threatened to resign if he was found in the least blameworthy. On March 29 he received a letter from Duke Karl-August of Weimar "accepting his resignation." Despite frantic efforts to repair the harm he had inflicted on himself — efforts that included the ill-advised publication of his *Juridical Defense Against the Charge of Atheism*[17] — and despite equally frantic efforts on his behalf by friends, colleagues, and students, Fichte failed to retain his position at the University of Jena. In June of 1799 he fled Jena for refuge in Berlin, where he largely remained for the rest of his life.

Of all the tracts written against Fichte during and following the Atheism Controversy, the one that undoubtedly wounded him most deeply was an "Open Letter to Fichte" published by one of the most distinguished men of letters in all of Germany, J. H. Jacobi, an author for whom Fichte himself had the highest personal regard and with whom he had corresponded for years.[18] In this document, published under the title *Jacobi to Fichte*, Jacobi characterized philosophy in general and Fichtean philosophy in particular as "nihilism," a quest for certainty that can end only in reducing all knowledge and all meaning to sheer "nothingness." Mortified by what he took to be Jacobi's utter misunderstanding of the basic character of transcendental philosophy and by his failure to appreciate the fundamental difference between the essentially theoretical task of philosophy

---

16. *J. G. Fichtes d. Phil. Doctors und ordentlichen Professors zu Jena Appellation an das Publikum über die durch ein Kurf. Sächs. Confiscationsrescript ihm beigemessenen atheistischen Aeusserungen.*

17. *Der Herausgeber des phil. Journals gerichtliche Verantwortungsschriften gegen die Anklage des Atheismus* (originally written and sent, along with other documents, to the Weimar authorities in March, but published in May of 1799).

18. *Jacobi an Fichte* originated as a long private letter Jacobi sent to Fichte in the spring of 1799 and later published, in an expanded form, in September of that same year (GA, III,3: 224–81; English trans. Diana I. Behler, "Open Letter to Fichte," in *Philosophy of German Idealism*, ed. Ernst Behler, pp. 119–41 [New York: Continuum, 1987]).

xviii   *Introductions to the Wissenschaftslehre*

(which occupies what Fichte calls the "standpoint of speculation") and the
practical business of everyday life (which occupies the "ordinary standpoint"), Fichte carefully deliberated how best to reply to Jacobi's stinging
public rebuke. Indeed, almost everything Fichte published during his first
year in Berlin, including *The Vocation of Man*, was designed not only to
demonstrate the falsity of the charge of atheism, but also to reveal the deep
confusion underlying *Jacobi to Fichte*.[19]

Though Fichte suspended publication of further installments of *An
Attempt at a New Presentation of the Wissenschaftslehre* in the spring of 1798,
he did not at that point abandon his intention of revising and publishing
the new presentation of the first principles of his system contained in his
lectures on *Wissenschaftslehre nova methodo*. Accordingly, one of the first
projects to which he turned his attention following his protracted self-
defense against the charge of atheism was that of preparing for publication
a "New Presentation" of the foundations of the *Wissenschaftslehre*, as is
indicated by the revealing announcement of the same, dated November 4,
1800 and published in several journals early the next year. The "New Presentation" is described in this announcement as a revision of the version of
the *Wissenschaftslehre* Fichte had been presenting "for the past five years"
in his classroom lectures — in other words, as a second attempt, following
the untimely suspension in 1798 of publication of any further installments
of the *Attempt at a New Presentation of the Wissenschaftslehre*, to publish a
revised version of the *Wissenschaftslehre nova methodo* lectures. According
to this announcement, Fichte anticipated that this (new) "New Presentation" would become available in the very near future.

The confidently announced "New Presentation" never appeared, however. Though Fichte worked diligently on this project during the fall of
1800, he was finally forced to abandon it once and for all — and this time
not for any external reasons, but for purely internal or systematic ones. As
the surviving manuscript of this incomplete revision[20] reveals, Fichte was
beginning to have serious second thoughts about several features of his

19. A more direct response to the charge of atheism — as well as to Jacobi's criticism — is contained in the essay entitled "From a Private Letter" (translated in
this volume), which was published almost simultaneously with *The Vocation of
Man*. See too the important unpublished manuscript from the spring of 1799,
"Rückerinnerungen, Antworten, Fragen" (GA, II,5: 103–86). A fragment from
this manuscript was appended by Fichte to his letters to Jacobi and Reinhold of
April 22, 1799 and is translated in EPW, pp. 432–37.

20. *Neue Bearbeitung der Wissenschaftslehre* (GA, II,5: 532–402).

earlier presentation and was finding it increasingly difficult to assimilate to the form of the latter some of the new results he had arrived at while working on *The Vocation of Man*. In the end, he seems to have concluded that he had no recourse but to begin completely anew. What was required was not yet another revision of the *Wissenschaftslehre nova methodo*, but a fresh start at an entirely new presentation of the *Wissenschaftslehre*, which is precisely what he attempted — though not for the last time — in the unpublished *Presentation of the Wissenschaftslehre from the Years 1801/02*.[21]

As is perhaps evident from the very title of the 1797/98 version — which modestly declares itself to be only a *Versuch* or "Attempt" at a new presentation — Fichte had begun, even while he was still in Jena, to doubt whether he would ever be able to publish a truly *definitive* presentation of the rudiments of his system. From the very start — that is, as early as 1794 — he had acknowledged that "it will be years before I can promise to be able to lay this system before the public in a worthy form";[22] and barely a year later he declared that, "As I see it, the presentation of the *Wissenschaftslehre* will require by itself an entire lifetime."[23] To be sure, Fichte never stopped trying to present his philosophy in private lectures; nor did he ever abandon his quest for an improved "presentation" of the same. He did, however, eventually conclude that he was simply incapable of producing a full, written exposition of the first principles of his system which could truly stand on its own as an independent publication and could "dispense with oral explanation." Making a virtue of necessity, he resolved, as he solemnly declared, "to confine himself to oral communication, so that misunderstanding can thereby be detected and eliminated on the spot."[24] Hence, though Fichte continued to lecture on the *Wissenschaftslehre* in Berlin, Erlangen, and Königsberg, on each occasion preparing a new, carefully composed manuscript for his lectures, it was only after his death, with the publication of his literary remains, that any of these later versions of the *Wissenschaftslehre* became available to a broader public.

21. *Darstellung der Wissenschaftslehre. Aus den Jahren 1801/02* (GA, II,6: 129–411).

22. Preface to the first ed. of *Concerning the Concept* (GA, I,2: 110; EPW, p. 95).

23. Letter to K. L. Reinhold, July 2, 1795.

24. From Fichte's *Pro memoria* to the Royal Cabinet, Berlin, January 3, 1804 (GA, III,5: 223; translated in full in the Editor's Introduction to Fichte, *Foundations of Transcendental Philosophy*, pp. 31–32).

In terms of content, most of the texts translated in this volume belong to
what Fichte called the "critique" of philosophy (which is not to be confused with "criticism" or Critical philosophy) and contrasted with philosophy per se (or "metaphysics").[25] Whereas the latter, according to
Fichte, has the task of providing a transcendental explanation of the possibility of ordinary knowledge and experience, critique, which resembles
what some twentieth-century philosophers would call "metaphilosophy,"
investigates the character and possibility of philosophy itself: "Critique is
related to metaphysics in exactly the same way that metaphysics is related
to the ordinary point of view of natural understanding. Metaphysics
explains the ordinary point of view, and metaphysics itself is explained by
critique. The object of genuine critique is philosophical thinking."[26]

Furthermore, Fichte distinguished between two sorts of critique. First
of all, there is the sort of critique, exemplified in *Concerning the Concept of
the Wissenschaftslehre*, that investigates the *content* of philosophical science
and explains the relationship between the latter and ordinary knowledge,
including all of those (empirical and formal) sciences that are possible from
the ordinary standpoint. Secondly, there is the sort of critique that ex-
plores and explains the differences between the *standpoint* of ordinary life
and the transcendental standpoint of philosophy itself. A critique of this
latter type investigates the distinctive character or *form* of philosophical
thinking: "It describes the point of view from which the transcendental
philosopher views all knowledge and his state of mind when he engages in

25. The distinction between "critique" and "metaphysics" is explained in the preface to the second ed. of *Concerning the Concept*. During the period of the Jena
Wissenschaftslehre, as broadly conceived, Fichte published three full-scale "critiques" or metaphilosophical works, in all of which he attempted to reflect upon
and to explain the distinctive character of his own approach to philosophy: (1)
Concerning the Concept of the Wissenschaftslehre (1794; 2nd ed., 1798); (2) the two
"Introductions" to *An Attempt at a New Presentation of the Wissenschaftslehre*
(1797); and (3) *Sonnenklarer Bericht an das grössere Publikum über das eigentliche
Wesen der neuesten Philosophie. Ein Versuch, die Leser zum Verstehen zu zwingen*
(written between August 1800 and March 1801 and published in April of 1801;
translated into English by John Botterman and William Rasch as "A Crystal Clear
Report to the General Public Concerning the Actual Essence of the Newest Philosophy: An Attempt to Force the Reader to Understand," in *Philosophy of German
Idealism*, ed. Behler, pp. 39–115).

26. GA, I,2: 159; EPW, p. 97. This and the following quotations are from the
preface to the second ed. of *Concerning the Concept*.

speculation." The latter is the sort of critique represented by the two introductions to *An Attempt at a New Presentation of the Wissenschaftslehre*, a type of critique that, as Fichte quite aptly noted, "contributes greatly toward forming a correct concept of our system, toward guarding against misunderstanding, and toward providing a means of entry into this system."[27]

To be sure, the distinction between metaphysics and critique, or between philosophy and metaphilosophy, is by no means as sharp and as unproblematic as the above description suggests, since, as Fichte himself noted, "a science and the critique of that science reciprocally support and explain each other."[28] Nevertheless, one has to start somewhere, and for a student of Fichte's Jena *Wissenschaftslehre* there is no better starting point than the two "Introductions" of 1797. While it is true and should never be forgotten that these texts were composed as introductions to a specific version of the *Wissenschaftslehre*, it is equally true that they can serve admirably as introductions to Fichte's overall project, at least during his Jena period — as introductions, if you will, to "the spirit of Fichte." Here, perhaps more clearly and successfully than anywhere else, he explains and defends his own understanding of the basic tasks, methods, and limits of philosophical speculation and attempts to answer such elementary but vital questions as: How does one raise oneself to the level of philosophizing; and, once there, on what basis does one select a particular deductive strategy and systematic starting point?

Fichte's answers to these questions, which culminate, in § 5 of the "First Introduction," in the celebrated dictum, "the kind of philosophy one chooses depends upon the kind of person one is," are elaborated in the context of a juxtaposition between "idealism" and "dogmatism," which are the names assigned by Fichte to what he describes as two mutually opposed systems of philosophy — and indeed, as the only two systems that are possible. Fichte's discussion of the relationship between these two systems, as well as of the "choice" between them, raises a number of central questions, not only concerning the character and starting point of philosophy, but also concerning the limits of rational argument and the true character of the dispute between determinists and proponents of human freedom. Not surprisingly, Fichte's discussion of these issues in his two "Introductions" has been the subject of much lively debate in recent

27. GA, I,2: 160; EPW, p. 98.
28. GA, I,2: 160; EPW, p. 98.

years.[29] Here, however, we will confine ourselves to a consideration of the contemporary background for Fichte's use of the terms "idealism" and "dogmatism."

In his first *Critique*, Kant frequently contrasted "dogmatism" in philosophy with "criticism," and he defined the former as "the presumption that it is possible to make progress with pure knowledge, according to principles, from concepts alone (those that are philosophical), as reason has long been in the habit of doing; and that it is possible to do this without having first investigated in what way and by what right reason has come into possession of these concepts." For Kant, therefore, "Dogmatism is the dogmatic procedure of pure reason, *without previous criticism of its own powers.*"[30] To be sure, once such a preliminary self-criticism of the power of cognition has been accomplished, then reason may and must proceed "dogmatically": that is, it may proceed to construct proofs on the basis of purely *a priori* principles.

For Kant, therefore, the contrast between dogmatism and criticism is primarily a *methodological* contrast between transcendental and non-transcendental approaches to philosophizing, between the sort of philosophy that explicitly poses the *quid juri* concerning its own claims and the sort that does not. What distinguishes dogmatism from criticism is thus not so much *what* the former affirms as *how* it affirms it; dogmatism (in the Kantian sense) poses for itself the metaphysical task of determining the true nature of God, freedom, and immortality, and "its procedure is at first dogmatic, that is, it confidently sets itself to this task without any previous examination of the capacity or incapacity of reason for so great an undertaking."[31] Because its procedure is in this sense "dogmatic," its conclusions are "dogmatic" as well, as is evidenced by the fact that such conclusions can always be opposed by "equally specious" opposing assertions.[32]

---

29. For orientation in this ongoing debate, see the works listed in Part IV of the Bibliography.

30. *Critique of Pure Reason*, Bxxxv. Trans. Norman Kemp Smith (London: Macmillan, 1929) [henceforth = KRV and cited according to the pagination of the first (= A, 1781) and second (= B, 1787) German editions]. For a critical examination of Kant's characterization of his rationalistic predecessors as "dogmatists," see Arthur O. Lovejoy, "Kant's Antithesis of Dogmatism and Criticism," *Mind* 15 (1906): 191–214.

31. KRV, A3/B7.

32. KRV, B23. This is, of course, well illustrated in Kant's discussion of "the antinomy of reason." Note, however, that in the course of this same discussion Kant employs the term "dogmatism" is a sense that is rather different from the one

A very different way of characterizing the distinction between dogmatism and criticism, not in *methodological* but rather in *metaphysical* terms, is prominent in the writings of another author who greatly influenced the early Fichte — Salomon Maimon. In Maimon's writings, dogmatism is identified with the position that "believes itself to be in possession of cognitions of *things in themselves*." It is thus synonymous with metaphysical realism, inasmuch as it "treats the objects of metaphysics as real objects."[33] Furthermore, Maimon often treated dogmatism as one of several possible types or systems of philosophy, and explicitly contrasted it with other possible systems, including criticism (by which he meant Kantianism as a philosophical system in its own right, rather than as a mere method of philosophizing), skepticism, and his own "coalition-system."

The influence of Maimon can be detected in a note to the preface to the first edition of Fichte's *Concerning the Concept of the Wissenschaftslehre* which begins as follows: "The real controversy between criticism and dogmatism concerns *the connection between our knowledge and a thing in itself.*"[34] This way of contrasting criticism and dogmatism is retained in the *Foundations of the Entire Wissenschaftslehre*, where Fichte follows Maimon in

---

discussed above, inasmuch as he characterizes the assertions that make up the "theses" side of the antinomies (e.g., the claim that the world has an intelligible beginning) as representing "dogmatism," and characterizes the opposing assertions on the side of the "antitheses" (e.g., the claim that the empirical series has no beginning) as representing "pure empiricism" (A466/B494).

In fact, both theses and antitheses are equally "dogmatic" in the sense that both sides have neglected the requisite preliminary critique of the power of cognition. Nevertheless, this implicit identification of dogmatism with rationalistic metaphysics had an important influence on subsequent discussions.

33. *Philosophisches Wörterbuch oder Beleuchtung der wichtigsten Gegenstände der Philosophie in alphabetischer Ordnung* (Brussels: Culture et Civilisation, 1970 [orig. 1791]), p. 22. See too *Versuch einer neuen Logik oder Theorie des Denkens* (Berlin: Reuther & Reichard, 1912 [orig. 1794], p. 342.

34. GA, I,2: 110n; EPW, p. 95n. To be sure, this way of characterizing dogmatism as the view that representations are produced by things in themselves is also anticipated in Kant. See, e.g., KRV, A389: "So long as we hold to the ordinary concepts of reason with regard to the communion in which our thinking subject stands with the things outside us, we are dogmatic, looking upon them as real objects existing independently of us, in accordance with a certain transcendental dualism which does not assign these outer appearances to the subject as representations, but sets them, just as they are given us in sensible intuition, as objects outside us, completely separating them from the thinking subject."

employing the term "dogmatism" as the name of a particular *metaphysical* position or system of philosophy rather than as denoting an "uncritical" method of philosophizing without a preceding critique of the power of cognition;[35] and often, in this same work, he juxtaposes such systematic dogmatism to another, opposing system (namely, Kant's transcendental idealism), which he too calls by the name "criticism." The difference between these two systems is described in the *Foundations* as follows: Criticism is the system that takes the pure I to be what is absolute and unconditioned, whereas any philosophy that resorts to an allegedly higher concept of a "Not-I" or independent thing is a form of dogmatism. "Critical philosophy is therefore *immanent*, because it posits everything in the I; dogmatism is *transcendent*, because it goes beyond the I."[36] But unlike Maimon, who often contrasted dogmatism with several other possible systems, including skepticism, Fichte does not view skepticism as a system of philosophy at all and limits the systematic options open to the philosopher to two and only two possibilities: *either* dogmatism *or* criticism.[37]

An important and novel feature of Fichte's discussion of the conflict between criticism and dogmatism, and one that is already present in the *Foundations*, is a strong emphasis on the *practical implications and presuppositions* of each system. For Fichte, the most important aspect of dogmatism as a philosophical system is that, if it is consistently developed, it cannot help but be a system of metaphysical determinism, or, as Fichte put it, "fatalism." Even in the 1794/95 *Foundations*, Fichte points to Spinozism as the most consistent expression of philosophical dogmatism, and interprets the latter as an unequivocal form of "fatalism."[38] Thus, by implication, if philosophy really is to be the "system of freedom" envisioned by the young Fichte, then it simply must be a system of criticism (or, as Fichte calls it in his later writings, "idealism").[39]

35. To be sure, there are still traces in Fichte's *Foundations* of Kant's methodological use of the term dogmatism to designate any position arrived at without a preliminary examination of its own possibility. See, e.g., the disparaging references to "dogmatic realism" and "dogmatic idealism" (GA, I,2: 310; Heath/Lachs, p. 147).

36. GA, I,2: 279; Heath/Lachs, p.117.

37. "There are only two systems: the critical and the dogmatic. Skepticism, as defined above, would be no system at all, since it denies the very possibility of any system" (GA, I,2: 280n; Heath/Lachs, p.118n).

38. GA, I,2: 279–80 and 310; Heath/Lachs, pp. 117 and 146.

39. Another feature of Fichte's later discussion which is already evident in the *Foundations* is his characteristic attempt to explain why someone might adopt one

Despite the undeniable influence of the writings of Maimon (and, of course, Kant) on Fichte's usage of the term "dogmatism," the more important and immediate influence upon his discussion of dogmatism and idealism in the two introductions to *An Attempt at a New Presentation of the Wissenschaftslehre* was Schelling's juxtaposition of "criticism" and "dogmatism" in two early works: *On the I as Principle of Philosophy, or, On the Unconditional in Human Knowledge*, published in the spring of 1795; and "Philosophical Letters on Dogmatism and Criticism," published in two installments in the *Philosophisches Journal* in 1795 and 1796.[40]

In *On the I*, Schelling (like Fichte) followed Maimon in describing the essence of dogmatism as lying in its allegiance to the thing in itself, but he went somewhat further in characterizing the difference between various systems of philosophy as a disagreement concerning the correct "absolute first principle" of philosophy. Dogmatism, the most perfect example of which is Spinozism,[41] begins with an "absolute substance" or "Not-I";

---

system or another, not by referring to arguments or indeed to any theoretical considerations, but rather by referring to purely *practical* considerations. Thus, for example, he explains the tendency toward dogmatism as arising, at least in part, from the practical "feeling" that the I is in fact not independent at all, but dependent on something outside of itself (GA, I,2: 281; Heath/Lachs, p. 118). See too the notorious footnote in which Fichte explains the *reluctance* of some people to accept idealism by asserting that "it would be easier to convince most people that they are a piece of lava on the moon than that they are an *I*" (GA, I,2: 326n; Heath/Lachs, p. 162n).

40. *Vom Ich als Princip der Philosophie, oder über das Unbedingte im menschlichen Wissen*, in Schelling's *Sämmtliche Werke*, ed. K. F. A. Schelling (Stuttgart: J. G. Cotta, 1856–61), vol. I, pp. 29–244; English trans. by Fritz Marti in Schelling, *The Unconditional in Human Knowledge. Four Early Essays (1794–1796)* (Lewisburg, Pa.: Bucknell University Press, 1980), pp. 63–128.

Philosophische Briefe über Dogmatismus und Kriticismus, in *Sämmtliche Werke*, vol. I, pp. 281–342; English trans., Marti, pp. 155–96. The first installment of Schelling's "Letters" (*Philosophisches Journal*, 1795, Heft 7, pp. 177–203) was titled "Philosophischen Briefen über Dogmaticismus und Kriticismus," whereas the second installment (1795, Heft 11 [though actually published in the spring of 1796], pp. 173–239) bore the more familiar title, which is also the title of the second edition, contained in vol. 1 of Schelling's *Philosophische Schriften* (1809). Interestingly, it was Niethammer, acting in his capacity as editor of the *Philosophisches Journal*, who changed the term "Dogmaticism" to "Dogmatism" in the title of Schelling's "Letters."

41. Though Fichte had already explicitly associated dogmatism with Spinozism, he was further influenced on this point by Schelling, whose knowledge of the

Introductions to the Wissenschaftslehre

criticism, the best examples of which, according to Schelling, are the philosophies of Kant and Fichte, begins with the "absolute subject" or "I." Accordingly, the former can also be described as "pure realism" and the latter as "pure idealism."[42] Schelling's juxtaposition of criticism and dogmatism, not merely as two rival systems but as proceeding from two different *philosophical starting points*, was explicitly taken up by Fichte in his "First Introduction" of 1797.

Though Schelling himself continued to juxtapose these two "exactly opposed"[43] systems to each other in his "Philosophical Letters on Dogmatism and Criticism," he also questioned the appropriateness of the terms "dogmatism" and "criticism" for naming the two systems in question. Instead, returning to Kant's original *methodological* use of the term, he proposes that it might be better to retain the term "criticism" not as the name for one of the two opposed systems of philosophy, but rather as designating a propaedeutic "critical" inquiry into the very possibility of any and all systems of philosophy ("metaphysics as a science"). "Criticism," so understood, "is destined to deduce from the essence of reason the very possibility of two exactly opposed systems; it is destined to establish a system of criticism (conceived as complete), or, more precisely, a system of idealism as well as and in exact opposition to it, a system of dogmatism or realism."[44] By the time he wrote the second installment to

---

history of philosophy was far superior to Fichte's. See Fichte's July 2, 1795 letter to Reinhold, where he remarks that "I am particularly fond of [Schelling's] references to Spinoza, on the basis of whose system mine can most properly be explained." Furthermore, the strategy of introducing students and readers to the *Wissenschaftslehre* by juxtaposing dogmatism and idealism is an idea that Fichte probably first picked up from Schelling's "Letters."

42. *Sämmtliche Werke*, vol. I, pp. 211–13; Marti, pp. 106–8.

43. Actually, in *On the I* at least, Schelling does not view criticism and dogmatism as the only two systematic possibilities; he also holds open the possibility of an intermediate system, which begins with the interaction between or mutual determination of the I and the Not-I. However, in that same text he also argues that such a system is actually a disguised form of dogmatism (*Sämmtliche Werke*, vol. I, p. 170; Marti, p.77).

44. Fifth Letter, *Sämmtliche Werke*, I, p. 303 (Marti, p. 169). In a note to this passage Schelling argues that it is time to replace "dogmatism" as the name of a system of philosophy with the more descriptive "objective realism" (= "subjective idealism") and "criticism" with "subjective realism" (= "objective idealism"). In this same spirit, Schelling also proposed a useful distinction between "dogmatism" as the system of objective realism and "dogmaticism" as the uncritical

his "Letters," Schelling was regularly referring to the two, opposed systems not as "criticism" and "dogmatism," but as "idealism" and "realism."

Moreover, whereas in *On the I* he had clearly suggested that only one system (namely, criticism) was theoretically tenable,[45] in his "Philosophical Letters on Dogmatism and Criticism" Schelling seems to view criticism and dogmatism (or idealism and realism) as equally unassailable (and also as equally indemonstrable) on purely theoretical grounds, and thus he writes that "which of the two we choose depends on the freedom of spirit which we ourselves have acquired."[46] Though such an assertion certainly appears to anticipate Fichte's famous dictum that the kind of philosophy one chooses depends on the kind of person one is, modern commentators are divided on the question of whether the similarity is more than superficial.[47]

---

procedure of reason when it erects a system — whether idealistic or dogmatic — without engaging in the requisite preliminary investigation of the cognitive faculty. Hence, "the *Critique of Pure Reason* has taught dogmaticism how it can become dogmatism, that is, a solidly established system of objective realism" (*Sämmtliche Werke*, I, p. 302; Marti, p. 169).

45. In a punning argument worthy of Hegel, Schelling had argued in *On the I* that dogmatism contradicts itself, since it takes as its "absolute" or "unconditioned" (*unbedingt*) starting point something that is precisely not "unconditioned" — namely, a "thing" (*Ding*) (see *Sämmtliche Werke*, vol. 1, p. 171; Marti, p. 77).

46. Sixth Letter, *Sämmtliche Werke*, vol. I, p. 308; Marti, p.173. See too Fourth Letter, *Sämmtliche Werke*, vol. I, p. 296; Marti, p. 165.

47. In his notes to the *Philosophisches Bibliothek* edition of Fichte's *Versuch einer neuen Darstellung* (Hamburg: Meiner, 1975), for example, Peter Baumanns consistently emphasizes the similarities between Fichte's position and Schelling's and corrects what he takes to be Fichte's misinterpretation of Schelling's "Letters." In contrast, the editors of GA, I,4 clearly share Fichte's view of the significant differences between his own view of the relationship between dogmatism and idealism and the contrast drawn by Schelling between dogmatism and criticism. Citing a later remark of Schelling's in which he himself interprets the "Letters" in a manner consistent with Fichte's criticisms, Fritz Marti, in the introduction to his English translation of Schelling's "Letters," concludes that "Schelling sees a relative right of dogmatism which Fichte denies, and he has a more positive view of nature" (Marti, pp. 154–55). For a reading of Schelling's essay which strongly supports Fichte's interpretation, see Reinhard Lauth, "Die erste philosophische Auseinandersetzung um das philosophische System," in Lauth, *Die Entstehung von Schellings Identitätsphilosophie in der Auseinandersetzung*

There is, however, no doubt concerning Fichte's own view of the matter: he disagreed, first of all, with what he understood to be Schelling's contention that criticism (idealism) and dogmatism (realism) were absolutely equivalent from a purely theoretical perspective and hence that one could simply "choose" between them as one wished. Moreover, he was concerned that readers of Schelling's "Letters" might confuse his position with Fichte's own, for he too, in his lectures on *Wissenschaftslehre nova methodo*, employed the opposition between these two systems (which, however, he called "dogmatism and idealism" rather than "dogmatism and criticism") to introduce his philosophy and to guide students toward the standpoint of the latter. Though Schelling is never mentioned by name in this context in either the first or second introduction to the *New Presentation*, Fichte's discussion of the opposition between dogmatism and idealism is in fact a critical reply to Schelling's "Philosophical Letters on Dogmatism and Criticism," and the differences between Schelling's position and that of Fichte's are worth noting.

What did Fichte object to in Schelling's "Letters"? A major source of dissatisfaction was surely Schelling's proposal to identify Fichte's *Wissenschaftslehre* not with systematic idealism but with mere methodological "criticism," and hence to lump it together with the *Critique of Pure Reason* as a philosophically neutral "canon of all possible systems." The sort of separation between epistemology and metaphysics, between a mere *Wissenschaftslehre* and a genuine system of philosophy, proposed by Schelling[48] thus represented for Fichte nothing less than a move toward a new type of dogmatism, one that sought to liberate the speculative task of

---

mit Fichtes Wissenschaftslehre (Freiburg: Alber, 1975), pp. 9–55.

Despite Fichte's published objections, Schelling continued to insist on the mutual autonomy — indeed, complementarity — of dogmatism and criticism (or of realism and idealism). Indeed, his subsequent "System of Identity" purports to discover and to proceed from the "point of indifference" that allegedly underlies and unites the opposing systems of "idealism" and "realism." (See Schelling's 1801 *Darstellung meines System der Philosophie*, in *Sämmtliche Werke*, vol. 4, pp. 105-212.) Ultimately, it is precisely this search for a higher "identity" of idealism and realism, spirit and nature, which most clearly distinguishes so-called absolute systems like those of Schelling and Hegel from a truly transcendental philosophy such as Fichte's.

48. "By itself the *Critique of Pure Reason* is or contains the genuine theory of science or *Wissenschaftslehre*, for it is valid for all *science*. Nevertheless, *science* may lift itself to an absolute principle; indeed, it must do this if it is to become a *system*. But it is

systematic philosophy from the strict requirements of transcendental grounding — which is, in fact, precisely what happened in the later thought of Schelling and Hegel. Thus the purpose of § 6 of the "Second Introduction" is not simply to defend Fichte's claims concerning the intimate relationship between Kant's philosophy and his own, but also to persuade readers that Kantianism is by no means neutral with respect to the dispute between idealism and dogmatism: though Kant himself may not have fully succeeded in constructing the complete philosophical system for which his *Critiques* paved the way, he certainly demonstrated that the system in question could only be transcendental idealism. Hence Fichte viewed Schelling's distinction between criticism and system as an attack upon the very foundations of his own project.

For the same reason, he was alarmed by what he took to be Schelling's insistence on the theoretical *equivalence* of idealism and realism, in the sense that neither possessed a more secure foundation or was in any sense better warranted than the other.[49] If, as Fichte believed, idealism is the only system that can withstand a transcendental critique, then the mutual irrefutability (which Fichte, of course, conceded) of the two systems does not necessarily imply that they are equally well grounded or equally tenable. What Fichte suspected was that Schelling's way of opposing idealism to realism was actually meant to lead to something else altogether, namely, toward a new dogmatism, a "philosophy of the absolute," which could claim to have overcome the opposition in question.[50]

---

impossible for the *Wissenschaftslehre* to establish an absolute principle and thereby to become a *system* (in the narrow sense of the word), because it is supposed to contain within itself, not an absolute principle nor a determinate, completed system, but rather, the canon of all principles and systems" (*Sämmtliche Werke*, vol. I, p. 304–5; Marti, p. 171).

49. That Schelling's way of contrasting the two systems was in fact a target of Fichte's "Introductions" is made clear by Fichte himself in the following passage from his May 31 – August 7, 1801 letter to Schelling: "I confess that the claims you once put forward in the *Philosophisches Journal* concerning two different philosophies — one idealistic and one realistic, both of them true and capable of subsisting alongside each other (an assertion that I immediately and gently refuted, since I viewed it as incorrect) — raised within me the suspicion that you had not completely penetrated the *Wissenschaftslehre*."

50. Schelling's own text provides ample support for such a suspicion. See, e.g., his Ninth Letter, where he remarks that "he who has reflected upon idealism and realism, the two most opposite theoretical systems, has found by himself that both can come to pass only in the approach to the absolute, yet that both must unite in

Such concerns may explain why Fichte, in the 1797 "Introductions," employed the peculiar terminology that he did: not, as in the *Foundations*, "criticism" vs. "dogmatism," nor, as in Schelling's "Letters" and elsewhere, "idealism" vs. "realism," but rather *idealism* vs. *dogmatism*, a formulation that cleverly conflates both of the preceding juxtapositions. Viewed in the light of the history we have just reviewed, what Fichte's new terminology suggests is the equivalence and inseparability of, on the one hand, idealism and criticism, and, on the other, realism and dogmatism.

To be sure, Fichte was anxious to give realism its due, and duly did so in a note to § 1 of the "Second Introduction"[51] (and elsewhere) by treating the difference between realism and idealism not as a difference between two different, equally tenable philosophical systems — there can be but *one* universally valid philosophy[52] — but as representing two entirely different "standpoints" or "points of view." Whereas the philosopher, from his speculative standpoint, is and must be a transcendental idealist, in his everyday life he, like everyone else, is and must be an empirical realist. So understood, there is no real opposition between "idealism" and "realism," and those who think there is have either, like Schelling, failed to appreciate the intimate connection between transcendental "criticism" and systematic "idealism," or, like Jacobi, failed to grasp the basic distinction between the "standpoint of philosophy" and the "standpoint of life." Everyday, empirical realism is simply not a philosophical theory (instead, it is an unavoidable standpoint, one that philosophy has to explain and to justify), and transcendental idealism is not and can never be an actual mode of thinking and living. Philosophy is not worldly wisdom, and common sense is not philosophy.

All of the translations included in this volume are based on the original

---

the absolute, that is, must cease as opposite systems" (*Sämmtliche Werke*, vol. I, p. 330; Marti, p. 188).

51. GA, I,4: 210–11n; trans. below, p. 38n. The note in question is clearly directed at Schelling.

52. Vigorous defense of the claim that all genuine philosophers are *AlleinPhilosophen*, committed to the proposition that there can be only one sole true system of philosophy (though there can, of course, be many different presentations of the same), is a prominent feature of many of the works Fichte wrote in response to Jacobi's "Open Letter." See, for example, in the present volume, "From a Private Letter" and "Public Announcement of a New Presentation of the *Wissenschaftslehre*."

editions, supplemented by later findings of the editors of the various editions of Fichte's collected writings. Philological and historical information concerning the composition and original publication of each text is provided in the notes. None of the texts present any special editorial problems.

I have tried to maintain as much consistency as possible in translating key terms into English, as indicated in the extensive German/English glossary. Though I have, as a general rule, tried to observe long-established conventions regarding the rendering of various technical terms (translating *Anschauung* as "intuition," *Vorstellung* as "representation," *Erkenntnis* as "cognition," etc.), there are some exceptions. I have not, for example, translated *das Ich* as either "the self" or "the ego," but always as "the I" — which sounds no more odd in English than does *das Ich* in German. Nor have I translated *Vermögen* as "faculty"; instead, I have rendered it as "power" (as in *Erkenntnisvermögen* = "power of cognition"). Finally, I have not translated the word *Wissenschaftslehre* at all, but have left it in German as a term of art designating Fichte's distinctive system of transcendental idealism. If it must be rendered into English, one can always substitute "doctrine of science" or perhaps "theory of scientific knowledge." "Science of knowledge," which has long been the accepted English translation of *Wissenschaftslehre*, is simply wrong.

On the whole, I have tried to convey in English some sense of Fichte's distinctive prose style. Though I have on occasion been forced to break some of his longer sentences into several shorter ones, I have tried to avoid doing so. Fichte's own paragraphing has been scrupulously observed, however. In addition, I have retained his characteristically German use of long dashes (*Gedankenstriche* or "thought strokes") to indicate parenthetical remarks, breaks, and subdivisions within paragraphs. Fichte's own, sometimes rather eccentric, use of italics has been retained, except in cases where German and English conventions clearly differ, as, for example, in the use of italics in cases of proper names, to indicate the "mention" of a term, or to signal a quotation.

The scholarly apparatus, which is devoted primarily to such matters as identifying persons, books, and events alluded to by Fichte himself, has been kept to a minimum. Fichte's own footnotes (which often contain important material) are always indicated by asterisks. All numbered notes have been added by the editor/translator. All material that appears within square brackets has also been added by the translator.

Fichte's thought is not easy to grasp, and the difficulties of understanding his various presentations of the same, including the ones in this

volume, are often compounded for contemporary readers by the vast con-
textual gulf separating his philosophical era from our own and by our
own historical ignorance — to say nothing of the gap between his late-
eighteenth-century German and our late-twentieth-century English. It is,
however, my belief, and certainly my hope, that such obstacles are not
insurmountable, and that one sign of any philosophy worthy of the name is
precisely its capacity to stimulate and to enlighten distant generations of
readers. While such a hope will surely seem forlorn to some, it is one that
was fully shared by Fichte himself, who occasionally consoled himself for
what he took to be his contemporaries' incomprehension of his philosophy
by imagining "some future age that might be able to understand it."[53]

I would like to thank Professor Reinhard Lauth for his initial encourage-
ment of this project and for his generosity in lending me his personal copies of the original issues of the *Philosophisches Journal* containing most of
the texts translated in this volume. Once again, I am greatly indebted to my
good friends Erich Fuchs and Wolfgang Natter for their expert and
indispensible assistance on a variety of philological, historical, and linguistic matters. Thanks are also due to Werner S. Pluhar for his many helpful
suggestions concerning specific points of translation. For proofreading and
editorial assistance, I thank David Wells, Yolanda Estes, and Lon Nease
(who also prepared the index), as well as the editorial and production staffs
at Hackett Publishing Company. I would also like to acknowledge the gen-
erous support I have received over the years from the Alexander von
Humboldt Foundation, under whose auspices I first began work on this
project. Finally, I would like to express my immense personal gratitude to
my wife and children, Viviane, Nicole, and Rebecca Breazeale; to acknowledge their heroic forbearance; and to dedicate this book to our unforget-
table year together at Schachstraße 6.

---

53. Preface to the second ed. of *Concerning the Concept* (GA, I,2: 163; EPW, p. 100).

German–English Glossary

abbilden	to portray
ableiten	to derive
die Absicht	intention (what one has in view)
die Agilität	agility
anerkennen	to acknowledge, to recognize
anknüpfen	to attach, to connect, to hold together
die Anlage	talent
annehmen	to assume, to recognize
anschauen	to intuit
das Anschauen	intuiting, act of intuiting
das Anschauende	the intuiting subject
die Anschauung	intuition
die Ansicht	view, point of view, opinion, way of looking at, appearance, aspect
der Anspruch	claim
der Anstoß	impact, check
auffassen	to grasp, to interpret, to construe
die Auffassung	comprehension
die Aufforderung	summons
der Aufgabe	task, assignment
aufheben	to cancel, to annul
die Aufmerksamkeit	attentiveness
aufstellen	to present, to exhibit, to display, to set up, to construct, to establish, to make (an assertion), to indicate, to propose, to state, to advance (an hypothesis)
aufweisen	to present
die Ausdehnung	extension
(sich) äussern	to express
der Ausspruch	dictum, pronouncement
das Beabsichtigte	what is intended

die Bedenklichkeit	difficulty
die Bedingung	condition (for the possibility of)
begreifen	to comprehend, to grasp, to grasp in or by means of a concept
das Begreifen	(act of) comprehending, comprehension
der Begriff	concept
beharrlich	constant
bekannt	well-known, familiar, known
bemerken	to observe
die Beschaffenheit	structure, constitution, (set of) properties
beschlossen	completed, finished
die Beschränktheit	(state of) limitation, limited state
die Beschränkung	limitation
beschreiben	to describe
bestehen	to subsist, to endure
das Bestehen	subsistence, continuing existence
bestimmbar	determinable
die Bestimmbarkeit	determinability
bestimmen	to determine, to specify
das Bestimmen	(act of) determining or specifying
bestimmt	determinate, determined, specific
die Bestimmtheit	determinacy, determinate state, precision
die Beweglichkeit	mobility
der Beweis	proof, argument
beweisen	to prove, to demonstrate
das Bewusstsein	consciousness
beziehen	to relate, to connect
das Bild	image
bilden	to form or entertain images: to shape or to form
binden	to constrain, to bind
die Causalität	causal power, causality

der Charakter	characteristic feature, feature, character, nature
darstellen	to present, to expound, to exhibit, to portray
die Darstellung	presentation, exposition, portrayal
die Denkart	way or manner of thinking
denken	to think, to conceive of
das Denken	thinking, act of thinking
das Denkende	the thinking subject
der Denkzwang	intellectual compulsion, feeling of being compelled to think in a certain way
die Einbildungskraft	imagination, power of imagination
einwirken	to exercise an effect on, to act efficaciously
die Einwirkung	effect, influence, efficacious action
empfinden	to sense, to have a sensation
die Empfindung	sensation
der Endzweck	final goal
entgegensetzen	to oppose, to posit in opposition
entschließen	to resolve, to decide
der Entschluß	decision, resolve
entwerfen	to construct, to project
erblicken	to view, to catch sight of, to observe
ergreifen	to apprehend
erkennen	to cognize, to recognize, to have a cognition of
das Erkennen	(act of) cognizing, cognition
die Erkenntnis	cognition
erklären	to explain, to explicate, to interpret, to account for, to state
erschöpfen	to complete, to exhaust
erweisen	to demonstrate, to show
das Factum	fact
finden	to find, to discover, to encounter
die Folge	sequence, consequence, result

das Fühlbar	what can be felt
für sich	for itself, by itself
das Gedachte	the object of thought, what is thought of
das Gefühl	feeling
der Gegensatz	opposite, opposition
gegensetzen	to oppose, to posit in opposition
der Gegenstand	object
der Geist	mind, spirit
das Gemüth	mind
geschieden	separate, separated
geschloßen	self-contained, brought to a close, concluded
die Gesellschaft	society, company
der Gesichtspunkt	viewpoint, point of view
die Gesinnung	disposition, character
die Gewalt	power
die Glaube	belief, faith, confidence
glauben	to believe, to have confidence in, to trust, to think
das Glied	element, member, term, link
der Grund	ground, foundation, basis, reason
grunden	to ground, to base upon, to found
gültig	valid
handeln	to act
das Handeln	acting (instance, mode, or type of acting)
die Handlung	action
hemmen	to curb, to obstruct, to restrict
hervorbringen	to produce, to generate
das Hinderniss	obstacle, hindrance
das Ich	the I
die Ichheit	I-hood
die Idee	Idea
die Intelligenz	intellect, intelligence

kennen	to be acquainted with, to know, to be aware of
die Kenntniß	cognizance, acquaintance, awareness
die Kraft	force, energy, power
die Lehre	theory, account
leiden	to be passively affected
das Leiden	passivity, passive state, state of passivity
losreisen	to wrench away, to tear away
machen	to produce, to make
das Mannigfaltige	manifold, multiplicity
das Material	material, content
das Materiale	the material aspect
die Materie	matter, content
das Merkmal	attribute, distinctive feature
die Moralität	morality
nachmachen	to imitate, to copy
nachweisen	to establish, to show
die Neigung	inclination
das NichtIch	the Not-I
das Objekt	object
ein Objektive	something objective, what is objective, an objective element
die Phantasie	imagination
philosophieren	to engage in philosophical inquiry, to philosophize
das Philosophieren	philosophical inquiry, philosophizing
das Räsonnement	argumentation, argument, line of reasoning, ratiocination
realisieren	to realize, to make real, to bring into being
das Recht	right
das Rechttun	right action, doing the right thing
reelle	real, genuine
die Reflexion	(act of) reflecting, (act of) reflection
die Rücksicht	respect, aspect

die Ruhe	state of repose
ruhend	in a state of repose, passive, stable
die Sache	content, matter, subject
der Satz	proposition, principle
schlechthin	simply, purely and simply, unconditionally
die Schwärmerei	fanaticism
die Selbstständigkeit	self-sufficiency
setzen	to posit
das Setzend	the (actively) positing subject
der Sinn	sense
die Sinnenwelt	sensible world
sinnlich	sensible, sensory
die Sinnlichkeit	sensibility, sensuousness
die Sitte	custom
die Sittenlehre	ethical theory, theory of ethics
die Sittlichkeit	morality
stehend	stable
die Stimmung	sentiment, disposition
der Stoff	matter, material, content, stuff
das Subjective	what is subjective, the subjective, the subjective element
die Summe	sum, total sum, totality
die Tat	deed
die Tathandlung	Act
tätig	active
das Tätiges	the active subject or agent
die Tätigkeit	activity
trennen	to separate, to divide
das Tun	doing, instance of doing, act of doing something
die Uebereinstimmung	agreement
das Uebergehen	movement of transition, passage, movement, transition
sich überlassen	to confine oneself (to)

übersinnlich	supersensible
umfassen	to comprise
unbestimmt	indeterminate
die Unbestimmtheit	(state of) indeterminacy
das Unvermögen	incapacity
die Verbindung	connection, bond
die Vereinigung	unification, union
das Verfahren	process, operation
das Verhältniss	relation, relationship
die Verhältnisse	conditions, circumstances, relations
verknüpfen	to connect, to tie together
das Vermögen	power
die Verwandlung	transformation
vernichten	to annihilate
die Vernunft	reason
versinnlichen	to make sensible, to sensibilize
der Verstand	understanding
verstandlich	intelligible
vorschweben	to hover before, to have (something) in mind
vorstellen	to represent, to have or to entertain representations
das Vorstellend	the representing subject
die Vorstellung	representation
wahrnehmen	to perceive
die Wahrnehmung	perception
wechselwirken	to interact, to stand in a relationship of mutual interaction
die Wechselwirkung	(reciprocal) interaction
das Wesen	being, essence, nature, creature, entity
wiederstehen	to resist
der Wille	will
ein Willen	a willing
die Willkür	choice, free choice, arbitrary choice, power of (free) choice

wirken	to act efficaciously, to operate, to have an effect on, to affect
das Wirken	efficacious acting, accomplishment
wirklich	actual
die Wirklichkeit	actuality, reality
wirksam	effective, effectively
die Wirksamkeit	efficacy, efficacious power
die Wirkung	effect
wissen	to know
das Wissen	knowing, knowledge
die Wissenschaft	science
die Wissenschaftslehre	*Wissenschaftslehre* (theory of scientific knowledge, or doctrine of science)
das Wollen	willing, act of willing
das Ziel	goal, object
(in sich selbst) zuruckgehen	to revert into itself
das Zusammenfassen	act of combining, combination
der Zusammenhang	combination, connection, context, interconnectedness
zusammensetzen	to combine, to assemble, to posit together, to compose
zusehen	to witness, to observe, to look at
der Zustand	state
der Zweck	goal, end, aim, purpose
zweckmässig	purposeful
zwingen	to compel, to constrain

Bibliography

I. Fichte's Works

Johann Gottlieb Fichtes sämmtliche Werke. Ed. I. H. Fichte. 8 vols. Berlin: Veit, 1845–46. Reprinted as vols. 1–8 of *Fichtes Werke.* Berlin: de Gruyter, 1971.

J. G. Fichte: Gesamtausgabe der Bayerischen Akademie der Wissenschaften. Ed. Reinhard Lauth, Hans Jacob, and Hans Gliwitzky. Stuttgart-Bad Cannstatt: Frommann, 1964 —.

Fichte, Johann Gottlieb. *Wissenschaftslehre nova methodo. Kollegnach- schrift Chr. Fr. Krause 1798/99.* Ed. Erich Fuchs. Hamburg: Meiner, 1982.

II. English Translations of Fichte's Early Writings

Attempt at a Critique of All Revelation. Trans. Garrett Green. Cam- bridge: Cambridge University Press, 1978.

Fichte: Early Philosophical Writings. Trans. and ed. Daniel Breazeale. Ithaca, N.Y. and London: Cornell University Press, 1988.

Science of Knowledge. Trans. and ed. Peter Heath and John Lachs. Cambridge: Cambridge University Press, 1982.

The Science of Rights. Trans. A. E. Kroeger. Philadelphia: J. B. Lippincott, 1869.

The Science of Ethics as Based on the Science of Knowledge. Trans. A. E. Kroeger. Ed. W. T. Harris. London: Kegan Paul, Trench, Trübner, 1897.

Foundations of Transcendental Philosophy (Wissenschaftslehre) nova methodo. Trans. and ed. Daniel Breazeale. Ithaca, N.Y. and London: Cornell University Press, 1992.

"On the Spirit and the Letter in Philosophy." Trans. Elizabeth Rubenstein. In *German Aesthetic and Literary Criticism: Kant, Fichte, Schelling, Schopenhauer, Hegel,* ed. David Simpson, pp. 74–93. New York: Cambridge University Press, 1984.

The Vocation of Man. Trans. Peter Preuss. Indianapolis, Ind.: Hackett, 1987.

"A Crystal Clear Report to the General Public Concerning the Actual Essence of the Newest Philosophy: An Attempt to Force the Reader to Understand." Trans. John Botterman and William Rasch. In *Philosophy of German Idealism*, ed. Ernst Behler, pp. 39–115. New York: Continuum, 1987.

III. Some General Works on Fichte

Adamson, Robert. *Fichte.* Edinburgh and London: Blackwood, 1881.

Baumanns, Peter. *Fichtes ürsprungliches System: Sein Standort zwischen Kant und Hegel.* Stuttgart–Bad Cannstatt: Frommann, 1972.

——————. *J. G. Fichte: Kritische Gesamtdarstellung seiner Philosophie.* Freiburg: Alber, 1990.

Breazeale, Daniel, and Tom Rockmore, eds. *Fichte: Historical Contexts/ Contemporary Controversies.* Atlantic Highlands, N.J.: Humanities Press, 1994.

Gardiner, Patrick. "Fichte and German Idealism." In *Idealism Past and Present*, ed. Godfrey Vesey, pp. 111–26. Cambridge: Cambridge University Press, 1982.

Gueroult, Martial. *L'evolution et la structure de la doctrine de la science chez Fichte.* 2 vols. Paris: Société de l'édition: les belles lettres, 1930.

Gurwitsch, Georg. *Fichtes System der konkreten Ethik.* Tübingen: Mohr, 1924.

Heimsoeth, Heinz. *Fichte.* Munich: Ernst Reinhardt, 1923.

Jacobs, Wilhelm G. *Johann Gottlieb Fichte.* Hamburg: Rowohlt, 1984.

Janke, Wolfgang. *Fichte: Sein und Reflexion — Grundlagen der kristischen Vernunft.* Berlin: de Gruyter, 1970.

Lauth, Reinhard. *Zur Idee der Transzendentalphilosophie.* Munich and Salzburg: Anton Pustet, 1965.

Neuhouser, Frederick. *Fichte's Theory of Subjectivity.* Cambridge: Cambridge University Press, 1990.

Pareyson, Luigi. *Fichte: Il sistema della libertá*, 2d ed. Milan: Musia, 1976.

Philonenko, Alexis. *La liberté humaine dans la philosophie de Fichte*, 2nd ed. Paris: Vrin, 1980.

_____. *L'Oeuvre de Fichte*. Paris: Vrin, 1984.

Pippin, Robert B. "Fichte's Contribution." *Philosophical Forum* 19 (1987–88): 74–96.

Rockmore, Tom. *Fichte, Marx, and the German Philosophical Tradition*. Carbondale: Southern Illinois University Press, 1980.

Rohs, Peter. *Johann Gottlieb Fichte*. Munich: Beck, 1991.

Royce, Josiah. "Fichte." In Royce, *The Spirit of Modern Philosophy*, pp. 135–63. Boston: Houghton Mifflin, 1893.

Seidel, George J. *Activity and Ground: Fichte, Schelling, Hegel*. Hildesheim: Olms, 1976.

Weischedel, Wilhelm. *Der Aufbruch der Freiheit zur Gemeinschaft: Studien zur Philosophie der jungen Fichtes*. Leipzig: Meiner, 1939.

Wood, Allen W. "Fichte's Philosophical Revolution." *Philosophical Topics* 19 (1991): 1–28.

Wundt, Max. *Johann Gottlieb Fichte*. Stuttgart: Frommann, 1927.

IV. Literature Pertaining to *An Attempt at a New Presentation of the Wissenschaftslehre*

Ameriks, Karl. "Kant, Fichte, and Short Arguments to Idealism." *Archiv für Geschichte der Philosophie* 72 (1990): 63–85.

Barion, Jacob. *Die intellektuelle Anschauung bei J. G. Fichte und Schelling und ihre religionsphilosophische Bedeutung*. Würzburg: Becker, 1929.

Baumanns, Peter. "Einleitung." In Fichte, *Versuch einer neuen Darstellung der Wissenschaftslehre*, pp. vii–xxvii. Hamburg: Meiner, 1975.

Bock, Kurt. "Das Verhältnis Fichtes zu Kant nach der Rezension des Aenesidemus und den beiden Einleitungen in die Wissenschafts-lehre." *Philosophisches Jahrbuch* 34 (1921): 50–63.

Brandt, Reinhard. "Fichtes 1. Einleitung in die Wissenschaftslehre (1798)." *Kant-Studen* 69 (1978): 67–89.

Breazeale, Daniel. "How to Make an Idealist: Fichte's 'Refutation of Dogmatism' and the Problem of the Starting Point of the *Wissen-schaftslehre*." *Philosophical Forum* 19 (1988): 97–123.

Cantoni, Alfredo. "La 'Teoria della Scienza' del 1798 di G. A. Fichte." *Pensiero. Rivista quadrimestrial di Folosofia* 3 (1958): 51–68.

Flach, W. "Fichte über Kritizismus und Dogmatismus." *Zeitschrift für philosophische Forschung* 18 (1964): 585–96.

Gram, Moltke S. "Intellectual Intuition: The Continuity Thesis." *Journal of the History of Ideas* 42 (1981): 287–304.

_____. "Things in Themselves: The Historical Lesson." *Journal of the History of Philosophy* 18 (1980): 407–31.

Griswold, Charles. "Fichte's Modification of Kant's Transcendental Idealism in the *Wissenschaftslehre* of 1794 and Introductions of 1797." *Auslegung* IV, 2 (n.d.): 132–51.

Gueroult, Martial. "L'Antidogmatisme de Kant et de Fichte." In Gueroult, *Etudes sur Fichte*, pp. 16–59. Paris: Aubier-Montaigne, 1974.

Henrich, Dieter. "Fichte's Original Insight." Trans. David Lachterman. *Contemporary German Philosophy* 1 (1982): 15–52.

Hickey, Lance P. "Fichte's Critique of Dogmatism: The Modern Parallel." *Philosophical Forum* 35 (2004): 65–80.

Hohler, Thomas. "Intellectual Intuition and the Beginning of Fichte's Philosophy: A New Interpretation." *Tijdschrift voor Filosofie* 37 (1975): 52–37.

Janke, Wolfgang. "Intellektualle Anschauung und Gewissen: Aufriß eines Begründungsproblems." *Fichte-Studien* 5 (1993): 21–55.

Koch, Reinhard. *Fichtes Theorie des Selbstbewußtseins: ihre Entwicklung von den "Eignen Meditationen über ElementarPhilosophie" 1793 bis zur "Neuen Bearbeitung der W.L." 1800.* Würzburg: Königshausen & Neumann, 1989.

Lachs, John. "Fichte's Idealism." *American Philosophical Quarterly* 9 (1972): 311–18.

_____. "Is There an Absolute Self?" *Philosophical Forum* 19 (1987–88): 169–87.

Lauth, Reinhard. *Die Entstehung von Schellings Identitätsphilosophie in der Auseinandersetzung mit Fichtes Wissenschaftslehre.* Freiburg: Alber, 1975.

Mandt, A. J. "Fichte's Idealism in Theory and Practice." *Idealistic Studies* 14 (1984): 127–47.

Martin, Wayne M. "Fichte's Anti-Dogmatism." *Ratio* 5 (1992): 129–46.

Omine, Akira. "Intellektuelle Anschauung und Mystik." *Fichte Studien* 3 (1991): 184–203.

Pareyson, Luigi. "Die Wahl der Philosophie nach Fichte." Trans. Horst Seidl. In *Epimeleia. Die Sorge der Philosophie um den Menchen*, ed. Franz Wiedmann, pp. 30–60. Munich and Salzburg: Anton Pustet, 1964.

Philonenko, Alexis. "Die intellektuelle Anschauung bei Fichte." In *Der transcendentale Gedanke. Die gegenwärtige Darstellung der Philosophie Fichtes*, ed. Klaus Hammacher, pp. 91–106. Hamburg: Meiner, 1981.

Rabb, J. Douglas. "Incommensurable Paradigms and Critical Idealism." *Studies in the History of the Philosophy of Science* 6 (1975): 343–46.

————. "J. G. Fichte: Three Arguments for Idealism." *Idealistic Studies* 6 (1976): 169–77.

————. "Lachs on Fichte." *Dialogue* 12 (1973): 480–85.

Römelt, Johannes. "'Merke auf dich selbst.' Das Verhältnis des Philosophen zu seinem Gegenstand nach dem *Versuch einer neuen Darstellung der Wissenschaftslehre* (1797/98)." *Fichte-Studien* 1 (1990): 73–98.

Salvucci, Pasquale. "Fichte interprete di Kant nella 'Seconda introduzione alla Dottrina della Scienza.'" In Salvucci, *Grand Interpreti di Kant, Fichte e Schelling*, pp. 9–84. Urbino: Pubblicazioni dell' Università di Urbino, 1958.

Snider, Eric. "Scientific Philosophy and Philosophical Method in Fichte." *Metaphilosophy* 20 (1989): 68–76.

Stolzenberg, Jürgen. *Fichtes Begriff der intellektuellen Anschauung: Die Entwicklung in den Wissenschaftslehren von 1793/94 bis 1801/02.* Stuttgart: Klett-Cotta, 1986.

Suber, Peter. "A Case Study in *Ad Hominem* Arguments: Fichte's *Science of Knowledge*." *Philosophy and Rhetoric* 23 (1990): 12–42.

Tilliete, Xavier. "Erster Fichte-Rezeption. Mit besonderer Berücksichtigung der intellektuellen Anschauung." In *Der transcendentalen Gedanke*, pp. 532–43.

Wundt, Max. "Die Wissenschaftslehre von 1797." In Wundt, *Fichte-Forschungen*, pp. 77–141. Stuttgart: Frommann, 1929.

V. Literature Pertaining to the Atheism Controversy and to Fichte's Early Philosophy of Religion

Baumgartner, Hans Michael. "Transcendentales Denken und Atheismus: Der Atheismusstreit um Fichte." *Hochland* 56 (1963/64): 40–48.

_____. "Ueber das Gottesverständnis der Transzendental-
philosophie: Bemerkungen zum Atheismusstreit von 1798–99."
Philosophisches Jahrbuch 73 (1965): 303–21.

Böckelmann, Frank, ed. *Die Schriften zu J. G. Fichtes Atheismusstreit.*
Munich: Rogner & Bernhard, 1969.

Breazeale, Daniel. "The 'Standpoint of Life' and the 'Standpoint of
Philosophy' in the Context of the Jena *Wissenschaftslehre* (1794–
1801)." In *Transzendentalphilosophie als System: Die Auseinandersetzung zwischen 1794 und 1806*, ed. A. Mues, pp. 212–41. Hamburg:
Meiner, 1989.

Coreth, Emerich, S. J. "Vom Ich zum absoluten Sein: Zur Entwicklung
der Gotteslehre Fichtes." *Zeitschrift für katholische Philosophie* 79
(1957): 257–303.

di Giovanni, George. "From Jacobi's Philosophical Novel to Fichte's
Idealism: Some Comments on the 1798–99 'Atheism Dispute.'"
Journal of the History of Philosophy 27 (1989): 75–100.

Hase, Karl. *Jenaisches Fichte-Büchlein.* Leipzig: Breitkopf und Härtel,
1856.

Hirsch, Emanuel. "Fichtes Gotteslehre 1794–1802." In Hirsch, *Die
idealistische Philosophie und das Christentum: Gesammelte Aufsätze*, pp.
140–290. Gütersloh: Bertelsman, 1926.

_____. "Fichtes Religionsphilosophie in der Frühzeit der
Wissenschaftslehre." *Zeitschrift für Philosophie und philosophische
Kritik* 163 (1917): 34–36.

Leighton, J. A. "Fichte's Conception of God." *Philosophical Review* 4
(1895) 143–53.

Lindau, Hans, ed. *Die Schriften zu J. G. Fichtes Atheismus-Streit.*
Munich: Müller, 1912.

Philonenko, Alexis. "Introduction et Commentaire" to his translation of
"Le Foundment de Notre Croyance en une divine providence." In
Fichte, *Ecrits de Philosophie Première. Doctrine de la Science 1801–
1802 et textes annexes*, Tome 2, commentaire analytique, pp. 209–28.
Paris: Vrin, 1987.

Rickert, Heinrich. "Fichtes Atheismusstreit und die Kantische
Philosophie." *Kant-Studien* 4 (1899/1900): 137–66.

Seidel, George J. "Fichte and Secular Christianity." *Antigonish Review* 1
(1970): 101–9.

Stadler, Robert, S. J. "Der neue Gottesgedanke Fichtes: Eine Studie zum 'Atheismusstreit.'" *Theologie und Philosophie* 54 (1979): 481–541.

Stine, Russell Warren. *The Doctrine of God in the Philosophy of Fichte.* Philadelphia: University of Pennsylvania, 1945.

Talbot, Ellen Bliss. "Fichte's Conception of God." *The Monist* 23 (1913): 42–58.

——————. "The Relation between Human Consciousness and the Ideal as Conceived by Kant and Fichte." *Kant-Studien* 4 (1900): 286–310.

Thomas, J. Heywood. "J. G. Fichte and F. W. J. Schelling." In *Nineteenth-Century Religious Thought in the West*, ed. Ninian Smart, John Clayton, Steven Katz, and Patrick Sherry, vol. 1, pp. 41–79. Cambridge: Cambridge University Press, 1985.

Vaihinger, Hans. "Forberg, the Originator of the Fichtean Atheism Controversy, and His Religion of As-If." In *The Philosophy of As If*, trans. C. K. Ogden, 2nd ed., pp. 319–327. London: Routledge & Kegan Paul, 1935.

VI. Other Works Cited

Allison, Henry E. *The Kant-Eberhard Controversy*. Baltimore: Johns Hopkins University Press, 1973.

Beiser, Frederick C. *Enlightenment, Revolution, and Romanticism: The Genesis of Modern German Political Thought 1790 – 1800*. Cambridge, Mass. and London: Harvard University Press, 1992.

——————. *The Fate of Reason: German Philosophy from Kant to Fichte*. Cambridge, Mass. and London: Harvard University Press, 1987.

Breazeale, Daniel. "Between Kant and Fichte: Karl Leonhard Reinhold's 'Elementary Philosophy.'" *Review of Metaphysics* 35 (1982): 785–821.

——————. "Fichte's *Aenesidemus* Review and the Transformation of German Idealism." *Review of Metaphysics* 34 (1981): 545–68.

Clark, Robert J. *Herder: His Life and Thought* Berkeley: University of California Press, 1969.

di Giovanni, George, and H. S. Harris, eds. and trans. *Between Kant and Hegel. Texts in the Development of Post-Kantian Idealism*. Albany: State University of New York Press, 1985.

Fichte, J. G. *Oeuvres Choisies de Philosophie Première*, trans. A. Philonenko, 2nd ed. Paris: Vrin, 1972.

Fuchs, Erich, ed. *J. G. Fichte im Gespräch: Berichte der Zeitgenossen*. 6 vols. Stuttgart-Bad Cannstatt: Frommann-Holzboog, 1978–92.

Herder, Johann Gottfried von. *Sämtliche Werke*. Ed. Heinrich Düntzer and Wollheim da Fonseca. Berlin: Hempel, 1869–79.

Jacobi, Friedrich Heinrich. *David Hume über den Glauben oder Idealismus und Realismus. Ein Gespräch* (orig. 1787). New York: Garland, 1983.

_____. "Open Letter to Fichte." Trans. Diana I. Behler. In *Philosophy of German Idealism*, ed. Ernst Behler, pp. 119–41. New York: Continuum, 1987.

_____. *Werke*. Ed. Friedrich Roth and Friedrich Köppen (orig. 1812ff.). Darmstadt: Wissenschaftliche Buchgesellschaft, 1976.

Kant, Immanuel. *Critique of Pure Reason*. Trans. Norman Kemp Smith. London: Macmillan, 1929.

_____. *Gesammelte Schriften*. Ed. Königliche Preußischen Akademie der Wissenschaften. Berlin: Walter de Gruyter, 1902 ff.

_____. *Kant: Philosophical Correspondence (1759–99)*. Ed. and trans. Arnulf Zweig. Chicago: University of Chicago Press, 1967.

_____. "On a Newly Arisen Superior Tone in Philosophy." Trans. Peter Fenves. In *Raising the Tone of Philosophy: Late Essays by Immanuel Kant, Transformative Critique by Jacques Derrida*, ed. Peter Fenves, pp. 51–81. Baltimore, Md. and London: Johns Hopkins University Press, 1993.

Lauth, Reinhard. *Die transzendentale Naturlehre Fichtes nach den Prinzipien der Wissenschaftslehre*. Hamburg: Felix Meiner, 1984.

Leibniz, Gottfried W. *The Monadology and Other Philosophical Writings*. Ed. and trans. Robert Latta. Oxford: Oxford University Press, 1898.

Lovejoy, Arthur O. "Kant's Antithesis of Dogmatism and Criticism." *Mind* 15 (1906): 191–214.

Maimon, Salomon. *Philosophisches Wörterbuch oder Beleuchtung der wichtigsten Gegenstände der Philosophie in alphabetischer Ordnung* (orig. 1791). Brussels: Culture et Civilisation, 1970.

_____. *Versuch einer neuen Logik oder Theorie des Denkens* (orig. 1794). Berlin: Reuther & Reichard, 1912.

Oesch, Martin, ed. *Aus der Frühzeit des deutschen Idealismus: Texte zur Wissenschaftslehre Fichtes 1794–1804*. Würzburg: Königshausen + Neumann, 1987.

Reinhold, Karl Leonard. *Auswahl vermischter Schriften*. Vol. 2. Jena: Mauke, 1797.

──────────. *Beyträge zur Berichtigung bisheriger Missverständnisse der Philosophen*, vol. 1. Jena: Mauke, 1790.

Richter, Jean Paul. *Jean Pauls Sämtliche Werke*. Vol. 9. Ed. Eduard Berend. Weimar: H. Böhlaus Nachfolger, 1933.

Schelling. F. W. J. *Ideas for a Philosophy of Nature*. Trans. Errol E. Harris and Peter Heath. New York: Cambridge University Press, 1988.

──────────. *Sämmtliche Werke*. Ed. K. F. A. Schelling. Stuttgart: J. G. Cotta, 1856–61.

──────────. *System of Transcendental Idealism (1800)*. Trans. Peter Heath. Charlottesville: University Press of Virginia, 1978.

──────────. *The Unconditional in Human Knowledge. Four Early Essays (1794–1796)*. Trans. Fritz Marti. Lewisburg, Pa.: Bucknell University Press, 1980.

Widmann, Joachim. "Exact Concepts: Fichte's Contribution on a Problem of Tomorrow." Trans. Joseph G. Naylor. *Idealistic Studies* 11 (1981): 41–48.

VII. Bibliographies

Baumgartner, Hans Michael, and Wilhelm G. Jacobs. *J. G. Fichte — Bibliographie*. Stuttgart–Bad Cannstatt: Frommann, 1968.

Breazeale, Daniel. "Bibliography [of English Translations of Fichte's Works and of Works in English about Fichte]." In *Fichte: Historical Contexts/Contemporary Controversies*, ed. Breazeale and Rockmore, pp. 235–63.

Doyé, Sabine, et al. *J. G. Fichte — Bibliographie (1969–1991)*. Amsterdam and Atlanta: Rodopi, 1994.

Key to Abbreviations and Symbols

BWL   *Ueber den Begriff der Wissenschaftslehre* (1794).

EPW   *Fichte: Early Philosophical Writings*. Ed. and trans. Daniel Breazeale. Ithaca, N.Y.: Cornell University Press, 1988.

GA   *J. G. Fichte: Gesamtausgabe der Bayerischen Akademie der Wissenschaften*. Ed. Reinhard Lauth, Hans Jacob, and Hans Gliwitzky. Stuttgart-Bad Cannstatt: Frommann, 1964—. (This definitive edition is published in four parts, each of which consists of many separate volumes. Cited by section, volume, and page number.)

GWL   J. G. Fichte. *Grundlage der gesamten Wissenschaftlehre* (1794/95).

KGS   *Kants gesammelte Schriften*. Ed. Königlich Preußischen Akademie der Wissenschaften. Berlin: Reimer/de Gruyter, 1902—. (Cited by volume and page number.)

KRV   Immanuel Kant. *Kritik der reinen Vernunft* (First ed. [A], 1781; second ed. [B], 1787).

SW   *Johann Gottlieb Fichtes sämmtliche Werke*. Ed. I. H. Fichte. Berlin: Veit, 1845–46. (Cited by volume and page number.)

WLnm   J. G. Fichte. *Wissenschaftslehre nova methodo* (1796/99). (Usually cited as K or H: K = the "Krause Nachschrift" of WLnm (1798/99): Johann Gottlieb Fichte. *Wissenschaftslehre nova methodo*. Kollegnachschrift K. Chr. Fr. Krause. Ed. Erich Fuchs. Hamburg: Meiner, 1982. H = the "Hallesche Nachschrift" of WLnm (1797/98?). In GA, IV,2.

[ ]   Everything within square brackets is added by the editor/translator.

*, †   Footnotes designated by asterisks or daggers are Fichte's own.

¹   Footnotes designated by a number are added by the editor/translator.

The numbers without parentheses in the margins refer to the page numbers of the German text as published in the appropriate volume of SW. Those within parentheses refer to the page numbers of the German text as published in the appropriate volume of GA.

1

An Attempt at a New Presentation

of the

Wissenschaftslehre

Published in four installments in the *Philosophisches Journal* 1797/98.

Preface

De re, quae agitur, petimus, ut homines eam non opinionem sed
opus esse cogitent, ac pro certo habeant, non sectae nos alicujus, aut
placiti; sed utilitatis et amplitudinis humanae fundamenta moliri.
Deinde ut suis commodis aequi, in commune consulant, et ipsi in
partem veniant.

— Baco de Verulamio[1]

A passing acquaintance with the philosophical literature that has appeared
since the publication of the Kantian *Critiques* quickly convinced the author

Fichte's *Versuch einer neuen Darstellung der Wissenschaftslehre* was first published,
in four installments, in the *Philosophisches Journal einer Gesellschaft Teutscher
Gelehrter*, of which Fichte and his colleague, F. I. Niethammer, were then co-
editors. The first installment, consisting of the "Vorerinnerung" and "[Erste]
Einleitung," was published in vol. V, no. 1 (first, defective printing [by Späth], end
of February 1797; second, corrected and slightly revised version [by Gabler], end
of March 1797). All philosophically significant differences between the first and
second printings are indicated in the notes. The second installment, consisting of
§§ 1–6 of the "Zweite Einleitung," was published in vol. V, no. 4 (which appeared
in August of 1797); the third installment, consisting of §§ 7–12 of the "Zweite
Einleitung," in vol. VI, no. 1 (November 1797); and the final installment, consisting of the "Erste Capitel," in vol. VII, no. 1 (March 1798).

The numbers without parentheses in the margins of this translation are the page
numbers of the German text of *Versuch einer neuen Darstellung der Wissenschafts-
lehre*, as published in vol. I of Fichte's *Sämmtliche Werke*, ed. I. H. Fichte (Berlin:
Veit & Comp., 1845/46) [henceforth = SW], pp. 419–518. Those within parenthe-
ses provide the pagination of the critical edition of the same text, as contained in
Series I, Volume 4 of *J. G. Fichte — Gesamtausgabe der Bayerischen Akademie der
Wissenschaften*, ed. Reinhard Lauth and Hans Gliwitzky (Stuttgart–Bad Cannstatt:
Friedrich Frommann, 1964 ff.) [henceforth = GA], pp. 183–281.

1. "In behalf of the business which is at hand I entreat men to believe that it is not
an opinion to be held, but a work to be done; and to be well assured that I am
laboring to lay the foundation, not of any sect or doctrine, but of human utility and
power. Next, I ask them to deal fairly by their own interests, [. . .] to join in
consultation for the common good; and [. . .] to come forward themselves and
take part in that which remains to be done." Francis Bacon, *Instauratio magna*
(1620), p. 12. English translation by James Spedding and Robert Leslie Ellis.

Note that this is the same passage from the Preface to Bacon's *Great Instauration*

[handwritten marginalia: misconstrue of Kant's problem]

of the *Wissenschaftslehre*[2] that this great man's intention of fundamentally revising the way in which our age thinks about philosophy and about science as a whole has miscarried completely, inasmuch as not one of his many followers seems to have noticed what Kant is really talking about. Believing himself to possess such knowledge, the author resolved to dedicate his life to presenting this great discovery in a manner entirely independent of Kant, and this is a decision he will never renounce. Time alone will tell whether or not he has been any more successful in making himself understood by his contemporaries. In any event, he knows that nothing true and useful that appears among human beings is ever really lost, though it may be that only a distant posterity will know how to make use of it.

In accordance with my profession as a teacher, I first prepared a text for the use of students attending my lectures, where I was able to continue with oral explanations until I had succeeded in making myself understood.

This is not an appropriate place to testify to the many reasons I have for being satisfied with my students and for cherishing the highest hopes con-

420
(184)

---

that Kant employed as the motto for the second edition of his *Kritik der reinen Vernunft* [henceforth = KRV]. See KRV, Bii. (As is customary, the *Critique of Pure Reason* is here cited throughout according to the pagination of both the first, 1781 edition [= A] and the second, 1787 edition [= B]. Fichte himself possessed and quoted from the third, 1790 edition, which is virtually identical to the second edition.) As Peter Baumanns has noted in his edition of the *Versuch einer neuen Darstellung der Wissenschaftslehre* (Hamburg: Meiner, 1975), the fact that the above citation from Bacon contains the same ellipses as Kant's suggests that Fichte took it directly from Kant.

2. *Wissenschaftslehre* ("Doctrine of Science" or "Theory of Scientific Knowledge") was Fichte's name for his entire system of philosophy and is not the name of any particular book. The general concept of such a system was first outlined in a short work entitled *Ueber den Begriff der Wissenschaftslehre* [hereafter = BWL] which Fichte published in 1794. (See SW, I, pp. 27–82 = GA, I,2: 107–63.) An English translation of *Concerning the Concept of the Wissenschaftslehre* by Daniel Breazeale may be found on pp. 94-135 of *Fichte: Early Philosophical Writings* (Ithaca, N.Y. and London: Cornell University Press, 1988) [henceforth = EPW].) The "first principles" of Fichte's new system were first presented and systematically developed in a work entitled *Grundlage der gesamten Wissenschaftslehre* (*Foundations of the Entire Wissenschaftslehre*) [henceforth = GWL], which Fichte first issued in installments in 1794/95. (In SW, I, pp. 83–328 = GA, I,2: 251–451; translated into English by Peter Heath as *Foundations of the Entire Science of Knowledge*, in J. G. Fichte, *Science of Knowledge* [Cambridge: Cambridge University Press, 1982].)

cerning the contributions I expect many of them to make to science. This same text[3] also became known outside of my lecture hall, and a wide variety of notions concerning this book have become current among scholars. Except from my own students, I have yet to read or to hear a single judgment of this work which even professes to be based upon any argument. To be sure, I have encountered plenty of ridicule and vituperation, as well as universal testimony to people's heartfelt aversion to this theory and to their failure to understand it. I am willing to bear all of the blame for the latter, until such time as people have had an opportunity to become familiar with the contents of my system in some other form, in which case they may find that the original presentation is not so totally inaccessible after all. Alternately, I will unconditionally and forever assume complete responsibility for this previous lack of understanding if by doing so I can entice the reader to give his attention to this new presentation, in which I shall take the utmost pains to achieve the greatest possible clarity. I will continue this presentation until I am convinced that I write entirely in vain. But I shall be writing in vain so long as no one cares to examine my arguments and reasons.

I still owe the reader the following remarks: I have always said, and here I repeat, that my system is none other than the Kantian system. I.e., it contains the same view of the subject, though it proceeds in a manner that is entirely independent of Kant's presentation. I have not said this in order to take upon myself the mantle of a great authority nor in order to obtain some sort of external support for my own theory, but merely in order to tell the truth and to render justice where it is due.

One might think that after the passage of almost twenty years it would be possible to prove this claim. With the exception, however, of a single recent hint,[4] which I shall discuss below, Kant has remained a closed book. Indeed, what people have purported to find in Kant's writings is the very thing that cannot be reconciled with them and that Kant himself wished to refute.

421   My writings are not meant to explain Kant's nor are they intended to be explained by his writings. They must stand on their own without any reference whatsoever to Kant. To state my own position as plainly as possible: I am not concerned to rectify nor to bring to completion any set of philo-

3. Viz., *The Foundations of the Entire Wissenschaftslehre* (GWL).

4. This is an allusion to J. S. Beck, whose interpretation of Kantianism is discussed and criticized below, in § 7 of the First Introduction and in § 6 of the Second Introduction.

sophical concepts that may already be in circulation — be they "anti-Kantian" or "Kantian." Instead, I desire to uproot current conceptions completely and to accomplish a complete revolution in the way we think about these issues, so that — in all seriousness and not simply as a figure of speech — the object will be posited and determined by our power of cognition,[5] and not vice versa. Accordingly, my system can be evaluated only *(185)* on its own terms and cannot be judged by the principles of any other philosophy. It only has to agree with itself. It can be explained only by itself, and it can be proven — or refuted — only on its own terms. One must either accept it completely or reject it in its entirety.

"If this system were true, then certain other propositions could not continue to be affirmed!" This objection amounts to nothing at all; for, in my opinion, no proposition whatsoever that is refuted by this system should continue to be affirmed.

"I do not understand this text!" To me, this means no more than what it says, and I consider such an admission to be supremely uninteresting and uninformative. No one can understand my writings, nor should anyone be able to understand them, without first having studied them. For, since Kant was not understood, my writings do not repeat any lesson that has already been conveyed somewhere else; instead, they contain something that is completely new to the present age.

Baseless criticism merely indicates to me that someone does not care for my theory; and again, such an admission is of the greatest insignificance. The question is by no means whether you care for this theory or not, but rather, whether or not it has been proven. In order to facilitate an examination of the foundations of this system, I intend, in this new presentation, to indicate every point at which this system must be attacked. I write only for readers who continue to harbor an inner[6] sense for the certainty or the dubitability, the clarity or the confusion, of their own cognition. I write for *422* readers for whom science and conviction still retain some meaning and who are themselves driven by a lively zeal to seek the same. I wish to have nothing to do with those who, as a result of protracted spiritual servitude, have lost their own selves and, along with this loss of themselves, have lost any feeling for their own conviction, as well as any belief in the conviction

5. "das ErkenntnißVermögen." Fichte follows Kant and Reinhold in using the term *Vermögen* (here translated as "power") to refer to each of the mind's various "capacities" or "faculties."

6. First printing has *immer* instead of *innerer*, which would make this clause read: "who still harbor a sense for the certainty [. . .]."

of others. To those for whom it is simply folly for anyone to seek truth on his own, for those who see in the sciences nothing but a comfortable livelihood, who shrink from any extension of the same, as from a new job, and for whom no means is shameful so long as it is employed in order to silence the person who disrupts their business as usual: to them I have nothing to say.

I would be sorry if I were understood by people of this sort. To date, this wish has been fulfilled so far as they are concerned; and I hope that, in the present case as well, these prefatory remarks will so confuse them that, from now on, they will be unable to see anything beyond the mere letters, inasmuch as what passes for spirit in their case will be yanked back and forth by the secret fury pent up within them.

[First]
Introduction

1.

Attend to yourself; turn your gaze from everything surrounding you and look within yourself: this is the first demand philosophy makes upon anyone who studies it. Here you will not be concerned with anything that lies outside of you, but only with yourself.

Even on the most cursory self-observation, everyone will perceive a remarkable difference between the various ways in which his consciousness is immediately determined, and one could call these immediate determinations of consciousness "representations."[1] Some of these determinations appear to us to depend entirely upon our own freedom, and it is impossible for us to believe that anything outside of us, i.e., something that exists independently of our own efforts, corresponds to representations of this sort. Our imagination and our will appear to us to be free. We also possess representations of another sort. We refer representations of this second type to a truth that is supposed to be firmly established independently of us and is supposed to serve as the model for these representa-

1. *Vorstellungen.* Throughout this translation, the noun *Vorstellung* is translated as "representation" whenever it occurs in an even vaguely technical context. In many ordinary expressions, however, the word has no special technical meaning at all, but is merely a vague term designating whatever one "has in mind," similar to the informal sense of words like "notion" and "idea" in contemporary English usage. Fichte's technical employment of this term is derived from Kant and Reinhold, for whom it is the most general term that can be employed to designate all the objects of our consciousness (viz., "intuitions," "concepts," "Ideas," etc.) *as* objects of consciousness. A "representation" is, quite literally, whatever is *vorgestellt*, or "placed before," the mind. It is important to remember that "representations" need not be thought of as copying (or "representing") anything outside of themselves, though this is certainly the way in which they are frequently thought of within ordinary consciousness. (In this technical sense, "representation" plays a role in the writings of the early transcendental idealists similar to that played by the term "idea" in the writings of Descartes, Locke, Leibniz, and Berkeley and the expression "perceptions of the mind" in the writings of Hume.) Similarly, the verb *vorstellen*, which is here somewhat awkwardly rendered as "to represent" or "to entertain representations," is the term that designates the activity of representing.

tions. When a representation of ours is supposed to correspond to this truth, we discover that we are constrained in determining this representation. In the case of cognition, we do not consider ourselves to be free with respect to the content of our cognitions. In short, we could say that some of our representations are accompanied by a feeling of freedom and others are accompanied by a feeling of necessity.

We cannot reasonably ask why the representations that depend upon our freedom are determined in just the way they are determined and not in some other way. For when we posit them to be dependent upon freedom, we deny that the concept of a "basis" (or "foundation" or "reason" or "ground")[2] has any applicability in this case. These representations are what they are for the simple reason that I have determined them to be like this. If I had determined them differently, then they would be different.

But what is the basis of the system of those representations accompanied by a feeling of necessity, and what is the basis of this feeling of necessity itself? This is a question well worth pondering. It is the task of philosophy to answer this question; indeed, to my mind, nothing is philosophy except that science that discharges this task. Another name for the system of representations accompanied by a feeling of necessity is "experience" — whether inner or outer. We thus could express the task of philosophy in different words as follows: Philosophy has to display the basis or foundation of all experience.

Only three objections can be raised against this conception of philosophy's task. On the one hand, one might deny that consciousness contains any representations that are accompanied by a feeling of necessity and that refer to a truth determined without any help from us. A person who denies this would either do so against his own better knowledge, or else he would have to be constituted differently than other human beings. If so, then in this case nothing would exist for him which he could deny, and thus there would be no denial. Consequently, we could dismiss his objection without any further ado. Or else, someone might contend that the question we have raised is completely unanswerable and that we are and must remain in a state of invincible ignorance on this point. It is superfluous to engage in reasoned debate with someone who makes this objection. The best way to refute him is by actually answering the question, in which case there will be nothing left for him to do but to examine our effort and to indicate where and why it seems to him to be insufficient. Finally, someone might lay a rival claim to the name "philosophy" and maintain

424
(187)

2. "des Begriffs vom Grunde." The term *Grund* is variously translated here as "foundation," "ground," "basis," and "reason."

that philosophy is something completely different or something more than what we have claimed. It would be easy to prove to anyone who raises this objection that this is precisely what all of the experts have at all times considered philosophy to be, that all the other things he might like to pass off as philosophy already possess other names of their own, and therefore, that if the word "philosophy" is to have any definite meaning at all, it has to designate precisely the science we have indicated.

We have no desire, however, to engage in a fruitless dispute over a word; and this is why we have long ceased to lay any claim to the name "philosophy" and have given the name *Wissenschaftslehre*, or "Theory of Scientific Knowledge," to the science that actually has to carry out the task indicated.

2.

One can ask for a basis or foundation only in the case of something one judges to be contingent, i.e., only if one presupposes that the thing in question could also have been different from the way it is, even though it is not something determined by freedom. Indeed, something becomes contingent for someone precisely insofar as he inquires concerning its basis. To seek a basis or reason for something contingent, one has to look toward something else, something determinate, whose determinacy explains why what is based upon it is determined in precisely the way it is and not in any of the many other ways in which it could have been determined. It follows from the mere thought of a basis or reason that it must lie outside of what it grounds or explains. The basis of an explanation and what is explained thereby thus become posited — as such — in opposition to one another,   *425* and are related to one another in such a way that the former explains the latter.

Philosophy has to display the basis or foundation of all experience. Consequently, philosophy's object must necessarily lie *outside of all expe- rience*. This is a principle that is supposed to be true of all philosophy, and it really has applied to all philosophy produced right up to the era of the Kantians, with their "facts of consciousness" and hence of "inner experi- ence.[3]

---

3. It is not Kant himself whom Fichte has in mind in this passage. This is, in- stead, a reference to the attempt by certain contemporary followers of Kant (whom Fichte often refers to as "so-called Kantians") to base philosophy solely on the "facts of consciousness" or "facts of (inner) experience." The first to propose this

No objection to its principle

(188)   No objection whatsoever can be made to the principle just advanced,
for the premise of our argument is derived simply from an analysis of the
F *Refers*
to Objection
3 or p.8-9
previously stipulated concept of philosophy, and our conclusion is merely
inferred from this premise. Naturally, we cannot prevent anyone who
wishes to do so from maintaining that the concept of a basis or foundation
has to be explicated in some other way, nor can we prevent him from employing this term to designate whatever he wishes. We, however, are fully
entitled to declare that we do not wish the preceding description of "philosophy" to be understood to include anything except what *we* have stated.
Accordingly, if one does not wish to accept this definition of philosophy,
then one has to deny the very possibility of philosophy in the sense we have
indicated, and we have already taken this objection into account.

3.

Finite rational being

A finite rational being possesses nothing whatsoever beyond experience.
The entire contents of his thinking are comprised within experience.
These same conditions necessarily apply to the philosopher, and thus it

---

strategy was Fichte's immediate predecessor at Jena, Karl Leonhard Reinhold
(1758–1823), who claimed to base his entire, systematic revision of Kant's Critical
philosophy on a single first principle ("the principle of consciousness"), a principle
he described as no more than an expression of an "immediate fact of consciousness." Reinhold first outlined his own "Elementary Philosophy" or "Philosophy of
the Elements" in his *Versuch einer neuen Theorie des menschlichen Vorstellungsvermögens* (1789) and then elaborated and revised it in two subsequent works:
Beyträge zur Berichtigung bisheriger Missverständnisse der Philosophen, vol. I (1790)
and *Ueber das Fundament des philosophischen Wissens* (1794). (A substantial excerpt
from the latter is translated by George di Giovanni as *The Foundations of Philosophical Knowledge*, in *Between Kant and Hegel: Texts in the Development of Post-
Kantian Idealism*, ed. George di Giovanni and H. S. Harris [Albany, N.Y.: State
University of New York Press, 1985], pp. 52–103.) For discussion of Reinhold's
crucial role in the development of transcendental idealism, see ch. 8 of Frederick C.
Beiser, *The Fate of Reason: German Philosophy from Kant to Fichte* (Cambridge:
Harvard University Press, 1987); and Daniel Breazeale, "Between Kant and
Fichte: Karl Leonhard Reinhold's 'Elementary Philosophy,'" *Review of Metaphys-
ics* 35 (1982): 785–821. For Fichte's critique of Reinhold's project, see his 1794
review of *Aenesidemus* (translated in EPW), as well as the illuminating letters from
Fichte to Reinhold (also translated in EPW).
     Another notable attempt to base philosophy on the "facts of consciousness" was
made by Fichte's colleague (and professional rival) at Jena, K. C. E. Schmid (1761–

appears incomprehensible how he could ever succeed in elevating himself
above experience.

The philosopher, however, is able to engage in abstraction. That is to
say, by means of a free act of thinking he is able to separate things that are
connected with each other within experience. The *thing*, i.e., a determinate
something that exists independently of our freedom and to which our cognition is supposed to be directed, and the *intellect*, i.e., the subject that is
supposed to be engaged in this activity of cognizing, are inseparably connected with each other within experience. The philosopher is able to abstract from either one of these, and when he does so he has abstracted from
experience and has thereby succeeded in elevating himself above experience. If he abstracts from the thing, then he is left with an intellect in itself   *426*
as the explanatory ground of experience; that is to say, he is left with the
intellect in abstraction from its relationship to experience. If he abstracts
from the intellect, then he is left with a thing in itself (that is, in abstraction
from the fact that it occurs within experience) as the explanatory ground of
experience. The first way of proceeding is called *idealism*; the second is
called *dogmatism*.[4]

As one will surely become convinced by the present account, these two
philosophical systems are the only ones possible. According to the former
system, the representations accompanied by a feeling of necessity are prod-
ucts of the intellect, which is what this system presupposes in order to
explain experience. According to the latter, dogmatic system, such representations are a product of the thing in itself, which is what this system
presupposes.

Anyone who wishes to dispute the claim that these two systems are the
only ones possible either must prove that there is some other way to elevate
oneself above experience except by means of abstraction, or else he must
prove that consciousness of experience contains some additional compo-   *(189)*
nent beyond the two already mentioned.

Regarding the first system, it will indeed become clear later on that
what is called "the intellect" is actually present within consciousness, al-

---

1812). For a detailed account of Schmid's variety of Kantianism and an even more
detailed statement of Fichte's objections to it, see the brilliant polemical essay of
1795, "Vergleich des von Herrn Prof. Schmid aufgestellten Systems mit der
Wissenschaftslehre." (In SW, II, pp. 420–58 = GA, I,3: 235–66; English translation
in EPW, pp. 316–35.)

4. For Fichte's use of these terms and the relation of the same to previous discussions by Kant and Schelling, see the editor's introduction.

beit under another designation, and is not, therefore, something produced purely by means of abstraction. We will also see, however, that our consciousness of the latter is conditioned by an act of abstraction, albeit one quite natural to human beings.

This is by no means to deny that it might very well be possible to construct a whole by fusing together fragments from each of these two very different systems. Nor would we deny that people have, in fact, very often engaged in just such an inconsistent enterprise. We do, however, deny that any system other than these two is possible so long as one proceeds consistently.

4.

427

We will employ the term "object of philosophy" to designate the explanatory ground or foundation a particular philosophy proposes to employ in order to account for experience, for such an "object" appears to exist only by means of and only for the philosophy that proposes it. With respect to their relationship to consciousness as a whole, there is a remarkable difference between the object of *idealism* and the object of *dogmatism*. Everything of which I am conscious is called an "object of consciousness." Such an object can be related to the representing subject in three different ways: It either appears to be something first produced by means of the intellect's representation of it, or else it appears to be something present without any help from the intellect. In the latter case, either the properties of this object appear to be determined along with the object itself, or else what is supposed to be present is the mere existence of the object, while its properties are determinable by the free intellect.

The first relationship between the object of consciousness and the representing subject gives us a purely "made up" or invented object — whether invented for any particular purpose or not. The second furnishes us with an object of experience. The third provides us with a unique type of object [viz., the I], the nature of which we wish to establish at once.

I can freely determine myself to think of this thing or that — of the dogmatist's "thing in itself," for example. If I now abstract from whatever it is I am thinking of and attend only to myself, then I myself become, in this object, the object of a determinate representation.[5] In my judgment, it

5. "so werde ich mir selbst in diesem Gegenstande das Object einer bestimmten Vorstellung." The German words *Gegenstand* and *Object* are both rendered here as "object." As a general rule, Fichte employs the latter term in more abstract contexts, such as the preceding discussion of the "object of philosophy," and limits the

is because of my own act of self-determination that I appear to myself in just this determinate manner and am not determined in some other way. In the present case, therefore, it is only because I have determined myself in precisely this way that I appear to myself to be engaged in thinking at all; and this is also the reason why, of all the possible thoughts I could be thinking, I am thinking precisely of the thing in itself. I have freely made myself into such an object. I have not, however, made myself "in itself"; instead, I am required to think of myself as what precedes and is to be determined by an act of self-determination.[6] I am, accordingly, an object for myself, an object whose properties, under certain conditions, depend upon the intellect alone, but whose existence must always be presupposed.

(190)

The object of idealism is precisely this I in itself.* The object of this system, moreover, actually appears within consciousness as something real, although not as a *thing in itself*; for were the I to appear within consciousness as a thing in itself, then idealism would cease to be what it is and would be transformed into dogmatism. Instead, the object of idealism appears within consciousness as an *I in itself*. It does not appear there as an object of experience, for it is nothing determinate, but is determined solely by me, and without this determination it is nothing whatsoever and does not exist at all. Instead, it appears within consciousness as something elevated above all experience.

428

In contrast, the object of dogmatism belongs to the class of those objects produced only by means of free thinking. The thing in itself is a pure invention which possesses no reality whatsoever. It certainly does not appear within experience. For the system of experience is nothing but thinking accompanied by a feeling of necessity, and not even the dogmatist, who, like every other philosopher, has the task of providing this system of experience with a foundation, can pretend that it is anything else. To be sure, the dogmatist wishes to guarantee the reality of this thing in itself; that is to say, he wants to establish the necessity of thinking of it as the basis

---

former to more concrete cases of "objects of experience" (*Gegenstände* — those things which appear to "stand over against" consciousness and to limit practical action). Fichte does not, however, adhere in any rigorous fashion to this terminological distinction.

6. "ich bin genöthigt, mich als das zu bestimmende der Selbstbestimmung voraus zu denken."

* I have hitherto avoided this expression in order not to occasion any representation of an I as a thing in itself. My concern was in vain; consequently, I will now employ this expression, because I do not see whom I have to spare.

or foundation of all experience. And he will have succeeded in doing just this if he can show that experience is really explained thereby and that it cannot be explained without thinking of this thing in itself. But this is precisely the point in question here, and one may not presuppose what has to be proven.

The object of idealism has an advantage, therefore, over that of dogmatism, for the former can be shown to be present within consciousness — not, to be sure, as the explanatory ground of experience, for this would be contradictory and would transform this system itself into a portion of experience; yet it can still be shown to be present, as such, within consciousness. In contrast, the object of dogmatism cannot be considered to be anything but a pure invention, which can be made into something real only by the success of this system.

The above remarks were added merely for the purpose of facilitating a clear understanding of the differences between the two systems and were not meant to imply anything against the latter system. It should by no means be held against a philosophical system that its object, considered as the explanatory ground of experience, must lie beyond experience; for this is true of every philosophy and is required by the very nature of philosophy itself. Nor have we yet encountered any reason why this object should, in addition to this, appear within consciousness in a particular manner.

Should anyone find these remarks to be unconvincing, this does not mean that it will be impossible for him to become convinced by our inquiry as a whole, for these are merely incidental remarks. Nevertheless, in keeping with my intention, I wish to take various possible objections into account here as well. Someone might deny, for example, that any immediate self-consciousness is involved in a free action of the mind. Once again, all we would have to do is to remind such a person of what we said above about the conditions under which such immediate self-consciousness is possible. Such self-consciousness does not impose itself upon anyone, and it does not simply occur without any assistance from us.[7] One must actually act in a free manner, and then one must abstract from the object and attend only to oneself. No one can be forced to do this. And if someone pretends to act in this manner, no one else can ever know whether he is proceeding correctly and in the manner requested. In a word: this type of consciousness cannot be proven to anyone. Everyone must freely generate it within himself. One could object to our second claim (viz., that the thing in itself is a

(margin handwritten note: Explanatory ground of exp. lies outside exp.)

_429_
_(191)_

7. "kommt nicht von selbst." I.e., self-consciousness, unlike our consciousness of objects, does not come before us on its own; it has to be produced. In order to be self-conscious we have to *do* something.

mere invention) only if one has misunderstood it. We would refer anyone
who raises such an objection to our earlier description of how this concept
is produced.

5.

Neither of these two systems can directly refute the opposing one; for the
dispute between them is a dispute concerning the first principle, i.e., concerning a principle that cannot be derived from any higher principle. If the
first principle of either system is conceded, then it is able to refute the first
principle of the other. Each denies everything included within the opposite system. They do not have a single point in common on the basis of
which they might be able to achieve mutual understanding and be united
with one another. Even when they appear to be in agreement concerning
the words of some proposition, they understand these same words to mean
two different things.*

    To begin with, idealism is unable to refute dogmatism. As we have al-
ready seen, the former does indeed have an advantage over the latter, in
that it is able to exhibit the presence within consciousness of the foundation
it wishes to employ in its explanation of experience, viz., the freely acting
intellect. Even the dogmatist must concede this fact, as such, for otherwise
he would render himself incapable of any further discussion with the idealist. By means of a correct inference from his own first principle, however,
the dogmatist transforms this fact into an illusion and a deception and

430
(192)

---

* This is why Kant was not understood and why the *Wissenschaftslehre* has found
no acceptance and is unlikely to find such acceptance anytime soon. Kant's system
and the *Wissenschaftslehre* are both *idealistic*, not in the ordinary, imprecise sense of
the term, but in the precise sense just indicated. Modern philosophers, however,
are as a whole *dogmatists* and are firmly resolved to remain so. The only reason that
they put up with Kant at all is that it was possible to make him out to be a dogmatist.
But these same sages necessarily find the *Wissenschaftslehre* to be unbearable, because it cannot be transformed in this way. The rapid diffusion of the Kantian
philosophy just as soon as it became interpreted in the [dogmatic] manner in which
it is now interpreted is no proof of the profundity of our age; on the contrary, it
testifies to the superficiality of the same. This form of "Kantianism" is the most
fantastic monster that human fantasy has ever engendered, and it does little credit
to the perspicuity of its defenders that they fail to realize this. Furthermore, it can
be easily proven that the only thing that recommends this philosophy is that it
allows people to dispense with all serious speculation and allows them to believe
that they have been granted a royal patent authorizing them to continue cultivating
their beloved and superficial empiricism.

thereby renders it incapable of serving as a basis for explaining anything else; for, within the context of the dogmatist's philosophy, this "fact" is not able to vouch for its own truth. According to the dogmatist, everything that occurs within consciousness is a product of a thing in itself, and therefore this must also be true of those determinations of our consciousness which are allegedly produced by freedom, as well as of our opinion that we are free. This opinion is produced within us by the efficacious action of some thing, and those determinations we think of as derived from our own freedom are also produced in this way. We do not realize this, however, and this is why we ascribe no cause to such determinations and attribute them, instead, to freedom. Every consistent dogmatist must necessarily be a fatalist. He does not deny, as a fact of consciousness, that we consider ourselves to be free; indeed, it would be quite unreasonable to deny this. Instead, he uses his own principle to prove the falsity of this claim. He entirely rejects

431   the self-sufficiency of the I, which the idealist takes as his fundamental explanatory ground, and he treats the I merely as a product of things, i.e., as an accidental feature of the world. A consistent dogmatist is also necessarily a materialist. He can be refuted only by postulating the freedom and self-sufficiency of the I. But this is precisely what he denies.

The dogmatist is equally incapable of refuting the idealist.

The dogmatist's principle, viz., the thing in itself, is nothing and, as even its exponent must concede, has no reality beyond that reality it is supposed to obtain by serving as the sole foundation for an explanation of experience. But the idealist undermines this proof to the extent that he is able to account for experience in a different way. In doing this, the idealist denies the very basis upon which the dogmatist proposes to erect his own

(193)   account of experience. The thing in itself thus becomes a complete chimera, and no further reason is evident why anyone should ever assume that a thing in itself exists at all. With this, the entire edifice of dogmatism comes crashing to the ground.

The absolute incompatibility of these two systems follows from what has already been said, for the implications of each nullify those of the other. Thus any system that tries to combine elements of both is necessarily inconsistent. Whenever this is attempted, the various components will not fit together, and at some point there arises an enormous gap. Anyone who wishes to challenge this claim must establish the possibility of such a combination, a combination that presupposes[8] a continuous transition from matter to mind or vice versa, or (what amounts to the same thing) a con-

---

8. Reading, with the text of the original edition and with GA, "zur Freiheit, voraussetzt, müßte" for SW's "zur Freiheit, müsste."

tinuous transition from necessity to freedom.

So far as we can see at this point, both of these systems appear to have the same speculative value, and yet they can neither co-exist with nor do anything to refute each other. Thus it is interesting to ask what might motivate anyone who understands this situation — and it is not at all difficult to understand — to prefer one of these systems to the other. Why does skepticism, i.e., the complete abandonment of any attempt to answer the question concerning the foundation of experience, not become universal? *432*

The dispute between the idealist and the dogmatist is actually a dispute over whether the self-sufficiency of the I should be sacrificed to that of the thing, or conversely, whether the self-sufficiency of the thing should be sacrificed to that of the I. What, therefore, could drive a rational person to declare himself in favor of either one of these two systems?

If a philosopher is to be considered a philosopher at all, he must necessarily occupy a certain standpoint, a standpoint that will sooner or later be attained in the course of human thinking, even if this occurs without any conscious effort on one's own part. When a philosopher considers things from this standpoint, all he discovers is that *he must entertain representations* both of himself as free and of determinate things external to himself.[9] It is impossible for a person simply to remain at this level of thinking. The thought of a mere representation is only half a thought, a broken fragment of a thought. We must also think of something else as well, namely, of something that corresponds to this representation and exists independently of the act of representing. In other words, a representation cannot subsist simply for itself and purely on its own. It is something only in conjunction with something else; by itself, it is nothing. It is precisely the necessity of thinking in this way that drives us from our initial standpoint and makes us ask: What is the basis of representations? Or, what amounts to exactly the same question: What corresponds to representations? *(194)*

The representation of the self-sufficiency of the I can certainly co-exist with a representation of the self-sufficiency of the thing, though the self-sufficiency of the I itself cannot co-exist with that of the thing. Only one of these two can come first; only one can be the starting point; only one can be independent. The one that comes second, just because it comes second, necessarily becomes dependent upon the one that comes first, with which it is supposed to be connected.

9. "*als daß er sich vorstellen müsse*, er sey frei, und es seyen außer ihm bestimmte Dinge." More freely: "he finds *that he must think* that he is free and that there are determinate things outside of him."

Which of these two should come first? This is not a question that can be decided simply by consulting reason alone. For what we are concerned with here is not how some member is to be connected to a series (which is the only sort of question that can be decided on the basis of rational grounds), but rather, with the act of beginning the entire series;[10] and since this act is absolutely primary, it can depend upon nothing but the freedom of thinking. Consequently, the decision between these two systems is one that is determined by free choice; and thus, since even a free decision is supposed to have some basis, it is a decision determined by *inclination* and *interest*. What ultimately distinguishes the idealist from the dogmatist is, accordingly, a difference of interest.

One's supreme interest and the foundation of all one's other interests is one's *interest in oneself*. This is just as true of a philosopher as it is of anyone else. The interest that invisibly guides all of his thinking is this: to avoid losing himself in argumentation, and instead to preserve and to affirm himself therein. But there are two different levels of human development, and, so long as everyone has not yet reached the highest level in the course of the progress of our species, there are two main sub-species of human beings. Some people — namely, those who have not yet attained a full feeling of their own freedom and absolute self-sufficiency — discover themselves only in the act of representing things. Their self-consciousness is dispersed and attached to objects and must be gleaned from the manifold of the latter. They glimpse their own image only insofar as it is reflected through things, as in a mirror. If they were to be deprived of these things, then they would lose themselves at the same time. Thus, for the sake of their own selves, they cannot renounce their belief in the self-sufficiency of things; for they themselves continue to exist only in conjunction with these things. It is really through the external world that they have become everything they are, and a person who is in fact nothing but a product of things will never be able to view himself in any other way. He will, furthermore, be correct — so long as he speaks only of himself and of those who are like him in this respect. The dogmatist's principle is belief in things for the sake of himself. Thus he possesses only an indirect or mediated belief in his own dispersed self, which is conveyed to him only by objects.

Anyone, however, who is conscious of his own self-sufficiency and independence from everything outside of himself — a consciousness that can be obtained only by making something of oneself on one's own and

10. Reading, with the text of the original edition and with GA, "von dem Anfangen der ganzen Reihe" for SW's "von dem Anfange der ganzen Reihe" ("with the beginning of the entire series").

independently of everything else — will not require things in order to support his self, nor can he employ them for this purpose, for they abolish his self-sufficiency and transform it into a mere illusion. The I that he possesses and that interests him cancels this type of belief in things. His belief in his own self-sufficiency is based upon inclination, and it is with passion that he shoulders his own self-sufficiency. His belief in himself is immediate.

434

(195)

This interest also permits us to understand why the defense of a philosophical system is customarily accompanied by a certain amount of passion. When the dogmatist's system is attacked he is in real danger of losing his own self. Yet he is not well prepared to defend himself against such attacks, for there is something within his own inner self which agrees with his assailant. This is why he defends himself with so much vehemence and bitterness. The idealist, in contrast, is quite unable to prevent himself from looking down upon the dogmatist with a certain amount of disrespect, since the dogmatist cannot say anything to him which he himself has not long since known and already rejected as erroneous. For one becomes an idealist only by passing through a disposition toward dogmatism — if not by passing through dogmatism itself.[11] Confounded, the dogmatist grows angry and, if it were only in his power to do so, would prosecute; while the

---

11. The autobiographical pathos of this observation is apparent from the following passage from Fichte's November 1790 draft of a letter to his friend H. N. Achelis in which he announces his rejection of metaphysical determinism (viz., "dogmatism") and espousal of a Kantian philosophy of freedom (viz., "idealism"):

"The influence that this philosophy, especially its moral part (though this is unintelligible apart from a study of the *Critique of Pure Reason*), exercises upon one's entire way of thinking is unbelievable — as is the revolution that it has occasioned in my own way of thinking in particular. I particularly owe it to you to confess that I now believe wholeheartedly in human freedom and realize full well that duty, virtue, and morality are all possible only if freedom is presupposed. I realized this truth very well before — perhaps I said as much to you — but I felt that the entire sequence of my inferences forced me to reject morality. It has, in addition, become quite obvious to me that very harmful consequences for society follow from the assumption that all human actions occur necessarily. [. . . .] If I have the time and the leisure, I will devote them for the present entirely to the Kantian philosophy. It would perhaps be of benefit to the world forcefully and vividly to urge Kant's first principles of morality upon the public in a popular presentation. This is a merit I would like to acquire for myself, especially in order to compensate for my having spread false first principles."

See too the even earlier remarks on this same subject in Fichte's August/September 1790 letter to F. A. Weisshuhn. (Both of these letters are translated in full in EPW.)

idealist remains cool and is in danger of ridiculing the dogmatist.

The kind of philosophy one chooses thus depends upon the kind of person one is. For a philosophical system is not a lifeless household item one can put aside or pick up as one wishes; instead, it is animated by the very soul of the person who adopts it. Someone whose character is naturally slack or who has been enervated and twisted by spiritual servitude, scholarly self-indulgence, and vanity will never be able to raise himself to the level of idealism.

As we will show in a moment, one can point out to the dogmatist the inadequacy and inconsistency of his system; one can confuse and worry him on every side; but one cannot convince him, for he is incapable of calmly and coolly listening to and evaluating a theory that he finds to be simply 435 unendurable. If idealism should prove to be the only true philosophy, then from this it would follow that in order to philosophize one must be born a philosopher, must be reared as a philosopher, and must educate oneself as a philosopher. But no application of human art or skill can make one into a philosopher. This science, therefore, does not expect to make many converts among people who are *already firmly set in their ways*. If it may entertain any hopes at all in this regard, these are pinned on the young, whose innate energy has not yet been ruined by the slackness of the present age.

6.

Dogmatism, however, is quite unable to explain what it is supposed to explain, and this demonstrates its inadequacy.

(196)   Dogmatism is supposed to explain representations, and it tries to make a particular representation comprehensible on the basis of an efficacious action of the thing in itself. The dogmatist, however, is not permitted to deny the testimony of immediate consciousness regarding representations. — What is this testimony? In answering this question, it is not my intention to attempt to formulate in concepts something accessible only to inner intuition, nor do I intend to engage here in an exhaustive discussion of a topic to which the greater portion of the *Wissenschaftslehre* is devoted. All I wish to do is to remind you of something everyone who has ever taken a hard look within himself must long since have discovered.

The intellect, as such, *observes itself*, and this act of self-observation is immediately directed at everything that the intellect is.[12] Indeed, the na-

12. "[. . .] and this act of self-observation is immediately united with everything that pertains to the intellect." [First printing.]

ture of the intellect consists precisely in this *immediate* unity of being and seeing. Everything included within the intellect exists *for* the intellect, and the intellect is *for itself* everything that it is; only insofar as this is true is the intellect what it is, *qua* intellect. Let us say that I think of this object or that: What does this mean? How do I appear to myself in this act of thinking? I appear to myself in this case only as follows: If the object in question is one I have merely imagined, then I produce certain determinations within myself. Or, if the object in question is one that is really supposed to exist, then these determinations are present within me without any assistance from me — *and I observe this production, this being.* These determinations exist within me only to the extent that I observe them; observing and being are inseparably united. — A thing, in contrast, may possess a variety of different features; but if we ask, *"For whom is it what it is?"* no one who understands our question will answer that "it exists for itself." Instead, an intellect also has to be thought of in this case, an intellect *for* which the thing in question exists. The intellect, in contrast, necessarily is for itself whatever it is, and nothing else needs to be thought of in conjunction with the thought of an intellect. When the intellect is posited to exist as an intellect,[13] then that for which it exists is already posited along with it. Accordingly, if I may speak figuratively, there is a double series within the intellect: a series of being and a series of observing, a series of what is real and a series of what is ideal. The essence of the intellect consists precisely in the indivisibility of this double series. (The intellect is synthetic.) In contrast, only a single series pertains to the thing, namely, the real series (a merely posited being). Thus the intellect and the thing are direct opposites of one another. They lie in two different worlds, between which there is no bridge.

Dogmatism wishes to use the principle of causality to explain the general nature of the intellect as such, as well as the specific determinations of the same. The intellect is in this case supposed to be something that has been caused; i.e., it is supposed to be the second member in a series.

436

13. "Durch ihr Gesetztseyn, als Intelligenz." *Gesetztseyn* ("posited being" or "being posited") is a word of Fichte's own coinage. For the intellect, all being is, initially anyway, simply "posited being" — i.e., the conscious representation or thought of being. What distinguishes the intellect from objects is that, in the case of the former, there can be no question of distinguishing its "being in itself" (*Sein für sich*) from its "posited being" (or "being for consciousness"). An intellect exists only insofar as it is posited (and indeed, posited by itself); and if it is posited, then it exists. Its *Sein an sich* = its *Gesetztsein*. This is what it means to say that the intellect exists *für sich* or "for itself."

But the principle of causality concerns a *real* series, not a double one. The force of an efficaciously acting cause is directed at another object lying *(197)* outside of and in opposition to itself.[14] This force produces a particular being within this other object, and this is all it can produce. The being produced in this way is a being that exists for a possible intellect outside of itself; it does not exist for itself. Moreover, if we assign a merely mechanical force to the object of this efficacious action, then it will, in turn, be able to transmit to an adjacent object any impression it itself has received. In this way, the movement that emanates from the first object may be transmitted through an entire series of any length you please, but nowhere within this series will you ever encounter a member whose efficacious acting reverts into itself.[15] Alternately, let us assign to the object of the first efficacious action the highest property one can assign to a thing, viz., irritability: In this case, the object would possess a force of its own and would be governed by laws of its own nature and not simply by a law assigned to it by something that affects it (which is what happens in the case of a merely mechanical series). Such an object will indeed be able to react upon an impact it receives; moreover, the being it assumes when it is affected is not determined by the particular cause, but is instead conditioned by the necessity of being something or other. Nevertheless, such an object is and remains nothing but a simple being, a being for a possible intellect outside of itself. You will not be able to obtain an intellect unless you also think of it as something primary and absolute, even though it may also be difficult for you to explain the connection between such an intellect and a being that is independent of it. — Even after such an explanation, the series is and remains a single one, and thus what was supposed to be explained has by no means been explained. The dogmatists were supposed to establish the transition from being to representing. They have not done this, nor can they, for their principle contains within itself only the ground of a being. It does not contain within itself the ground of what is directly opposed to being, viz., representing. They make an enormous leap into a world completely alien to their own principle.

437

14. *ihm entgegengesetztes.* As this passage indicates, Fichte frequently uses this term to mean simply "not identical to" or "different from," rather than "formally opposed." It is in this quite informal sense that red and yellow (or bears and tigers) can be said to be "opposites"; i.e., what one is (e.g., a bear) the other (e.g., a tiger) is not. Much confusion can be avoided by remembering that, in referring to "opposites," Fichte is *not* always (or even usually) talking about *polar opposites* or *logically contradictory* terms such as "A" and "Not-A" or "I" and "Not-I."

15. "das in sich selbst zurückgehend wirke."

They try to disguise this leap in a variety of different ways. Strictly speaking, the soul must not be any special sort of thing at all; it must be nothing whatsoever but a product of the interaction between things. This is the path followed by consistent dogmatism, which simultaneously turns into materialism.

But all that can come into being in this way is something within things, and never anything separate from them — unless, that is, we also supply the thought of an intellect that observes these things. The analogies dogmatists introduce in order to make their system comprehensible — e.g., the analogy of the harmony arising from the combined sound of several different instruments — only make it easier to comprehend how contrary to reason their system actually is. The harmony, like the combined sound, does not lie in the instruments themselves. It lies only in the mind of the listener who unifies this manifold; and if such a listener is not thought of in addition, then this harmony does not exist at all.

Yet who can prevent the dogmatist from assuming that the soul is one of the things in themselves? If this is the case, then the soul is one of the things he postulates in order to carry out his task. Indeed, it is only in this way that the principle of the efficacious action of things upon the soul can be applied — for the only sort of interaction materialism allows is the interaction of things among themselves, by means of which thoughts are supposed to be produced. In their attempt to think the unthinkable, some dogmatists have wanted to presuppose that either the efficaciously acting thing or the soul — or both of them — is of such a nature that representations could be produced as a result of efficacious action. [On the one hand, one may presuppose that] the *thing that exercises an effect* is of such a nature that its effects would be representations — perhaps somewhat like *God* in Berkeley's system (which is a dogmatic system and by no means an idealistic one).[16] But this proposal does not help us at all; for the only kind of efficacious action we understand is the mechanical kind, and it is simply impossible for us to think of any other way one thing could exercise an effect upon another. This presupposition therefore turns out to consist of nothing but empty and meaningless words. On the other hand, one may presuppose that the soul is of such a nature that every efficacious action that is directed at it turns into a representation. But with this assertion we

438
(198)

16. In George Berkeley's phenomenalist system God is conceived to be an infinite, active cause who produces representations (or, in Berkeley's vocabulary, "ideas") in our finite minds. See *A Treatise Concerning the Principles of Human Knowledge* (1710), pars. 146–49.

are in the same situation as we were with the first one: we are simply unable to understand it.

This is how dogmatism always proceeds in all the various guises in which it appears. It leaves an enormous gap between things and representations, and it fills this gap, not with any explanation, but with a few empty words. One can, of course, memorize these words and repeat them to others, but no person has ever been able to think of anything in conjunction with these words, nor will anyone ever be able to do so. For whenever one attempts to consider precisely *how* this alleged transition between things and representations is supposed to occur, the whole concept vanishes into an empty froth.

Thus dogmatism can do no more than repeat its principle over and over again and in various different forms. It can state it and restate it, but it can never proceed from this principle to a derivation of what needs to be explained. But philosophy consists precisely in such a derivation. It follows that, even viewed from the side of speculation, dogmatism is not a philosophy at all, but is nothing more than a helpless affirmation and assurance. The only type of philosophy that remains possible is idealism.

439   What is here asserted is not intended as a reply to any objections of the reader, for there is simply nothing that can be said against it. Instead, these remarks concern the absolute incapacity of many people to understand this point. No one who understands the mere words can deny that all efficacious action is mechanical in character and that no representation can be produced merely by means of mechanical action. But this is precisely where the difficulty lies; for a certain level of self-sufficiency and spiritual freedom is already required if one is to be able to comprehend the nature of the intellect as we have just portrayed it, and it is upon this that our entire refutation of dogmatism is based. Many people have simply not progressed in their own thinking past the point of being able to grasp the single series constituted by the mechanism of nature. So long as this single series is the

(199)   only one present in their minds, then, naturally enough, even if they should desire to think about representations, they will consider them too to be part of this same series. For such people, a representation becomes a particular sort of thing — a most remarkable error, of which we can find traces in even the most celebrated philosophical authors. Dogmatism is quite adequate for such people. Nor are they aware that anything is lacking in their system, for the opposed world [of representations] is not present for them at all. — This is why one is unable to refute a dogmatist by means of the proof just stated — no matter how clear this proof may be. For the dogmatist cannot be led to accept this proof, since he lacks the power or ability that is required in order to grasp its premises.

The manner in which we have dealt with dogmatism here also offends against the indulgent mode of thinking that is so characteristic of our present age. To be sure, such a mode of thinking has been extraordinarily widespread in every age, but only in our own has it become elevated to a maxim that can be expressed in the following words: "One must not be so *critical* strict in one's inferences, nor should philosophical proofs be required to be *non-* as precise as, say, those of mathematics." All that people who think in this *non-* lenient manner have to do is to catch sight of a few links in a chain of *rigorous* argument and of the rule of inference that applies in this case: their power *φ* of imagination immediately supplies them with the rest — wholesale, as it were, and without asking any further questions about its origin. Suppose that someone such as Alexander von Joch[17] says: "All things are determined by natural necessity; our representations depend upon the properties of things, and our will depends upon our representations; therefore, our entire will is determined by natural necessity, and our opinion that we   *440* possess free will is only a delusion." They find this uncommonly easy to understand and very clear to boot, despite the fact that it contains not an ounce of human understanding; and they go away convinced of this point and astonished at the rigor of this demonstration. I must remind you that the *Wissenschaftslehre* does not proceed from such an easy-going way of thinking, nor does it expect to be judged by such an indulgent standard. If even a single link in the long chain of argument it has to construct is not securely fastened to the one that follows, then this system will not have succeeded in proving anything at all.

7.

As we said above, idealism explains the determinations of consciousness by *intellect is* referring them to the acting of the intellect, which it considers to be some- *active* thing absolute and active, not something passive. The intellect cannot be anything passive, because, according to the postulate of idealism, it is what   *(200)* is primary and highest and is thus preceded by nothing that could account

17. Karl Ferdinand Hommel (1722–81) was a jurist and professor of law at Leipzig. In 1770, Hommel published a book entitled *Alexander von Joch beyder Rechte Doctor über Belohnung und Strafe nach Türkischen Gesezen*, in which he not only argued forcefully in favor of a system of metaphysical determinism, but also maintained that he himself possessed no personal sense of his own freedom. In 1793 Fichte included a criticism of Hommel's "Turkish fatalism" in the second edition of his own *Versuch einer Kritik aller Offenbarung*. (SW, V, p. 22 = GA, I,1: 139; English translation by Garrett Green, *Attempt at a Critique of All Revelation* [Cambridge: Cambridge University Press, 1978], p. 45.)

for its passivity. For the same reason, no real *being, no subsistence or continuing existence*, pertains to the intellect; for such being is the result of a process of interaction, and nothing yet exists or is assumed to be present with which the intellect could be posited to interact. Idealism considers the intellect to be a kind of *doing* and absolutely nothing more. One should not even call it an *active subject*, for such an appellation suggests the presence of something that continues to exist and in which an activity inheres. But idealism has no reason to make such an assumption, for it is not included within the principle of idealism, and anything not included within this principle must first be derived. What has to be derived now are *determinate* representations of a material, spatial, etc. world, one which is present without any help from us — for representations of this sort are notoriously present within consciousness. But nothing determinate can be derived from what is indeterminate, for in that case the formal principle of all derivation, i.e., the principle of sufficient reason or "grounding principle,"[18] could not be applied. Consequently, the acting of the intellect which is supposed to serve as the foundation of these determinate representations must be a determinate mode of acting; and, since the intellect itself is the ultimate ground of all explanation, this must be a type of acting which is determined by the intellect itself and by its own nature, not by anything outside of the intellect. Accordingly, what idealism presupposes is the following: The intellect acts; but, as a consequence of its very nature, it can act only in a certain, specific manner. If one considers the intellect's necessary modes of acting in isolation from any [actual] acting, then it is quite appropriate to call these the "laws of acting." Hence there are necessary laws of the intellect. — At the same time, the feeling of necessity accompanying these determinate representations is also made comprehensible in this way: For what the intellect feels in this case is not, as it were, an external impression; instead, what it feels when it acts are the limits of its own nature. Insofar as idealism presupposes the existence of such necessary laws of the intellect (which is the only rational thing it can suppose, since this is the only way it can explain what it is supposed to explain) it is called "Critical" or "transcendental" idealism.[19] A system of transcendent

441

18. *der Satz des Grundes*. This is the ordinary German name for what is called in English "the principle of sufficient reason."

19. The name "Critical idealism" (or elsewhere, "Critical philosophy") is employed by Fichte to refer to the Kantian system, not as interpreted by contemporary "Kantians" (for whom Fichte demonstrates a scarcely veiled contempt), but rather as presented in Kant's own *Critiques* — as interpreted by Fichte. The term "Critical" is here capitalized whenever it is employed in this specific, Kantian sense.

Transcendent Idealism – self-contradictory

idealism would be one that purports to derive determinate representations from the free and completely lawless acting of the intellect — which is an utterly self-contradictory supposition, since, as we just noted, the principle of sufficient reason is certainly not applicable to completely free and lawless acting.

Just as surely as the intellect's assumed laws of acting are supposed to have their basis in the unitary nature of the intellect itself, these laws must constitute a single system. This means that the reason why the intellect must act in certain precise ways under certain specific circumstances is because it has certain modes of acting under any circumstances whatsoever, and the former can be derived from the latter. These general modes *(201)* of acting can, in turn, be further explained by referring to a single, fundamental law. Whenever it acts, the intellect assigns a law to itself, and this act of legislation occurs in conformity with an even higher, necessary way of acting or representing. For example, the law of causality is not a primary or original law; instead, it is only one of the various ways in which a manifold can be combined. The law of causality can therefore be derived from the fundamental law governing such combination, which, in turn — along with the manifold itself — can be derived from still higher laws. *442*

It follows from what has just been said that Critical idealism can set to work in two different ways. On the one hand, it may actually derive from *Fichte's C.I.* the fundamental laws of the intellect the system of the intellect's necessary modes of acting and, along with this, the objective representations that come into being thereby. By proceeding in this way, Critical idealism allows the entire range of our representations to come into being gradually before the eyes of the reader or listener. On the other hand, it may attempt to grasp these same laws in the form in which they are already immediately *Kant's C.I.* applied to objects in any particular case; i.e., it may attempt to grasp them at their lowest level (in which case they are called "categories"). Critical idealism then asserts that the objects are determined and ordered by these categories.

To a Critical idealist of the latter sort, i.e., one who does not derive the *F3 ? to Kant* presumed laws of the intellect from the very nature of the intellect, one may address the following question: How did you obtain any material acquaintance with these laws? I.e., how did you become aware that the laws of the intellect are precisely these laws of substantiality and causality? (For I do not yet wish to trouble such an idealist by asking him how he knows that these are really nothing but immanent laws of the intellect.) Since the laws in question are ones that are immediately applied to objects, our idealist can only have obtained these laws by abstraction from the objects in question. In other words, he can only have drawn them from experience. It does not matter at all that in the course of obtaining them he may have, as it were, taken a detour through logic. For logic itself arises for him only by means of an act of abstracting from objects; and thus, by proceeding in this way he succeeds merely in accomplishing indirectly something that would be all too obvious if he were to do it directly. Consequently, he has no way to confirm that the laws of thought he postulates actually are laws of thought and that they are really nothing else but the immanent laws of the intellect. In opposition to a Critical idealist of this sort, the dogmatist will assert that the idealist's "categories" are general properties of things, the basis for which is to be found within the very nature of these things themselves; and it is hard to see why we should place any more credence in the unproven assertions of the one than in the unproven assertions of the other. — This way of proceeding does not provide us with any understanding of precisely how the intellect acts and why it must act in precisely this way. In order to obtain an understanding of this, we must specify within the premises themselves something that can pertain only to the intellect, and the laws of thinking must then be derived from these premises before our very eyes.

(202)
443

   The former mode of proceeding makes it especially difficult to see how the object itself could come into being. Even if one is willing to grant the unproven postulate made by this type of Critical idealism, it is still able to explain nothing more than the *properties* and the *relations* of the thing: e.g., that it is in space, that it expresses itself in time, that its accidents must be referred to something substantial, etc. But what is the origin of that which possesses these particular relations and properties? What is the origin of the content that assumes this form? Dogmatism takes refuge in this content, and a Critical idealism of this sort simply makes a bad situation worse.

   We know very well that the thing does indeed arise through an instance of acting in accordance with these laws. The thing is nothing whatsoever but *the sum of all of these relations as combined by the power of imagination*, and all of these relations, taken together, constitute the thing. The object is indeed the original synthesis of all of these concepts. Form and content are not two separate elements. Form in its entirety[20] is the content, and it is only by means of analysis that we first obtain individual forms. But the Critical idealist who proceeds in the way we described above can do no more than assure us that this is the case. Indeed, it is something of a mystery how he himself knows this — if, indeed, he knows it at all. So long as one does not allow the thing in its entirety to come into being before the

20. "Die gesammte Formheit."

eyes of the thinker, dogmatism has still not been pursued into its final hiding-place. But it is possible to do this only if one allows the intellect to act in total — and not merely in partial — conformity with the laws of the same.

An idealism of this sort is, therefore, both unproven and unprovable. The sole weapon it can wield against dogmatism is to issue assurances that it is right; and the only weapon it can wield against the higher, complete form of idealism is helpless rage, coupled with the claim that no one can proceed any further in this direction than it itself has already gone, the mere assurance that no territory remains to be explored beyond the territory it itself has already explored, and the assertion that anything anyone says beyond this point becomes unintelligible *to it*, etc. — all of which means nothing at all.

444

Finally, the only laws established within a system of this sort are laws that determine only the objects of outer experience and do so by means of the purely subsumptive power of judgment.[21] But this is far and away the smallest portion of the system of reason. Consequently, since it lacks any understanding of the overall operation of reason, this sort of half-Critical idealism gropes around just as blindly in the realm of practical reason and reflective judgment as do those who merely parrot what others have said; and — with equal ingenuousness — it copies down remarks that it itself finds to be completely unintelligible.*

(203)

21. Reading, with the original edition and with GA, *Urtheilskraft* for SW's *Wechselkraft* ("reciprocal force").

* A Critical idealism of this sort has been propounded by Prof. Beck in his *Only Possible Standpoint*.[22] Despite the fact that I find his approach to be deficient in the manner just criticized, I do not wish to allow this to prevent me from testifying publicly to the high and well-earned respect I have for this man who, completely on his own, has managed to raise himself above the confusion of his age and to understand that the Kantian philosophy is not any variety of dogmatism, but is instead a transcendental idealism according to which the object is given neither entirely nor in part but is produced. I expect, moreover, that in time he will be able to raise

22. J. S. Beck (1761–1840) was a professor of philosophy at Halle and one of the more original early expositors and interpreters of Kant. Beck's major work is his *Erläuternder Auszug aus den critischen Schriften des Herrn Prof. Kant, auf Anrathen desselben*, which appeared in three independently published volumes in 1793, 1794, and 1796. It is in vol. 3 of this work, entitled *Einzig möglicher Standpunkt aus welchem die Kritische Philosophie zu beurtheilen ist*, that Beck develops his own version of transcendental idealism, the so-called Standpoint Theory. (In English, see the excerpt from Beck's *The Standpoint from Which Critical Philosophy Is to Be Judged*, translated by George di Giovanni, in *Between Kant and Hegel*, pp. 204–49.)

445   I have, on a previous occasion, already provided a clear discussion of the
(204)   method followed by a complete transcendental idealism of the sort estab-
           lished by the *Wissenschaftslehre*.* I cannot understand why people seem
           not to have understood this account: Suffice it to say that I have been
           assured that it was not understood.

           Thus I am obliged to repeat what I have said before and to remind the
           reader that everything within this science depends upon an understanding
           of this point.

           This type of idealism begins with a single basic law of reason, which it
           immediately establishes within consciousness. In order to do this, it pro-
           ceeds as follows: It summons the listener or the reader to think freely of a

---

himself to an even higher standpoint. I consider the book in question to be the most
appropriate gift one could lay before the present age, and to anyone who wants to
study the *Wissenschaftslehre* as presented in my own writings, I recommend Prof.
Beck's book as the best preparation for the same. It does not conduct one along a
path to my system, but it does succeed in overcoming the most serious obstacle
barring this path for so many people. — Some people have professed to be
wounded by the tone of Prof. Beck's book, and an esteemed reviewer, writing in a
famous journal, has recently demanded in no uncertain terms: "*crustula, elementa
velit ut discere prima.*"[23] For my part, I find his tone to be, if anything, too tolerant.
For I honestly do not understand what sort of thanks is owed to certain authors
who, for more than a decade, have done nothing but confuse and demean the most
spiritual and exalted theory; nor do I see why anyone should have to beg their
permission to be right. — For his own sake, I can only lament the hastiness with
which this same author [i.e., Beck], writing in the company of others for whom he
is far too good, has inveighed against books that his own conscience should have
told him that he did not understand, just as it should also have told him that he was
unable to gauge accurately the potential depth of the issues involved.[24]

* In the book *Concerning the Concept of the Wissenschaftslehre* (Weimar, 1794).

---

23. "Crumbs! Would that he would learn first principles." (Or, more freely: "Rubbish! He ought to learn his abc's!") The comment to which Fichte alludes concerning the offensive "tone" of Beck's writings was contained in a review of the
Erläuternder Auszug published by J. B. Erhard in the November 28, 1796 issue of
the *Allgemeine Literatur-Zeitung*. Johann Benjamin Erhard (1766–1827) was a phy-
sician and philosopher from Nürnberg whose writings Fichte had mentioned fa-
vorably in the Introduction to his *Grundlage des Naturrechts* (see SW, III, p.12 =
GA, I,3: 323).

24. This is a reference to a disparaging review of Fichte's BWL and GWL published by Beck in the *Annalen der Philosophie und des philosophischen Geist* in February of 1795. (It is probable that Beck was also the author of the anonymously
published reviews of Fichte's *Vorlesungen, etc.* and *Grundlage des Naturrechts*,
which appeared in the same journal in April of 1795 and in 1796.)

certain concept. If he indeed does this, he will discover that he is obliged to
proceed in a certain way. Here we have to distinguish between two different things: [1] The requested act of thinking, which can only be performed
freely. The person who does not perform this act on his own will not be
able to see any of the things set forth in the *Wissenschaftslehre*. [2] The
necessary manner in which this free act of thinking has to be performed if
it is to be performed at all. The basis for this necessity lies in the very
nature of the intellect itself and is not a matter of free choice. This is something *necessary*, even though it only occurs in and by means of a free action.
It is something *discovered*, even though its discovery is conditioned by freedom.

To this extent, idealism establishes within immediate consciousness   *(205)*
what it asserts. Nevertheless, it remains merely a presupposition that this
constitutes the necessary and fundamental law of reason as a whole, a law
from which we can derive the entire system of our necessary representations — not merely our representations of a world in which objects are
determined by the subsumptive and reflective power of judgment, but also
our representations of ourselves as free, practical beings subject to laws. A
complete transcendental idealism has to demonstrate the truth of this presupposition by actually providing a derivation of this system of represen-   *446*
tations, and precisely this constitutes its proper task.

It does this by proceeding as follows: *It shows that what is postulated as
the first principle and immediately established within consciousness is not possible unless something else occurs as well, and that this second thing is not possible
apart from the occurrence of some third thing. It continues in this manner until
all of the conditions of the first principle have been completely exhausted and its
possibility has become completely comprehensible.* It proceeds in an uninter-
rupted progression from what is conditioned to the condition of the same.
Each condition becomes, in turn, something that is itself conditioned and
whose condition has to be discovered.

If the presupposition idealism makes is correct, and if it has inferred
correctly in the course of its derivations, then, as its final result (i.e., as the
sum total of all of the conditions of that with which it began), it must arrive
at the system of all necessary representations. In other words, its result
must be equivalent to experience as a whole — though this equation is not
established within philosophy itself, but only subsequently.

This is because experience is not something with which idealism is, as
it were, acquainted in advance and which it keeps in view as the goal at
which it has to arrive. In the course of its derivations, idealism knows nothing of experience and takes no heed of it whatsoever. It commences from

its own starting point, and it proceeds in accordance with its own rule, without the slightest concern for what may ultimately result. The correct angle from which it has to begin drawing its straight line is given to it. Does it also require some point toward which this line should be directed? I believe that all of the points that lie along this line are also given to idealism along with its original task. Suppose that a determinate number is given to you, and that you surmise that this number is a product of certain factors. All that you have to do in this case is to determine the product of these factors by applying a rule with which you are already quite familiar. Only after you have determined this product will you be able to tell whether it agrees with the number in question. [In the case of transcendental philosophy] the given number is experience as a whole; the factors are what is established within consciousness, plus the laws of thinking; and the act of multiplying is the act of philosophizing. Those who advise you to keep your eye constantly fixed upon experience when you philosophize are advising you to fudge the factors a little and to engage in a bit of faulty multiplication in order to be sure of obtaining numbers that will agree with each other — a procedure as dishonest as it is superficial.

447
(206)

To the extent that these final results of idealism are viewed as results, i.e., to the extent that they are viewed as conclusions of a chain of argument, they are "*a priori*" and contained within the human mind. To the extent, however, that argument and experience actually coincide and one views these same results as something given within experience, then they can be called "*a posteriori*." For a full-blown idealism, *a priori* and *a posteriori* are not two different things, but are one and the same thing, simply looked at from two different sides, and they can be distinguished from each other only in terms of the different means one employs in order to arrive at each. Philosophy anticipates experience in its entirety; it *thinks* of experience only as something necessary, and to this extent the experience of which philosophy thinks is — in comparison with actual experience — *a priori*. Insofar as it is given, a given number is something *a posteriori*. The same number is *a priori* insofar as it is treated as the product of its factors. Anyone who is of a different opinion does not know what he is talking about.

If the results of some philosophy do not agree with experience, then the philosophy in question is surely false, for it has not succeeded in doing what it promised to do: that is to say, it has not provided a derivation of experience as a whole, and it has failed to explain experience in terms of the necessary acting of the intellect. In this case, either the presupposition of transcendental idealism is totally incorrect, or else it has simply been dealt

with incorrectly in the particular faulty presentation that has failed to
achieve what it was supposed to achieve. Since the task of explaining the
foundations of experience is one that is simply present within human reason itself; since no rational being will assume that reason could contain
within itself a task simply impossible to discharge; since there are only two
ways to discharge this task, viz., in the manner of dogmatism and in that of
transcendental idealism; and since it can be shown without any further ado
that the former is unable to do what it promises to do: for all of these
reasons, the resolute thinker will always decide in favor of the latter alter-   *448*
native. I.e., he will always conclude that the error lies only in the inferences
made within transcendental idealism and not in what it presupposes, which
must surely be correct in itself. He will not allow any unsuccessful attempt
to prevent him from making another attempt, until success has finally been
attained.

As one can see, the path followed by this type of idealism is one that
begins with something present within consciousness, though it is present
there only as a result of a free act of thinking, and proceeds from there to
experience as a whole. What lies between these two extremes constitutes
the proper territory of this system. This is not the domain of "facts of
consciousness"; it is not part of the realm of experience. How could anything that limited itself to experience be called philosophy? For it is precisely the task of philosophy to indicate the basis or foundation of
experience, and the foundation of anything must necessarily lie outside of
that for which it provides the foundation. It is something produced by a
free, but law-governed, act of thinking. This will become clearer when we   *(207)*
look more closely at the fundamental assertion of idealism.

Idealism demonstrates that what is purely and simply postulated is not
possible except on the condition of something else, which in turn is impossible without some third something, etc. Thus none of the individual
things it postulates is possible on its own; each is possible only in combination with all of the others. It thus follows from idealism's own claim that
nothing is actually present within consciousness but this entire whole, and
this whole is precisely experience. The idealist wishes to become better
acquainted with this whole, and in order to do so he must analyze it — not,
to be sure, by blindly groping around, but rather by proceeding in accordance with a specific rule of composition and in such a way as to enable this
whole to come into being before his own eyes. He is able to do this because
he is capable of abstraction; i.e., by engaging in an act of free thinking he is
indeed able to grasp the elements of this whole individually and alone. For
the sheer necessity of representations is not the only thing present within

consciousness; the freedom of representation is present there as well. And
this freedom, in turn, can operate either in accordance with laws or in
accordance with free choice.[25] It is from the standpoint of necessary consciousness that the whole [of experience] is given to the idealist. He discovers this whole in the same way he discovers himself. But the series that
comes into being in the act of assembling this whole from its elements is a
series produced only by freedom. Anyone who performs this free act becomes conscious of it and thereby, as it were, stakes out a new region within
his own consciousness. Similarly, what is conditioned by this act is simply
not present at all for someone who does not perform it. The chemist com-
pounds a body — a specific metal, for instance — from its elements. The
ordinary person sees a metal with which he is quite familiar, whereas what
the chemist sees is the connection between these specific elements.[26] Do
they see two different things? I think not; they both see the same thing, but
they view it in two different ways. The chemist sees what is *a priori*; he sees
the individual elements. The ordinary person sees what is *a posteriori*; he
sees the whole. — There is, however, the following difference between the
procedure of the chemist and that of the philosopher: The chemist must
first analyze the whole before he can compose it, for he is dealing with an
object with whose rule of assembly he cannot be acquainted prior to this
analysis; whereas the philosopher can engage in an act of composition without first having to engage in any analysis, since he is already acquainted
with the rule governing his object, that is, with the rule governing reason.

On the condition, therefore, that one wishes to think of something as
the foundation of experience, the only sort of reality that pertains to the
content of philosophy is the reality of necessary thinking. Philosophy asserts that the intellect can be conceived of only as active, and indeed, can be
conceived of as active only in a certain specific manner. Philosophy finds

449

(208)

25. Fichte actually writes ". . . und diese Freiheit hinwiederum, kann entweder
gesetzmäßig oder nach Regeln verfahren" (". . . this freedom, in turn, can operate
either in accordance with laws or in accordance with rules"). Alexis Philonenko,
the French translator of Fichte's "First Introduction," suggests amending this
passage by substituting *nach Willkür* ("in accordance with free choice," or "arbitrarily") for Fichte's own *nach Regeln* ("in accordance with rules"). This proposal
seems to make good sense in the present context, in which Fichte is contrasting the
spontaneity of free thinking ("the freedom of representation") with the kind of
constrained thinking normally involved in the constitution of experience. It has
therefore been incorporated in the English translation.

26. "[. . .] whereas what the chemist sees is the connection between the body and
the specific elements." [First printing.]

this type of reality to be quite adequate, for philosophy shows that there is no other type of reality at all.

The *Wissenschaftslehre* wishes to establish a complete transcendental idealism of the sort we have now described. These last remarks serve to specify the concept of the *Wissenschaftslehre*, and I do not have to consider any objections to this concept, since no one else can know better than I myself what it is I want to accomplish. It is simply laughable when someone tries to demonstrate the impossibility of something that will actually be accomplished, and, in part, already has been. All one has to do is attend to the following presentation of the argument and inquire whether or not it actually accomplishes what it has promised to accomplish.[27]

27. With the remark "(To be continued in the following issues)," the first published installment of *An Attempt at a New Presentation of the Wissenschaftslehre* concludes at this point.

Second Introduction to the
Wissenschaftslehre
For Readers Who Already Have a
Philosophical System of Their Own

1.

I believe that the introduction provided in the first installment of this journal is quite sufficient for unprejudiced readers, i.e., for those willing to
submit themselves to an author without any preconceived opinions, neither assisting nor resisting him. But the situation is different in the case of
readers who already possess a philosophical system of their own. In the
course of constructing their system they have abstracted certain maxims,
which have become first principles for them; consequently, whatever has
not been produced in accordance with these rules is, so far as they are
concerned, simply false. Nor do they have to engage in any additional inquiry in order to reach this conclusion; they do not even have to read the
presentation of a different system. Indeed, any other system has to be false,
precisely because it has been produced in accordance with a method opposed to what they take to be the only valid one. Unless we are to give up
on such people altogether — and why should we? — then the first thing we
have to do is to try to eliminate this obstacle that robs us of their attention.
In order to do this, we must get them to distrust their own rules.

   This type of preliminary methodological investigation is especially necessary in the case of the *Wissenschaftslehre*, since the entire structure and
meaning of the *Wissenschaftslehre* is completely different from that of any
of the philosophical systems that have preceded it. The exponents of the
other systems to whom I am here referring all begin with one concept or
another, and they are quite unconcerned with where they have obtained
this concept and from what they have assembled it. They then proceed to
analyze this concept and to combine it with others, to whose origins they
show an equal indifference. Their philosophy consists entirely in these
arguments they themselves construct. Accordingly, theirs is a philosophy
that exists only within their own thinking. The situation is quite different
in the case of the *Wissenschaftslehre*. What it takes as the object of its think-

ing is not some dead concept that is related only passively to the inquiry in question and obtains its significance only through this very act of thinking. Instead, the object reflected upon within the *Wissenschaftslehre* is something vital and active, something that generates cognitions out of itself and by means of itself, while the philosopher merely observes what happens. The part played by the philosopher in this process is no more than this: His task is to engage this living subject in purposeful activity, to observe this activity, to apprehend it, and to comprehend it as a single, unified activity. He conducts an experiment. It is up to him to place what is to be investigated in a position that will allow him to make precisely the observations he wishes to make. It is also up to him to attend to these appearances, to survey them accurately and to connect them with one another. But it is not for him to decide how the object should manifest itself. This is something determined by the object itself; and he would be working directly counter to his own goal were he not to subordinate himself to this object, and were he instead to take an active role in the development of what appears. In contrast, the philosopher of the previously mentioned sort is engaged in the manufacture of an artificial product. All that concerns him is the material of which the object upon which he is working consists; he is not at all concerned with any inner, self-active energy or force[1] of this object itself. Indeed, any such inner force must be killed before he can set to work, for otherwise it would resist his efforts. He succeeds in manufacturing something from this dead mass only by employing his own energy, guided solely by a concept he himself has previously constructed. The *Wissenschaftslehre* contains two very different series of mental acting: that of the I the philosopher is observing, as well as the series consisting of the philosopher's own observations. The opposed manner of philosophizing to which I have just referred contains but a *single* series of thinking, namely, the series of the philosopher's own thoughts, for the content or object of his thinking is not presented as something that is itself engaged in thinking. Many people fail to distinguish these two series from each other at all, or else they confuse them with one another and assign to one of these series something that really pertains to the other. This is one of the main reasons why the *Wissenschaftslehre* has been

---

1. "nicht auf eine innere selbstthätige Kraft desselben." The adjective *selbstthätige* ("self-active") is employed by Fichte to designate an action that is spontaneously originated and not determined by something else. Accordingly, *Selbstthätigkeit* or "self-activity" is the power to initiate and to accomplish an action entirely on one's own or "spontaneously" — i.e., to act *freely*.

455   misunderstood, and it is also a major source of many of the inappropriate objections that have been raised against this system. A person who makes this mistake does so because he encounters only one series within his own philosophy. The action of the philosopher who manufactures an artificial product is, to be sure, identical with that of the appearance itself, since the object he is considering does not act on its own. But what is reported by the philosopher who has conducted an experiment [in the manner described above] is not itself identical with the appearance he is investigating, but is merely the concept of the latter.*

(211)

2.

Following this preliminary remark, the broader implications of which will be explained within the present treatise, let us ask: How does the *Wissenschaftslehre* propose to go about accomplishing its task?

As we know, the question the *Wissenschaftslehre* has to answer is the

---

* This same confusion of the two series of thinking contained within transcendental idealism would also underlie any claim that, *alongside of* and *in addition to* this system, another, realistic system, which is just as well grounded and just as coherent as the idealistic system, is also possible.[2] The type of realism that presses itself upon all of us — including the most resolute idealist — when it comes to acting, i.e., the assumption that objects exist outside of and quite independently of us, is contained within idealism itself and is explained and derived within idealism. Indeed, it is the sole aim of all philosophy to provide a derivation of objective truth — within the world of appearances as well as within the intelligible world. — It is only in *his own* name [i.e., from the standpoint of philosophy] that the philosopher asserts that "everything that exists for the I exists by means of the I." The I that is described within his philosophy, however, asserts that "just as truly as I exist and live at all, there also exists something outside of me, something that does not owe its existence to me." Basing his account upon the first principle of his philosophy, the philosopher explains how the I comes to make such an assertion. The philosopher occupies the standpoint of pure speculation, whereas the I itself occupies the standpoint of life and science ("science," that is, in the sense in which science itself is to be contrasted with the "*Theory* of science" or "Wissenschafts*lehre*"). The standpoint of life is comprehensible only from the standpoint of speculation. In addition to this, however, realism certainly has some basis, since it forces itself upon us as a consequence of our own nature, but this is not a basis that is *known* and *understandable* [from within the standpoint of life]. The standpoint of speculation exists only in order to make the standpoint of life and science comprehensible. Idealism can never be a *way of thinking*; instead, it is nothing more than *speculation*.

2. This is an allusion to Schelling's *Philosophische Briefe über Dogmatismus und Kriticismus*, which is discussed in the Editor's Introduction.

following: What is the origin of the system of representations accompanied
by a feeling of necessity? Or, how do we come to ascribe objective validity   *456*
to something purely subjective? Or — since objective validity is designated by the term "being" — how do we come to assume the existence of
any being? Since this last question is one that arises as a result of introspec-
tion, i.e., from noticing that the immediate object of consciousness is nothing but consciousness itself, it follows that the type of "being" that is here
in question can only be a being for us. It would be completely absurd to
consider this question to be the same as the question concerning the existence of a being that has no relation to any consciousness. Yet it is precisely
what is most absurd that is most commonly encountered among the philosophers of our own philosophical era.

The question now raised — viz., how is a being for us possible? —
abstracts from all being. This does not mean that one must think, so to
speak, of a non-being; for by doing so one would succeed only in negating
the concept of being, not in abstracting from it. Instead, the concept of
being is here not thought of at all — either positively or negatively. This is
a question that inquires concerning the ground of the predicate of being as
such, whether this predicate is attributed or denied in any particular case.
But a ground always lies outside of what it grounds; i.e., it is contrasted
with or opposed to it. Thus, if one is really to address and to answer *this*
question, then one's answer must also abstract from all being. To maintain
on *a priori* grounds and in advance of the experiment that the sort of abstraction that would be required for such an answer is impossible — for the
reason that it is simply impossible as such — is also to maintain that no
such abstraction is possible in the question either; in other words, it is to
claim that it is impossible even to raise the question that has here been
raised, and from this it follows that the task of constructing a metaphysics
in the sense indicated is not a task contained with the nature of reason itself   *(212)*
— since this is a task that inquires concerning the foundation or ground of
being for us. No objective grounds can be adduced to demonstrate that this
is a question that is contrary to reason, for those who raise this question
maintain that its possibility and necessity are based upon the supreme law
of reason, i.e., the law of self-sufficiency (practical legislation),[3] to which

---

3. "das [Gesetz] der Selbständigkeit (die praktische Gesetzgebung)."
Selbständigkeit, here translated as "self-sufficiency," is employed by Fichte as a
virtual synonym for *Autonomie* ("autonomy") and designates the I's power to determine itself freely, rather than to be determined by some external "being." According to Fichte, any time we treat ourselves as free and autonomous
("self-sufficient") agents, we are already tacitly "abstracting from being."

all the other laws of reason are subordinate and which provides the foundation for all of these other laws, at the same time that it determines them and limits them to the particular spheres in which they are valid. Those who raise this question concerning the ground of being are willing to concede their opponent's arguments; however, they will then go on to deny that these objections apply to this case. Their opponent can judge the correctness of this contention only if he too can raise himself to the level of their highest law. But if he succeeds in doing this, he will at the same time have succeeded in raising himself to the point where he too requires an answer to the question in dispute — and, with this, he will have ceased to be their opponent. The roots of this controversy can, therefore, lie only in a subjective incapacity, i.e., in our opponents' consciousness that they have never personally raised this question and have never felt any need to obtain an answer to it. Nor, from our side, can we object to their position on any objective, rational grounds. For the state of mind in which such doubt [concerning the ground or foundation of being] automatically occurs is a state that is based upon preceding acts of freedom, and this is not something that can ever be compelled by any demonstration.

3.

Who is it then who undertakes the required abstraction from all being? In which of the two series does this act of abstracting lie? Obviously, it lies within the series of philosophical argumentation, for no other series is yet present.

The sole thing to which the person who undertakes this act of abstraction continues to cling and proposes to employ as the basis for explaining everything that has to be explained is the conscious subject. Consequently, he must grasp this subject entirely apart from any representation of being, for only in this way will he then be able to show that this subject contains within itself the ground of all being — "being for this subject," as goes without saying. But if we abstract from all being of and for this conscious subject, then nothing pertains to it but acting. More specifically, in relationship to being, the subject in question is the acting subject. The philosopher therefore has to apprehend this subject while it is engaged in acting. This is the point at which the previously mentioned double series first arises.

The fundamental claim made by the philosopher as such is the following: Insofar as the I exists only for itself, a being outside of the I must also necessarily arise for the I at the same time. The former contains within itself the ground of the latter; the latter is conditioned by the former. Our

self-consciousness is necessarily connected with a consciousness of some-   *458*
thing that is supposed to be something other than ourselves. The former,
however, is to be viewed as what provides the condition and the latter must
be viewed as what is conditioned thereby. In order to prove this contention
— not as something established, as it were, by argumentation and sup-   *(213)*
posed to be valid for a system of things existing in themselves, but rather,
as something that has to be established by observing the original operation
of reason and is valid for reason — the philosopher must first show how the
I exists and comes into being for itself. Secondly, he must show that this
being of the I for itself would not be possible unless a being outside of the
I also arose for the I at the same time.

Thus the first question would be: What is the I for itself? And our first
postulate would be the following: Think of yourself; construct the concept
of yourself and take note of how you do this.

The philosopher maintains that anyone who does even this much will
discover that when he thinks of this concept of himself his activity as an
intellect turns back upon or reverts into itself, and thus makes itself into its
own object.

If this is correct and is conceded to be so, then we may suppose that
we are already familiar with the manner in which the I is constructed, i.e.,
with the sort of being that it has for itself (which is the only sort of being we
are ever concerned with). The philosopher can now proceed from this
point and go on to show that this action would not be possible without
another action, by means of which a being outside of the I comes into being
for the I.

The various inquiries that make up the *Wissenschaftslehre* are connected
to one another in the manner we have just described. We must now consider the justification for proceeding in this manner.

4.

To begin with, what part of the described act should be ascribed to the
philosopher *qua* philosopher, and what part of it pertains to the I he is
supposed to be observing? All that pertains to the I is the act of turning
back upon itself. Everything else belongs to the philosopher's account of
this act. The system of experience as a whole is already present as a mere
fact for the philosopher; and it is this system of experience that now has to
be produced before the philosopher's eyes by the I, for this is how the
philosopher is supposed to become acquainted with the manner in which
experience arises.

459   We asserted that the I reverts *into itself*. Does this not imply that the I is already present for itself, in advance of and independently of this act of self-reversion? In order for the I to be able to act upon itself,[4] must it not already be present for itself in advance? And if this is so, doesn't your philosophy presuppose what it is supposed to explain?

To this objection I would reply: By no means! The I *originally* comes into being for itself by means of this act, and it is only in this way that the I comes into being at all, i.e., by means of an acting that is itself directed at acting; and this specific, determinate way of acting is not preceded by any sort of "acting as such" or "in general."[5] It is only *for the philosopher* that the I can be said to be already present in advance, as a fact; for the philosopher has already constituted experience in its entirety. Simply in order to make himself understood, he has to express himself as he does; and he is able to express himself in this way because he has long since grasped all of the concepts required for this purpose.

(214)   Let us begin by looking at the I that is being observed. What is this self-reverting act of the I? Among which class of modifications of consciousness should it be posited? It is not an act of comprehending anything by means of concepts.[6] It first becomes an act of comprehension only when it is opposed to a Not-I and only insofar as the I itself is determined within this opposition. Consequently, the act in question is a mere intuition.[7] —

4. "um sich zum Ziele eines Handelns machen zu können." More literally: "in order for the I to be able to make itself into the goal or intended object of an instance of acting."

5. "Erst durch deisen Act und lediglich durch ihn, durch ein Handeln auf ein Handeln selbst, welchem bestimmten Handeln kein Handeln überhaupt vorhergeht, wird das Ich *ursprünglich* für sich selbst." *Ein Handeln* = "an acting," "an instance of acting," or "a type of acting." ("An action" = *ein Act* or *eine Handlung*.)

6. "Es ist kein Begreifen."

7. "eine bloße Anschauung." *Anschauung* is one of the fundamental terms in Fichte's technical vocabulary, and, like his use of the term *Vorstellung* ("representation"), it too is directly derived from Kant. In the first *Critique* Kant defines "intuition" as the means by which objects are directly "given" to us, and thus as the means by which our knowledge or cognition is "immediately related to objects." Like Kant as well, Fichte sometimes uses "intuition" to designate a particular mental content or type of representation and at other times employs this same term to designate the mental power or "faculty" (*Vermögen*) by virtue of which we are able to engage in particular "acts of intuition" and hence to obtain particular "intuitions." (See the introductory paragraphs of the "Transcendental Aesthetic" in Kant's *Critique of Pure Reason*, A19/B33 ff.)

Accordingly, it also produces no consciousness, not even self-conscious-ness. It is precisely because no consciousness is produced by this act, con-sidered purely on its own, that we may proceed to infer the occurrence of another act, by means of which a Not-I comes into being for us. Only in this manner is it possible to advance our philosophical argument and thereby to accomplish the desired derivation of the system of experience. The described act of the I merely serves to put the I into a position in which self-consciousness — and, along with this, all other consciousness — be-comes possible. But no actual consciousness has yet arisen at this point. The act in question is merely a part of the entire action through which the intellect brings its own consciousness into being. Though the philosopher has to isolate this act, it is not originally a separate part of this whole.

How is this act related to the philosopher as such?

This self-constructing I is none other than the philosopher's own I. He can intuit the indicated act of the I only within himself; and in order to be able to intuit this act, he must perform it. He freely chooses to produce this act within himself.

But in connection with this, the following question can be and has been asked: If this entire philosophy is constructed upon something brought into being by an act of sheer, arbitrary free will,[8] does this not mean that it is nothing more than a figment of the imagination, a pure invention? How does the philosopher propose to ensure the objectivity of this merely sub-jective action? How does he propose to guarantee the primordial original-ity of an act that is obviously only empirical and occurs at a specific time, viz., at the time when he himself is engaged in philosophizing? How does he intend to demonstrate that his present act of free thinking, an act that occurs in the midst of the series of his own representations, corresponds to the necessary act of thinking by means of which he came into being for himself in the first place and which initiates the entire series of his repre-sentations? To this I reply: This action is, by its very nature, objective. I am for myself; this is a fact. But I can only have occurred for myself by means of acting,[9] for I am free. It is, moreover, only by acting in this spe-cific, determinate way that I can have occurred for myself; for it is by

460

---

8. "durch einen Act der bloßen Willkür."

9. "Ich bin für mich; dies ist Factum. Nun kann ich mir nur durch ein Handeln zu Stande gekommen seyn." Here, as well as in the following sentences, Fichte employs the expression *zu Stande kommen* ("to occur," "to take place," or "to come about") as a way of talking about the I's original presence to itself — a presence that indicates the occurrence of an act and is logically prior to any sort of "being" (*Sein*).

means of this same specific mode of acting that I occur for myself at every instant, whereas something quite different occurs for me through every other mode of acting. This acting is precisely the concept of the I, and the concept of the I is the concept of this acting. These are one and the same, and when we think of this concept, we do not and cannot think of anything but what has just been described. It *is* so, because I *make* it so. The philosopher merely makes clear to himself what he is actually thinking — and has always been thinking — whenever he thinks of *himself*. But that he actually

(215)   does think of himself is, for him, an immediate fact of consciousness. — This question concerning objectivity is based upon the remarkable presupposition that the I is something other than its own thought of itself, and that, in addition to and underlying this thought of the I, there is also something else — God knows what! — whose real nature one desires to fathom. If some people wish to raise such questions about the objective validity of thinking and want to ask about the connection between this object and the [thinking] subject, then I must confess that the *Wissenschaftslehre* will be

461   unable to provide them with any information concerning this topic. Let them seek to discover on their own such a connection in this case or any other. In attempting to do this, they may eventually come to realize that this unknown "something" they are seeking is, once again, nothing but something they themselves are thinking of, and that whatever they may, in turn, suppose to underlie this thought, this too is nothing but another one of their thoughts, and so on, *ad infinitum*. By continuing in this manner, they may perhaps finally come to realize that they are quite unable to ask or to speak about anything at all without actually thinking of it.

For the philosopher as such, this act is one he has freely willed and one that occurs within time. For the I that the philosopher — quite rightfully, as we have just seen — constructs in order to be able to observe it and draw inferences from it, however, this same act is necessary and original. In this act the philosopher observes himself: he immediately intuits his own acting. He knows what he does, because it is *he* who *does* it.

Does any consciousness arise for the philosopher when he does this? Undoubtedly, for he is not only engaged in intuiting, he is also engaged in *comprehending*. He comprehends his act as an instance of *acting as such* or *acting in general*, of which, as a result of his previous experience, he already possesses a concept; moreover, he also comprehends the act in question as this *specific, self-reverting mode of acting*, which is how he intuits it within himself. It is this characteristic difference that allows the philosopher to single out, within the general sphere of "acting as such," this specific type of acting. — What "acting" is is something that can only be intuited; such knowledge cannot be developed from concepts nor can it be communicated thereby. But what is contained within this intuition becomes comprehended through its opposition to mere *being*. "Acting is not being, and being is not acting": this is the only definition of acting one can obtain from its mere concept. In order to understand the true nature of acting, one has to turn to intuition.

This entire manner in which the philosopher proceeds seems *to me* at least to be something that is quite possible, very easy to accomplish, and entirely natural; and I can scarcely imagine how it could appear otherwise to my readers and how they could discover anything strange and mysterious within this procedure. One would hope that every person will be able to think of *himself*. One would hope as well that every person will become aware that, insofar as he is summoned to think of himself, he is summoned to engage in a type of *inner acting* that depends upon his own self-activity and will realize that, in accomplishing what is thus requested of him, he actually affects himself through his own self-activity; i.e., he *acts*. It is also to be hoped that anyone will be able to distinguish *this* way of acting from the *opposite* sort of acting in which he engages when he thinks of an object outside of himself; and presumably, he will discover that in the latter case the thinking subject and the object of thought are posited in opposition to one another and that, consequently, his activity is directed at something other than himself. In the case of the kind of acting now requested of him, however, the act of thinking and what is thought of within this act are one and the same, and thus his activity must here turn back upon or revert into itself. Since it is *only* in this manner that he can obtain the thought of himself (for, as he has discovered, an entirely different thought arises for him when he thinks in an opposite manner), one might also hope that he will be able to understand that his thought of himself is nothing other than the thought of this action and that the word "I" is nothing more than a way of designating the latter: i.e., that he will come to see that "I" and "self-reverting acting" are completely identical concepts. Let us assume that he goes along with transcendental idealism in presupposing — albeit in a purely problematic way — that all consciousness is based upon and conditioned by self-consciousness. (He must presuppose this in any case, just as surely as he turns his attention back upon himself at all and thereby raises himself to the point where he acquires the need for a philosophy — though the correctness of this presupposition will be categorically substantiated for him only within philosophy itself, insofar as the latter provides a complete deduction of experience in its entirety from the possibility of self-consciousness.) Insofar as he makes this assumption, he will, it is to be hoped, realize that he must *think* of this act of returning into himself as

462

(216)

Transc.
Ideals
assumption

preceding and conditioning all other acts of consciousness, or, what amounts to the same thing, that he must think of this act of self-reversion as the original act of the subject. Since, moreover, nothing exists for him which is not contained within his consciousness, and since everything else within his consciousness is conditioned by this very act and thus cannot in turn — at least not in one and the same respect — be a condition for the possibility of this act, he must therefore think of this act as an act that is *for him* entirely unconditioned and thus absolute. Accordingly, he will again discover that the *presupposition that self-consciousness is the foundation of all consciousness* completely coincides with the *thought of the I as originally posited by itself*. One would hope that everyone will be able to grasp this as well and will be able to see that if transcendental idealism is to set to work

463   in a systematic fashion, it can proceed in no other way than the way in which it proceeds in the *Wissenschaftslehre*.

Should someone subsequently wish to offer some objection to this way of proceeding, his blows will be less likely to fall upon thin air if I simply refer him to the description that has just been provided and ask him to tell me the specific step to which he wishes to object.

5.

"Intellectual intuition" is the name I give to the act required of the philosopher: an act of intuiting himself while simultaneously performing the act
(217)   by means of which the I originates for him. Intellectual intuition is the immediate consciousness that I act and of what I do when I act. It is be-cause of this that it is possible for me to know something because I do it. That we possess such a power of intellectual intuition is not something that can be demonstrated by means of concepts, nor can an understanding of what intellectual intuition is be produced from concepts. This is some-thing everyone has to discover immediately within himself; otherwise, he will never become acquainted with it at all. For anyone to demand that we establish this by means of argument is far more extraordinary than it would be if someone who was blind from birth were to demand that we explain to him what colors are without his having to see.

To be sure, anyone can be shown, within his own acknowledged expe-rience, that this intellectual intuition is present in every moment of his consciousness. I cannot take a single step, I cannot move my hand or foot, without the intellectual intuition of my self-consciousness in these actions. It is only through such an intuition that I know that *I* do this. Only in this way am I able to distinguish my own acting (and, within this acting, my own self) from the encountered object of this acting. Every person who ascribes an activity to himself appeals to this intuition. It contains within itself the source of life, and apart from it there is nothing but death.

Like sensory intuition, which never occurs by itself or constitutes a complete state of consciousness, this intellectual intuition never occurs alone, however, as a complete act of consciousness. Both types of intuition must also be grasped by means of concepts, or "comprehended."[10] Nor is this all. In addition, intellectual intuition is always conjoined with some *sensory* intuition. I cannot discover myself to be acting without also discovering some object upon which I act; and I discover this object by means of sensory intuition, which I grasp by means of a concept. Moreover, I cannot discover myself to be acting unless I also construct an image or a picture of what it is I want to produce [by acting], which image I also grasp by means of a concept. For how do I know what it is I want to produce? How could I possibly know this unless I had immediately observed myself engaged in the act of constructing a concept of a goal, that is, in a type of acting? — Consciousness is a complete whole only in this state in which the manifold in question is unified. I become conscious only of the concepts involved, that is, the concept of the object and the concept of the goal, not however of the two intuitions that lie at the basis of these concepts.

Perhaps it is no more than this which the zealots wish to urge against intellectual intuition: viz., that it is possible only in connection with a sensory intuition. In any case, this is an important point and one that is certainly not disputed by the *Wissenschaftslehre*. But anyone who believes that this entitles him to deny the existence of intellectual intuition could, with the same right, also deny the existence of sensory intuition; for sensory intuition is possible only in conjunction with intellectual intuition, since everything that is supposed to be *my* representation must be referred to me; but consciousness of the I[11] comes only from intellectual intuition. (It is a remarkable fact about the recent history of philosophy that people have failed to realize that everything that can be said against the claim that intellectual intuition exists applies equally against the claim that sensory intuition exists, and thus the blows one directs at one's opponent strike oneself as well.)

If, however, it must be conceded that there is no immediate, isolated consciousness of intellectual intuition, then where does the philosopher obtain his acquaintance with intellectual intuition and his isolated representation of the same? I answer this question as follows: He undoubtedly

---

10. "beide müssen *begriffen* werden."

11. Reading, with the original text and with GA, "das Bewusstseyn Ich," for SW's "das Bewusstseyn (Ich)."

465

obtains this in the same way he obtains his acquaintance with and his isolated representation of sensory intuition: namely, by means of an inference
from the obvious facts of consciousness. The philosopher bases his claim
concerning intellectual intuition upon the following inference: First I resolve to think of some determinate thing, and then the desired thought
ensues; I resolve to do some determinate thing, and the representation of
its occurrence then ensues. This is a fact of consciousness. Insofar as we
regard this fact in accordance with the laws of purely sensory consciousness, it contains within itself nothing more than has already been indicated: viz., a sequence of specific representations. All I would be conscious
of in this case would be a particular temporal sequence of representations,
and this would be all I could claim to be conscious of. I would then be
permitted to say no more than this: "I know that the representation of this
specific thought, characterized as something that was supposed to come
into existence, was immediately succeeded in time by another representation of this same thought, now characterized as something that actually
does exist; i.e., I know that the representation of this determinate appearance as one that ought to exist was immediately succeeded by the representation of this same appearance as one that actually does exist." But this
would not provide me with any warrant for advancing the totally different
claim that the first representation contains within itself the *real ground* of
the latter and that the latter *came into being* for me as a result of my thought
of the former. I remain purely passive, a quiet stage upon which certain
representations are succeeded by other ones; but I am not the active principle that might have produced these representations. Yet I make precisely
this latter assumption, and I cannot abandon this assumption without
abandoning myself. Why do I make this assumption? No basis for it can be
found among the sensory ingredients we examined above. Accordingly, it
must have its basis in a special type of consciousness, indeed, in an immediate consciousness, and hence, in an intuition. The intuition in question
certainly cannot be a sensory intuition directed at some materially subsisting thing; instead, it must be an intuition of a sheer activity — not an
activity that has been brought to a halt, but one that continues; not a being,
but something living.

(219)

Hence the philosopher discovers this intellectual intuition as a fact of
consciousness. (It is a fact for him; for the original I it is an Act.[12]) He does

12. "für ihn ist es Thatsache; für das ursprüngliche Ich ThatHandlung."
Thathandlung (which is here always translated as "Act" and capitalized) is a term of
Fichte's own coinage, constructed by combining the word for "fact" (= *Thatsache*)
with the word for "action" (= *Handlung*). It is a term employed to designate the

not, however, discover it immediately, as an isolated fact within his consciousness, but only insofar as he introduces distinctions into what is present as a unity within ordinary consciousness and thereby dissolves this whole into its components.

We have here presupposed the fact of this intellectual intuition so that we could then proceed to explain its *possibility* and, by explaining its connection to the system of reason as a whole, defend it against the suspicion of falseness and deception it brings upon itself because it opposes the dogmatic way of thinking (which also possesses a foundation of its own within reason). It is, however, an entirely different undertaking to confirm, on the basis of something even higher, the *belief* in the reality of this intellectual intuition, with which, according to our explicit admission, transcendental idealism must commence, and to show the presence within reason itself of the very interest upon which this belief is based. The only way in which this can be accomplished is by exhibiting the ethical law within us, within the context of which the I is represented as something sublime and elevated above all of the original modifications accomplished through this law and is challenged to act in an absolute manner, the sole foundation of which should lie in the I itself and nowhere else. It is in this way that the I becomes characterized as something absolutely active. Our intuition of self-activity and freedom has its foundation in our consciousness of this law, which is unquestionably not a type of consciousness derived from anything else, but is instead an immediate consciousness. Here I am given to myself, by myself, as something that is obliged to be active in a certain way. Accordingly, I am given to myself, by myself, as "active in an overall sense" or "as such." I possess life within myself and draw it from myself. It is only through the medium of the ethical law that I catch a glimpse of *myself*; and insofar as I view myself through this medium, I necessarily view myself as self-active. In this way an entirely alien ingredient, viz., my consciousness of my own real efficacy, arises for me within a consciousness that otherwise would be nothing but a consciousness of a particular sequence of my representations.

Intellectual intuition provides the only firm standpoint for any philoso-

446

Ethical law [margin annotation]

---

type of originally productive act that is, at the same time, its own product and/or object (in contrast with an ordinary *Handlung*, which is directed at an object outside of itself). In other words, it designates the original, productive activity of the I itself and thus provides the starting point for a transcendental deduction of experience. Fichte first introduced this term in 1794 in his "Review of *Aenesidemus*" (see SW, I, p. 8 = GA, I,2: 46; English translation in EPW) and employed it extensively in GWL.

phy. Everything that occurs within consciousness can be explained upon the basis of intellectual intuition — and only upon this basis. Without self-consciousness there is no consciousness whatsoever, but self-consciousness is possible only in the way we have indicated: I am only active. I cannot be driven from this position. This is the point where my philosophy becomes entirely independent of all arbitrary choice and becomes a product of iron necessity — to the extent, that is, that free reason can be subject to necessity; i.e., it becomes a product of *practical* necessity. I *cannot* go beyond this standpoint, because I am not *permitted* to go beyond it. With this, transcendental idealism simultaneously reveals itself to be the only type of philosophical thinking that accords with duty. It is the mode of thinking in which speculation and the ethical law are most intimately united. I *ought* to begin my thinking with the thought of the pure I, and I ought to think of this pure I as absolutely self-active — not as determined by things, but rather as determining them.

The concept of acting, which becomes possible only by means of this intellectual intuition of the self-active I, is the sole concept that unites the two worlds that exist for us: the sensible world and the intelligible world. The sensible or sensory world is what stands in opposition to my acting; and since I am finite, I have to posit something in opposition to my acting. The intelligible world is what ought to come into being through my acting.

I would very much like to know what those who assume a familiar air of superiority whenever they encounter any mention of "intelligible intuition"* imagine our consciousness of the ethical law to be like, or how they are able to construct for themselves concepts such as "right," "virtue," and the like — concepts that they certainly do possess. According to them, there are but two *a priori* intuitions: time and space. They undoubtedly construct the [ethical] concepts in question within time, which is the form of inner sense. But they undoubtedly do not consider these concepts to be

---

* This is what is done, for example, by the Raphael of book reviewers in his review of Schelling's *On the I as the Principle of Philosophy*.[13]

13. This is a reference to J. B. Erhard's review of Schelling's 1795 treatise, *Vom Ich als Princip der Philosophie*, a work written during the period when Schelling was most directly under the influence of Fichte's *Wissenschaftslehre* (in Schelling, *Sämmtliche Werke*, ed. K. F. A. Schelling [Stuttgart: J. G. Cotta, 1856–61], vol. 1, pp. 149–244; English translation by Fritz Marti, *On the I as the Principle of Philosophy*, in *The Unconditional in Human Knowledge* [Lewisburg, Pa.: Bucknell University Press, 1980], pp. 63–149). Erhard's patronizing and critical review of Schelling's book appeared in the October 11, 1796 issue of the *Allgemeine Literatur-Zeitung*.

identical to time itself; they are only a certain way of filling time. With what then do they fill time in this case, and what underlies their construction of these concepts? The only *a priori* intuition that remains for them is space. Consequently, their "right" would have to turn out to be, let us say, square, while their "virtue" would perhaps have to be circular, in the same way that all of the concepts they construct on the basis of sensory intuition — the concept of a tree, for example, or of an animal — are nothing but certain ways of limiting space. But they do not really conceive of right or   *468* virtue in this manner. What then is it that underlies their construction of these concepts? If they observe correctly, they will discover that what underlies these concepts is acting as such, i.e., freedom. Both concepts, the   *(221)* concept of right as well as that of virtue, are for them determinate limitations of acting as such, just as all sensory concepts are for them determinate limitations of space. But how have they arrived at this foundation that underlies their construction of these concepts? One would hope that they have not inferred acting from the dead inertia of matter, nor freedom from the mechanism of nature. They must have obtained this by means of immediate intuition; consequently, in addition to the two intuitions they recognize, there must also be a third.

   Accordingly, the question of whether philosophy should begin with a fact or with an Act (i.e., with a pure activity that presupposes no object but, instead, produces its own object, and therefore with an *acting* that immediately becomes a *deed*)[14] is by no means so inconsequential as it may seem to some people to be. If philosophy begins with a fact, then it places itself in the midst of a world of being and finitude, and it will be difficult indeed for it to discover any path leading from this world to an infinite and supersensible one. If, however, philosophy begins with an Act, then it finds itself at the precise point where these two worlds are connected with each other and from which they can both be surveyed in a single glance.

6.

Neither the *Wissenschaftslehre* nor its author is in the habit of seeking protection by appealing to any sort of authority. There are, of course, people who are unwilling to allow themselves to be persuaded by this theory until

14. "ob die Philosophie von einer ThatSache ausgehe, oder von einer ThatHandlung (d.i. von reiner Thätigkeit, die kein Object voraussetzt, sondern es selbst hervorbringt, und wo sonach das *Handeln* unmittelbar zur *That* wird)." Reading, with the original text and GA, "reiner Thätigkeit" for SW's "einer Thätigkeit" ("an activity").

they have first determined whether it accords with what has been taught by someone else, rather than asking whether it accords with the dictates of their own reason. The *Wissenschaftslehre* does not address itself to readers of this sort, for they are lacking in absolutely spontaneous self-activity, i.e., that completely independent confidence in themselves which this philosophy presupposes. Thus it is not in order to recommend his own theory, but for an entirely different reason, that the author of the *Wissenschaftslehre* has prefaced his presentation with the claim that this philosophy is in complete

469 accord with Kant's and is nothing other than the Kantian philosophy properly understood. This is an opinion that has grown stronger and stronger as he has continued to elaborate his system and has had occasion to apply the principles of the same in a variety of different ways. Yet all of the recognized experts on Kant's philosophy who have expressed an opinion

(222) on this topic — be they friends or foes of the *Wissenschaftslehre* — have unanimously affirmed just the opposite;* and, *at their suggestion*, this has even been asserted by Kant himself, who must surely understand his own philosophy better than anyone else.† The author of the *Wissenschaftslehre*

---

* The ingenious reviewer of the first four volumes of this philosophical journal, writing in the *Allgemeine Literatur-Zeitung*,[15] also demands some proof of this claim, but he does not express any opinion of his own concerning the agreement or lack of agreement between these two systems. Accordingly, he is not one of the authors whom I am here discussing.

15. This is an allusion to a review of the *Philosophisches Journal* that Friedrich Schlegel (1772–1829) published in the *Allgemeine Literatur-Zeitung* in March of 1797, i.e., while Schlegel himself was a colleague of Fichte's at Jena. In discussing the controversy over Fichte's claim that the *Wissenschaftslehre* deals with the same questions as Kant's philosophy and answers them in the same way as Kant, Schlegel remarked that it would take an entire book to examine this claim and expressed his hope that Fichte himself "will very soon find the leisure and the inclination to provide a *complete proof* of this claim."

† Thus Herr Forberg,[16] whom the *Allgemeine Literatur-Zeitung* and the Salzburg *Literatur-Zeitung*, as well as other sources, have identified as the author of *Fragments from My Papers* (Jena 1796), can (on p. 77) "assert on the *best* authority" (presumably from a letter he received from Kant himself) "that it is Kant's opinion that Fichte's system is completely different from the Kantian system." To be sure, I myself have hitherto found it impossible — whether on the "best authority" or any other — to determine Kant's opinion of the *Wissenschaftslehre*. Nor do I at all expect that this venerable elder, who has certainly earned his present position, will now immerse himself in a completely new train of thought, one that is quite foreign to him and departs completely from his own manner of presentation, simply so that he will then be able to deliver a judgment that time itself will undoubtedly deliver without any word from him. Furthermore, I know very well that Kant is not in the

would be happy to share this opinion — if only he could. For he does not   *470*
think there is anything shameful about having failed to understand Kant
correctly; indeed, he predicts that the opinion that there is nothing shameful about this will soon become quite widespread. Hence he could put up
with the minor embarrassment involved in having once interpreted Kant
incorrectly and would, in return, obtain for himself the honor of being   *(223)*
considered the originator of a view that will surely become universal and
will produce the most beneficial revolution within humanity. It is almost
impossible to explain why both the supporters and the opponents of the
Wissenschaftslehre have contested this claim so vigorously and why they
have so earnestly entreated the author of the *Wissenschaftslehre* to produce
some proof of this claim — a task that he never pledged himself to assume
and has expressly declined to undertake, and one that, properly considered, constitutes a part of the eventual history of the *Wissenschaftslehre* and
does not belong to the actual presentation of the same. It is certainly not
out of any tender concern for the honor of its author that the opponents of
the *Wissenschaftslehre* make such a demand, and its supporters can dispense with any such concern, since I myself have no desire to acquire any

---

habit of passing judgment upon any work he himself has not read.[17] Nevertheless,
in all fairness and until such time as I can prove the opposite, I must take Herr
Forberg at his word on this. Kant may very well have expressed such an opinion;
but if he has, this raises the question of whether he *has really read and really understood* the *Wissenschaftslehre*, or whether he may not instead have been referring to
those monstrosities the originator of the "standpoint theory" has been pleased to
present under the name *"Wissenschaftslehre"* to the readers of the *Annalen der
Philosophie und des philosophischen Geistes* — a journal which, according to its editor, has called attention to the alleged weaknesses of the *Wissenschaftslehre*.[18]

16. Friedrich Karl Forberg (1770–1848) was for several years a colleague of
Fichte's at Jena, and his anonymously published *Fragmente aus meinen Papieren*
(1796) offers readers a fascinating glimpse of the philosophical climate in Jena just
prior to and during Fichte's first years there, as well as several engaging descrip-
tions of Fichte himself.

17. See Kant's May 12, 1793 letter to Fichte, in which Kant excused himself from
passing judgment on the *Attempt at a Critique of All Revelation* on the grounds that
any such judgment would require a careful and time-consuming study of Fichte's
text.

18. The "originator of 'the standpoint theory'" is J. S. Beck, who, in 1795 and
1796, published several harshly critical reviews of Fichte's writings. Beck's reviews
appeared in the *Annalen der Philosophie*, which was the more or less "official" organ
of orthodox Kantianism and whose editor during this period was L. H. Jacob
(1759–1827), professor of philosophy at Halle.

such honor for myself. The honor I recognize and seek lies elsewhere. Is it perhaps possible that all of these people have misunderstood Kant's writings and that I can avoid their reproach in this way? This suggestion constitutes no reproach — not, at least, when it comes from the author of the *Wissenschaftslehre*, who acknowledges as openly as possible that he too failed to understand Kant's writings and found them to possess a valuable and internally consistent meaning only after he had already discovered the *Wissenschaftslehre* in his own way. Furthermore, one would hope that it will soon become impossible for anyone to view such a failure of understanding as a matter for reproach. My opponents will be particularly anxious to defend themselves against the charge of having failed to recognize their own theory, the very theory they themselves have been defending with all their might, when it was presented to them in an unfamiliar form. And I too would prefer to spare them this rather severe reproach, were it not that I have an interest that seems to me to be higher than theirs, an interest to which their interest *ought* to be sacrificed: for I do not wish, even for a single instant, to be considered to be anything more than I am, nor will I permit myself to be credited with any merit that I do not deserve.

471
(224)

Consequently, I must at some point provide the proof that has been so frequently demanded of me, and thus I propose to take advantage of the present opportunity for this purpose.

As we have just seen, the *Wissenschaftslehre* proceeds from an intellec-

---

Fichte's conjecture concerning Kant's lack of first-hand acquaintance with the published *Wissenschaftslehre* was quite correct; however, it appears that it was not Beck's reviews on which Kant relied in forming his opinion of the *Wissenschaftslehre*, but rather the long, omnibus review of Fichte's writings published by K. L. Reinhold in the *Allgemeine Literatur-Zeitung* in January of 1798. (See Kant's revealing letter of April 5, 1798 to J. H. Tieftrunk, in which, after confessing his lack of any first-hand acquaintance with the *Wissenschaftslehre*, Kant then proceeds to express a quite low opinion of it.)

Eventually, Kant published a rather harsh "Declaration" in the August 29, 1799 issue of the *Allgemeine Literatur-Zeitung*, in which he made public his disagreement with Fichte's claims concerning the similarities between their systems and unequivocally repudiated the *Wissenschaftslehre*. (For an English translation of this remarkable document, as well as of the letter to Tieftrunk, see Kant's *Philosophical Correspondence 1759–99*, trans. Arnulf Zweig [Chicago: The University of Chicago Press, 1967], pp. 249–50 and 253–54.) For Fichte's reply to Kant's "Declaration," see his September 1799 letter ("Concerning Kant's Declaration") in GA, III,4: 75–76, and his November 4, 1800 "Public Announcement of a New Presentation of the *Wissenschaftslehre*" (translated below).

tual intuition, namely, an intellectual intuition of the absolute self-activity of the I.

Yet it certainly cannot be denied and is unmistakably obvious to every reader of Kant that there is nothing against which Kant has declared himself more decisively and, one might say, disparagingly than against the claim that we possess a power of intellectual intuition.[19] This, moreover, is a declaration that is so deeply rooted in the very nature of Kant's philosophy that, despite all of the further elaboration his system has undergone since the first appearance of the *Critique of Pure Reason* — thanks to which the principles of this system have obviously assumed in his own mind a much higher degree of clarity and a more finished form (as will become apparent to anyone who carefully compares Kant's more recent writings with his previous ones) — he has nevertheless repeated this assertion as forcefully as ever in one of his most recent writings ("Concerning a Superior Tone in Philosophy," in the May 1796 issue of the *Berlinische Monatsschrift*).[20] In this essay he treats the delusion that we possess a power of intellectual intuition as the source of that style of philosophizing that scorns all labor and produces nothing but the worst sort of fanaticism.

If a philosophy is built upon precisely what the Kantian philosophy unequivocally repudiates, what further evidence could be required in order to show that the philosophy in question is the complete opposite of the Kantian system and is precisely the sort of deplorable and absurd system discussed by Kant in this essay? But before anyone advances such an argument, he should first inquire whether these two systems may not be employing one and the same word to express two very different concepts. In Kant's terminology every intuition is directed at some being (a posited being, something fixed and enduring). Accordingly, "intellectual intuition" would, in this case, have to be a consciousness of a non-sensible being, an immediate consciousness of the thing in itself, and indeed, a consciousness made possible by thought alone. I.e., it would amount to a *472* creation of the thing in itself simply from the concept of the same (similar to the way in which those who demonstrate the existence of God from the

19. See, e.g., KRV, Bxln, B68–72, B158–59, and A251–56/B307–14.

20. "Von einem neuerdings erhobenen vornehmen Ton in der Philosophie." In *Kants gesammelte Schriften*, ed. by the königliche Preußischen Akademie der Wissenschaften (1902–10; rpt., Berlin: de Gruyter, 1968) [henceforth = KGS], vol. VIII, pp. 387–406. English translation by Peter Fenves, "On a Newly Arisen Superior Tone in Philosophy," in *Raising the Tone of Philosophy: Late Essays by Immanuel Kant, Transformative Critique by Jacques Derrida*, ed. Peter Fenves (Baltimore and London: Johns Hopkins University Press, 1993), pp. 51–81.

(225)

mere concept thereof must view God's existence as nothing more than a
consequence of their own thinking). It may well be that, because of the
particular path followed in its presentation, the Kantian system had to
ward off the thing in itself in this particular way. The *Wissenschaftslehre*,
however, has disposed of the thing in itself in another way; it recognizes
the concept of a thing in itself to be a complete perversion of reason, an
utterly unreasonable concept. Since the *Wissenschaftslehre* derives the
entire concept of being only from the form of sensibility, it follows that,
for it, all being is necessarily *sensible* being. Within this system, therefore,
one is completely protected against any claim that the concept of being is
somehow related to the thing in itself. From the standpoint of the *Wissenschaftslehre*, therefore, "intellectual intuition" in the Kantian sense is
something impossible, something that slips between our fingers whenever
we try to think of it and does not even merit a name. The intellectual
intuition of which the *Wissenschaftslehre* speaks is not directed toward any
sort of being whatsoever; instead, it is directed at an acting — and this is
something that Kant does not even mention (except, perhaps, under the
name "pure apperception"). Nevertheless, it is still possible to indicate the
exact place within Kant's system where he should have discussed this. For
Kant would certainly maintain that we are conscious of the categorical
imperative, would he not? What sort of consciousness is this? Kant neglected to pose this question to himself, for nowhere did he discuss the
foundation of *all* philosophy. Instead, in the *Critique of Pure Reason* he
dealt only with theoretical philosophy, within the context of which the
categorical imperative could not appear; and in the *Critique of Practical
Reason* he dealt only with practical philosophy and discussed only the content of this sort of consciousness, and thus the question concerning the
very nature of this sort of consciousness could not arise within the context
of the second *Critique*. — Our consciousness of the categorical imperative
is undoubtedly immediate, but it is not a form of sensory consciousness. In
other words, it is precisely what I call "intellectual intuition"; and, on the
assumption that there are no classical authors in philosophy,[21] I have just as

---

21. This is an apparent allusion to Kant's remark in his 1790 polemic against
Eberhard, *Ueber eine Entdeckung nach der alle neue Kritik der reinen Vernunft durch
eine ältere entbehrlich gemacht werden soll*, that "*What is philosophically correct* is
something one neither can nor must learn from Leibniz. Instead, the test of this is
our commonly shared human understanding, and this is just as available to one
person as it is to another. There are no *classical authors* in philosophy." (KGS, VIII,
p. 219n. A complete English translation of Kant's text, along with a great deal of
interesting supplementary material, is contained in Henry E. Allison, *The Kant-
Eberhard Controversy* [Baltimore: The Johns Hopkins University Press, 1973].)

much right to use this term to designate this type of consciousness as Kant has to use it to designate something else, something that is actually nothing at all. This same right also entitles me to demand that anyone who passes judgment upon my system should first become familiar with the meaning I assign to this term. *473*

A noteworthy passage on this topic may be found in the writings of my esteemed friend Court Chaplain Schulz, with whom I once shared my then still vague Idea[22] of constructing philosophy in its entirety upon the basis of the pure I. This was long before I had become clear about this in my own mind, and I found Herr Schulz to be closer to this Idea and less opposed to it than anyone else. On p.159 of Part Two of his *Examination of the Kantian Critique of Pure Reason*,[23] he writes: "Just because it can and must instruct us in an immediate manner, we must not for this reason confuse the pure, active self-consciousness, of which every I actually consists, with the *power* *(226)* *of intuition*; nor should one conclude from this that we possess a *non-sensory power of intellectual intuition*." (This is quite correct, as has since been affirmed by the *Wissenschaftslehre*.) "For an *intuition* is a *representation* that is *immediately* related to its object. Pure self-consciousness, however, is not a representation at all; but rather it is *that* whereby every representation first becomes an actual representation." — "When I say that I entertain a representation of something, this is simply another way of saying that I am conscious of having a representation of this object," etc. Thus, according

---

22. "meine noch unbestimmte Idee." Though sometimes employed by Fichte in an uncritical manner and with the everyday meaning of a "notion" or "mere idea," the term *Idee* has an important technical meaning within the context of Kantian philosophy, where it designates what Kant calls the "transcendental Ideas or pure concepts of reason." (See, e.g., KRV, A338/B396: "Although a purely transcendental Idea is, in accordance with the original laws of reason, a quite necessary product of reason, its object, it may yet be said, is something of which we possess no concept.") An *Idee*, unlike a *Begriff* (or "concept of the understanding"), does not, therefore, determine any sensible object, but instead sets a *task* for reason itself; i.e., *Ideen* (or "Ideas") possess a "regulative" rather than a "constitutive" function. *Idee* is here always rendered as "Idea" and capitalized.

23. Johann Friedrich Schultz (sometimes spelled "Schulz") (1739–1805) was *Hofprediger* and professor of mathematics at Königsberg, as well as a close personal friend of Kant's. The conversation with Schultz to which Fichte here refers must have occurred during Fichte's visit to Königsberg during the summer of 1791 (where he became personally acquainted with Kant and also composed his first book, the *Critique of All Revelation*). Schultz's own *Prüfung der Kantischen Critik der reinen Vernunft* was published in two volumes in 1789 and 1792. In a published "Declaration" dated May 29, 1797 Kant identified Schultz as the most accurate expositor of his philosophy (KGS, XII, p. 367).

to Herr Schulz, a representation is a possible object of consciousness. —
But Herr Schulz himself was just talking about pure self-consciousness.
He undoubtedly knows what it is he is talking about when he speaks in this
way, and thus, at least insofar as he is a philosopher, he does indeed possess
a representation of pure self-consciousness. But he too neglects to discuss
this consciousness that the philosopher himself possesses; instead, he dis-
cusses only original consciousness. Accordingly, the meaning of his claim
is as follows: Originally, that is to say, within ordinary consciousness, unaccompanied by any philosophical reflection, mere self-consciousness does
not, taken by itself, constitute a complete consciousness; instead, it is only
a necessary component of the latter, albeit a component that makes a complete consciousness possible in the first place. But does *sensory* intuition
constitute a complete consciousness? Is it not also simply that whereby a
representation first becomes a representation? Intuitions without concepts
474   are indeed blind.[24] In what sense, therefore, is Herr Schulz entitled to call
(sensory) intuition, considered apart from self-consciousness, a "representation"? As we have seen, from the philosopher's standpoint self-consciousness is just as much a representation as is sensory intuition; but from
the standpoint of the original, representing subject, *sensory intuition* is no
more a representation than is self-consciousness. Or does a concept constitute a representation? Concepts without intuitions are empty indeed.
Taken in isolation, neither self-consciousness, a sensory intuition, nor a
concept constitutes a representation; they are only that whereby represen-
(227)   tations become possible. According to Kant, according to Schulz, and according to me, three elements are required for a complete representation:
[1] There is that whereby the representation obtains a relation to an object
and thus becomes a representation of *something*. We all agree in calling this
"sensory intuition." (This remains true even when the object of representation is I myself. In this case I become for myself something that endures
through time.) [2] There is that whereby the representation is related to a
subject and thus becomes *my* representation. This, according to Kant and
Schulz, should not be called "intuition." I, however, call it by this name,
for it bears the same relationship to a complete representation that sensory
intuition does. [3] Lastly, there is that whereby the first two elements are
united and thus become a representation. Here again, we all agree in designating this a "concept."

24. This is an allusion to Kant's oft-(mis)quoted remark: "thoughts without content are empty; intuitions without concepts are blind." (KRV, A51/B75.)

What then is the overall gist of the *Wissenschaftslehre*, summarized in a few words? It is this: Reason is absolutely self-sufficient; it exists only for itself. But nothing exists for reason except reason itself. It follows that everything reason is must have its foundation within reason itself and must be explicable solely on the basis of reason itself and not on the basis of anything outside of reason, for reason could not get outside of itself without renouncing itself. In short, the *Wissenschaftslehre* is transcendental idealism. And what, summarized in a few words, is the gist of the Kantian philosophy? How may Kant's system be characterized? I confess that I find it impossible to conceive how anyone could understand even a single sentence of Kant's and reconcile it with all the others unless he makes the same presupposition the *Wissenschaftslehre* makes. I believe that this presupposition manifests itself on every page of Kant's writings, and I confess that one of the reasons why I have heretofore declined to provide the proof demanded of me is because it seemed to me to be a bit ridiculous, as well as boring, to demonstrate the presence of a forest by counting the individual trees.

475

Here I will quote only one central passage from Kant. On p. 136 of the new edition of the *Critique of Pure Reason* he states: "The supreme first principle of the possibility of all intuition, in its relation to understanding, is this: that the entire manifold should be subject to the conditions of the original unity of apperception."[25] In other words, it is possible to *think of* what has been intuited only on the condition that this is compatible with the possibility of the original unity of apperception. Furthermore, according to Kant, an intuition is possible only insofar as it is thought of and comprehended, since, according to him, intuitions without concepts are blind, i.e., are nothing at all; and thus, intuition itself is subject to the conditions that make thinking possible. According to Kant, therefore, not only is thinking immediately subject to the conditions of the original unity of apperception, but, since it is mediated by thinking, the act of intuiting that is conditioned thereby — and hence *all consciousness* — is also subject to these same conditions.

(228)

What is this condition? (Though Kant admittedly talks about "conditions" in this passage, he nevertheless puts forward only a single funda-

---

25. KRV, B136. Fichte quotes (as usual) from the third, 1790 edition of the *Critique of Pure Reason*, which has the same pagination and, except for some minor corrections of printers' errors and some (controversial) changes in the use of italics, is identical to the second edition = B. As usual, Fichte's citation is not exact.

mental condition.) According to § 16, the condition in question is this: that my representations should be *capable* of being accompanied by the "*I* think."[26] (Indeed, on p. 132, l. 14, the only word in italics is the word "I," and this is significant.) In other words: *I am the thinking subject* in this act of thinking.

What "I" is Kant talking about in this passage? Is this perhaps the I that the Kantians have so confidently pieced together from the manifold of representations, an I that is not contained in any of these individual representations but is contained within all of them taken together? If this were so, then the words we have quoted from Kant would mean *this*: "I who am thinking of D am the same I who previously thought of C, B, and A; and it is by thinking of my various acts of thinking that I first become for myself an I — i.e., that which remains identical within this manifold." If this is what Kant means, then he too would be as wretched a babbler as the "Kantians" whom we are discussing; for he would then be contending that the very possibility of all thinking is itself conditioned by another act of thinking, and indeed, by the act of thinking of this act of thinking. If so, then I should like to know how we are ever supposed to be able to

476

---

26. "The '*I* think' must be capable of accompanying all of my representations; for otherwise something would be represented which could not be thought at all, and this is equivalent to saying that the representation would be impossible, or at least would be nothing for me. That representation which can be given prior to all thought is entitled 'intuition.' All the manifold of intuition has, therefore, a necessary relation to the 'I think' in the same subject in which this manifold is found. But this representation is an act of *spontaneity*; that is, it cannot be regarded as belonging to sensibility. I call it 'pure apperception,' in order to distinguish it from *empirical* apperception; or again, I call it 'original apperception,' because it is that self-consciousness which, while generating the representation 'I think' (a representation which must be capable of accompanying all other representations, and which in all consciousness is one and the same), cannot itself be accompanied by any further representation. The unity of this apperception I likewise entitle the '*transcendental* unity of self-consciousness,' in order to indicate the possibility of *a priori* cognition arising from it. For the manifold representations, which are given in an intuition, would not be one and all *my* representations, if they did not all belong to one self-consciousness. As my representations (even if I am not conscious of them as such) they must conform to the conditions under which alone they *can* stand together in one universal self-consciousness, because otherwise they would not all without exception belong to me. From this original combination many consequences follow" (KRV, B131–33; Kemp Smith translation, with minor changes). Note that the "significant" use of italics in the phrase "*I* think" occurs only in the third ed. of KRV.

accomplish a single act of thinking!*

We do not, however, here wish to limit ourselves simply to drawing inferences; instead, let us cite Kant's own words. On p. 132 he writes: "This representation 'I think' is an act of spontaneity; that is, it cannot be regarded as belonging to sensibility." (And consequently, I would add, neither can it be ascribed to inner sensibility, to which the sort of identity of consciousness described above does indeed pertain.) "I call it 'pure apperception,' to distinguish it from (the just mentioned) empirical apperception; because it is that self-consciousness which, while generating the representation '*I* think' (a representation which must be capable of accompanying all other representations, *and which in all consciousness is one and the same*), cannot itself be accompanied by any further representation." Here we have a clear description of the nature of pure self-consciousness. This pure self-consciousness is the same in all consciousness, and thus it is not determinable by anything contingent within consciousness. The I that appears within pure self-consciousness is determined by nothing but itself, and it is determined absolutely. It also follows, therefore, that Kant cannot understand pure apperception to be the same as our consciousness of our individuality, nor can he combine the latter with the former. For consciousness of one's own individuality is necessarily accompanied by another sort of consciousness, namely, consciousness of a "you," and it is possible only on this condition.

    Thus we quite definitely encounter within Kant precisely the same concept of the *pure* I that is presented in the *Wissenschaftslehre*. — What, according to the quoted passage, is the relationship Kant thinks this pure I bears to all consciousness? The pure I *provides the conditions for all consciousness*. Thus, just as in the *Wissenschaftslehre*, so too for Kant as well: the possibility of all consciousness is conditioned by the possibility of the I, or of pure self-consciousness. An act of thinking of something conditioned presupposes whatever it is that conditions this something, for this is precisely what the relationship in question means. It therefore follows that even according to Kant a systematic derivation of consciousness as a whole (or, what amounts to the same thing, a philosophical system) would have to begin with the pure I — which is precisely how the *Wissenschaftslehre* does begin — and that the Idea of such a science has already been provided by Kant himself.

(229)

477

---

* Even if one were willing to overlook this difficulty (as bad as it is), all that could be produced by the act of combining these many different representations would be a manifold *act of thinking*, which appears as *a single act of thinking as such*, but by no means a *thinking subject* who engages in this manifold act of thinking.

One may, however, wish to weaken the force of this argument by making the following distinction: It is one thing to be *conditioned*; to be *determined* is something else altogether.

According to Kant, all consciousness is merely conditioned by self-consciousness; i.e., the contents of consciousness can still be grounded by or have their foundation in something or other outside of self-consciousness. Things that are grounded in this way must simply not *contradict* the conditions of self-consciousness; that is to say, they must simply not annul the possibility of self-consciousness, but they do not actually have to be *generated* from self-consciousness.

According to the *Wissenschaftslehre*, all consciousness is determined by self-consciousness; i.e., everything that occurs within consciousness has its foundation in the conditions that make self-consciousness possible — that is to say, is given and is produced thereby and possesses no foundation whatsoever outside of self-consciousness. — I must show that in our case the *determinacy* follows from the *conditionality*, and thus that the distinction in question is not present in this case and makes no difference at all. If

(230)   a person says "All consciousness is conditioned by the possibility of self-consciousness *and from now on I wish to view it in just this manner*," then, as he proceeds in his investigation of consciousness, he will never know anything more about consciousness than this, and he will abstract from everything else he may otherwise believe that he knows about consciousness. He will derive everything required from the postulated principle, and only the consciousness he has *derived* in this manner will count for him as consciousness at all. Everything else is and remains nothing whatsoever. Thus, for a person who is examining consciousness in this manner, derivability from self-consciousness *determines* the scope of what he will consider to be

478   consciousness; and this occurs precisely because he starts with the presupposition that all consciousness is *conditioned* by the possibility of self-consciousness.

I know full well that Kant has by no means actually *constructed* a system of this sort; for if he had, then the author of the *Wissenschaftslehre* would have excused himself from this particular effort and would have chosen to apply his energies to the cultivation of some other branch of human knowledge. I also know that Kant has by no means *proven* that the categories he has postulated are conditions for the possibility of self-consciousness, but has merely asserted that this is so. Nor has he provided any derivation whatsoever of space and time and of what fills them both and is *inseparable* from them within original consciousness; i.e., he has not provided a deduction of them as conditions for the possibility of self-con-

sciousness. Indeed, unlike the case of the categories, he has not even explicitly and directly asserted that space, time, and what fills them both are
supposed to be conditions for the possibility of consciousness; instead,
this is a conclusion one can reach only by means of the inference indicated
above. Nevertheless, I am equally certain that Kant has entertained the
thought of such a system, that all of the things he has actually presented are
fragments and results of this system, and that his assertions make coherent sense only on this assumption. Perhaps he himself has not thought this
system through with sufficient precision and clarity to be *able* to present
it to others; or perhaps he has indeed done so, but simply did not *wish* to
present it to others (as is suggested by certain hints that appear in his   *479*
writings):* This, it seems to me, is a question that can be left entirely   *(231)*
unexplored; or, if it is to be explored, let someone else undertake this
investigation, for I have never made any claims concerning this point.
Whatever might be unearthed by such an investigation, this worthy man
will still retain the *sole* credit for having been the first person who consciously attempted to divert the attention of philosophy away from external objects and to direct it within ourselves. This is the spirit† and the

---

* See, for example, the following passage from p. 108 of the *Critique of Pure Reason*: "In this treatise, I purposely omit the definitions of the categories, *even though
I may now be in possession of them.*" The categories can be defined only *by showing
how each category is determinately related to the possibility of self-consciousness*, and
anyone who is in possession of these definitions is necessarily in possession of the
Wissenschaftslehre. "Definitions of them" (i.e., of these categories) "would rightly
be demanded *in a system of pure reason*, but *here* such definitions would only divert
attention from the main point."[27] In this passage Kant draws a contrast between the   *(231)*
"system of pure reason" and "here" (viz., the *Critique of Pure Reason*), and he does
not claim that the latter constitutes the former. To be sure, it is not easy to understand how the *Critique*, simply by virtue of its sheer age, should have been transformed into a system, particularly after Reinhold publicly raised the question of
the foundation and the completeness of Kant's enterprise and since Kant himself
did not publish any system of pure reason. Nor is it any easier to understand why   *479*
the additional questions authorized by the passage just quoted were rather harshly
dismissed once they had actually been raised. — In my opinion, the *Critique of Pure
Reason* by no means lacks a foundation. Such a foundation is very plainly present;
but nothing has been constructed upon it, and the construction materials — though
already well prepared — are jumbled together in a most haphazard manner.

27. KRV, A82/B108 (Kemp Smith's translation, with modifications). The emphasis is Fichte's, whose quotation from Kant is, once again, inexact.

† When one is unable to make satisfactory progress in one's interpretation by ap-   *(231)*
pealing to the *letter*, then one certainly has to interpret in accordance with the *spirit*.

innermost soul of Kant's entire philosophy, and it is also the spirit and
soul of the *Wissenschaftslehre*.

480
(232)
   I will, nevertheless, be confronted with what is alleged to be a fundamental difference between Kant's system and the *Wissenschaftslehre*. Indeed, this difference has quite recently been cited once again by a man
who, more than perhaps anyone else, has long enjoyed a well-deserved
reputation for understanding Kant and who has recently demonstrated a
grasp of the *Wissenschaftslehre* as well. I am referring to Reinhold, who
(233)
wishes to maintain that, in advancing the claim I have just reiterated and
proven, the author of the *Wissenschaftslehre* is guilty of an injustice *to him-*

---

(232)
Kant himself, by modestly acknowledging that he is not aware of possessing any
particular talent for clarity, shows that he attaches no great value to the letter of his
own presentation. On p. xliv of the preface to the second edition of the *Critique of
Pure Reason* he himself recommends that one interpret his writings in their *inter-
connection* with one another and in accordance with the *Idea* contained within this
whole — i.e., in accordance with the *spirit and the intention* that may be contained
within the individual passages. Indeed, he himself (in *On a Discovery According to
Which Any New Critique of Pure Reason Has Been Made Superfluous by an Earlier
One*,[28] p. 119 ff.) provides a noteworthy demonstration of how to interpret a text in
accordance with its spirit. This occurs in his interpretation of Leibniz, every sentence of which proceeds from the following premise: Is it really credible that
Leibniz could have wished to say this, and this, and this? On p. 122 of the same
essay he states that one must not allow oneself to be misled by the account (which
Leibniz provides in his own explicit words) of *sensibility as a confused mode of representation*, but should, instead, *replace it* with a view that is in keeping with
Leibniz's intention — *since otherwise Leibniz's system would not be internally consistent*. Similarly, he contends that one would entirely misunderstand Leibniz's claim
concerning the innateness of certain concepts *if one were to take it literally*. The
latter are Kant's own words. — From this one can certainly infer that, in the case
of original philosophical authors, one should interpret their writings in accordance
with the spirit *that is really present within them*, which, however, does not mean that
one should interpret them in accordance with some "spirit" that *allegedly should be
present within them*. (We certainly cannot be speaking here of the writings of mere
interpreters, since one can always compare these with the actual writings of the
author whom they are expounding, assuming that the latter have not yet disap-
peared.)

28. *Ueber eine Entdeckung nach der alle neue Kritik der reinen Vernunft durch eine
ältere entbehrlich gemacht werden soll* (1790). In KGS, VIII, pp. 185–251. Fichte's
page numbers refer to the second, 1791 edition (which is virtually identical to the
first edition). The specific passage concerning the legitimacy of some interpretations that violate the letter of a philosophical text may be found on pp. 248–49 of
KGS, VIII. (English translation in *The Kant-Eberhard Controversy*, pp. 157–58.)

self and (as of course follows from this) *to other authorities on Kant's writings as well*. On p. 341 of Part Two of his *Selected Miscellaneous Writings* (Jena: Mauke, 1797) he states: "According to the *Critique of Pure Reason* as well, the foundation for the claim that our representations correspond to something outside of us is, to be sure, present within the *I*, but only to the extent that *empirical cognition* (experience) occurs within the I as a fact. With respect to its *transcendental* content (which constitutes only the *form* of empirical cognition), such cognition has its foundation *solely* within the *pure* I; but with respect to its *empirical content*, by means of which it possesses objective reality, it must be grounded within the I *by something different* from the I. But philosophy could not obtain a scientific form so long as *what is distinct from the I* and provides the foundation for the objective reality of what is transcendental had to be sought *outside of the I*."[29]

I will have succeeded neither in convincing my reader nor in completely *(234)* proving my claim until I have overturned this objection.

The (purely historical) question is this: Did Kant really base the empirical content of experience upon *something distinct from the I*?

I am quite well aware that this is how Kant has been understood by every "Kantian," with the sole exception of Herr Beck, whose book dealing with this subject, the *Only Possible Standpoint*, appeared after the publication of the *Wissenschaftslehre*.* This is also the way in which Kant is *481* understood by the interpreter who has recently been authorized by Kant himself, viz., Herr Schulz, whom I mention in this context only for this reason. Over and over again, he expresses his agreement with Herr Eberhard's[30] assertion *that the objective ground of appearances lies in something that is a thing in itself* and that it is only for this reason that phenomena are *bene fundata*.[31] (See, e.g., p. 99 of Part Two of Schulz's *Examination of the Kantian Critique of Pure Reason*.) We have already seen how Reinhold, right up to this very moment, continues to interpret Kant.

---

29. K. L. Reinhold, *Auswahl vermischter Schriften*, vol. 2 (1797), pp. 341–42.

* I do not include Herr Schelling among the expositors of Kant, nor have I myself ever laid any claim to this title, beyond asserting the claim that is here under discussion and beyond my present remarks on this topic.

30. Johann August Eberhard (1739–1809) was a professor of philosophy at Halle and a defender of the Leibnizian-Wolffian system. It was Eberhard's public attack on the Critical philosophy that provoked Kant's wrath in the previously mentioned *Ueber eine Entdeckung*. (For a discussion of Eberhard's views, see Allison's introduction to *The Kant-Eberhard Controversy*.)

31. "well grounded." This sentence is a free quotation from Schulz's *Prüfung*, Part Two, p. 99, where Schulz explicitly cites (and concurs with) Eberhard's view.

It may seem presumptuous and belittling of others when an individual
steps forward and says, "Until this moment, every one of the many worthy
scholars who have devoted their time and energies to the interpretation of
a certain book has understood it completely incorrectly. The system they
have purported to find within this book is, in fact, directly the opposite of
the system actually presented therein: viz., dogmatism instead of tran-
(235)   scendental idealism. I alone understand it correctly." In fact, however, the
presumption this seems to imply may only be apparent, for one may hope
that others too will subsequently come to understand the book in question
in the same way, and thus, that this lone individual will not remain alone.
There are also additional reasons why it should not be considered presumptuous of anyone to dare to contradict every single one of these
"Kantians," but I do not wish to mention these reasons here.

Most amazing of all, however, is that the discovery that Kant has no
knowledge of any "something" distinct from the I should be treated as
news. For ten years now the most thorough and complete proof of this has
been available for anyone to read. It is contained in Jacobi's *Dialogue on
Idealism and Realism* (Breslau, 1787), in the appendix entitled "Concerning Transcendental Idealism," pp. 207 ff.[32] Jacobi himself has already collected and cited Kant's most decisive and striking assertions on this point,
and he has quoted them in Kant's own words. I have no desire to redo what
has already been done and cannot very well be improved upon; thus I will
482   refer the reader to this book, and I do so all the more readily, since, like all
of Jacobi's philosophical writings, this entire book is one that can still be
read with profit by contemporary readers.

32. Friedrich Heinrich Jacobi (1743–1819) was a well-known novelist and man of
letters, as well as the author of several original and influential philosophical treatises. The work to which Fichte here refers, *David Hume über den Glauben oder
Idealismus und Realismus. Ein Gespräch* (1787), is one of Jacobi's most important
theoretical works. The body of this text consists of a long dialogue in which Jacobi
develops a general critique of philosophy and attempts to show that true "knowledge" is unobtainable and that what human beings require instead is "belief." The
appendix, "Ueber den transcendentalen Idealismus," which consists largely of
quotations from and paraphrases of Kant's writings, presents a searching and detailed critique of transcendental idealism. Fichte cites the first edition of *David
Hume*, which has recently been reprinted, with an introduction by Hamilton Beck,
as vol. 11 in a series entitled "The Philosophy of David Hume" (New York: Garland Publishing, 1983). (A revised edition is included in Jacobi's *Werke*, vol. II, pp.
1–310 [Leipzig: Gerhard Fleischer, 1815].) For an account of Jacobi's crucial role
in the development of post-Kantian philosophy, see chs. 2 and 3 of Beiser, *The Fate
of Reason*.

If I may, I would like to address a few questions to the previously mentioned interpreters of Kant: How far, according to Kant, does the applicability of the categories, and especially of the category of causality, extend? It extends only to the realm of appearances; i.e., the categories apply only to what already exists for us and within ourselves. How then could anyone ever assume that the foundation or ground of the empirical content of cognition lies in something distinct from the I? I think that one can make such an assumption only by means of an inference from what is grounded to something else that serves as its ground, and thus, only by applying the concept of causality. This is also the way in which Kant himself views this matter (see p. 211 of Jacobi's book),[33] and for this reason alone he rejects the assumption that *things in themselves exist outside of us*. His interpreters, however, would at this point permit Kant to forget his own system's fundamental claim concerning the overall validity of the categories and would permit him to employ a bold inference from the world of appearances in order to arrive at things that exist in themselves outside of us. This utter inconsistency has been denounced loudly enough by Aenesidemus,[34] who   *(236)* also, admittedly, interprets Kant in this way himself and whose skepticism, just like the philosophy of these Kantians, posits the truth of our

33. "For if we regard outer appearances as representations produced within us by their objects, and if we regard these objects as things existing in themselves outside of us, then it is indeed impossible to see how we could have any cognition of the existence of these objects except by means of an inference from the effect to the cause; and this being so, it must always remain doubtful whether the cause in question lies within us or outside of us." *David Hume*, p. 211. (This is a direct quotation from KRV, A372.)

34. "Aenesidemus" is the spokesman for "Humean skepticism" in a long, anonymously published attack on Kant and Reinhold entitled *Aenesidemus oder über die Fundamente der von dem Herrn Professor Reinhold in Jena gelieferten Elementar-Philosophie. Nebst einer Vertheidigung des Skepticismus gegen die Anmassungen der Vernunftkritik* (1792), whose author was Gottlob Ernst Ludwig Schulze (1761–1833), professor of philosophy at Helmstädt. A short excerpt from *Aenesidemus, or Concerning the Foundations of the Philosophy of the Elements Issued by Prof. Reinhold in Jena, Together with a Defence of Skepticism against the Pretensions of the Critique of Pure Reason*, translated by George di Giovanni, is included in *Between Kant and Hegel*, pp. 104–35. In 1794 Fichte himself published a major review of *Aenesidemus* in which he first announced his new philosophical strategy (in SW, I, pp. 3–25 = GA, I,2: 44–67; English translation in EPW, pp. 59–77). For further information, see Daniel Breazeale, "Fichte's *Aenesidemus* Review and the Transformation of German Idealism," *Review of Metaphysics* 34 (1981): 545–68, as well as ch. 9 of Beiser, *The Fate of Reason*.

cognition as consisting in its agreement with things in themselves. How
have these interpreters of Kant replied to this indictment? — Doesn't Kant
himself, they reply, talk about a "thing in itself"? What sort of thing is this,
according to him? As we can read on many pages of his writings, it is a
noumenon.[35] This is also what the thing in itself is according to Reinhold
and Schulz: a mere noumenon. But what is a "noumenon"? According to
Kant, Reinhold, and Schulz, a noumenon is something that, in obedience
to certain laws of thinking (which themselves have to be established and
have been established by Kant), we merely *think of* in addition to the appearances, and something that, in conformity with these same laws, we
must think of and add to the appearances.* Consequently, a noumenon is
something *produced only by our own thinking*. It is, however, not produced
by a *free* act of thinking, but rather by an act of thinking that is *necessary* —
necessary, that is, if I-hood is to exist at all. Accordingly, it is something
that exists only *for our thinking* and is present only for us as thinking beings.
But what additional use do these interpreters of Kant wish to make of this
"noumenon" or "thing in itself"? The thought of a thing in itself is based
upon sensation; but then, in turn, they want sensations to be based upon
the thought of a thing in itself. Their earth rests upon the back of the great

483
(237)

35. See, e.g., KRV, A289/B345–46 and B306–9.

* This is the cornerstone of Kantian realism. — From the viewpoint of life, within
which I appear only as something empirical, *I must* think of something as a thing in
itself, i.e., as present independently of *me as an empirical [I]*.[36] I have no knowledge
of the activity in which I am engaged when I think in this manner, precisely *because
it is not a free activity*. It is only from the philosophical viewpoint that I am able to
infer the presence of this activity within my thinking. A failure to make clear the
distinction between these two different points of view may explain why the clearest
thinker of our era,[37] in the work to which I have already referred, did not accept the
transcendental idealism that he grasped so correctly, and indeed, believed that he
had succeeded in destroying it merely by providing an exposition of it. For he
supposed that the manner of thinking that is characteristic of idealism is also required *within life* — a requirement, by the way, that really does only have to be
stated in order to be destroyed. — In my opinion, this same confusion explains why
others who are themselves adherents of idealism also wish to admit, *in addition to*
the idealist system, the existence of another, realistic system to which they will
never obtain entry.

36. "Etwas als Ding an sich, d.i. unabhängig von *mir, dem empirischen*, vorhan-
denes, *muß ich* mir auf dem Gesichtspunkte des Lebens, wo ich nur das Empirische
bin, denken."

37. Viz., Jacobi.

elephant; and the great elephant itself? — it stands upon their earth![38] Their thing in itself, which is nothing more than a mere thought, is supposed to *have an effect* upon the I! Have they already forgotten what they themselves just said, and is their thing in itself, which only a moment ago was nothing but a thought, now supposed to be something other than a mere thought? Or do they seriously wish to ascribe efficacy, a predicate that belongs only to reality, to a mere thought? Is this the astonishing discovery of that great genius whose torch illuminated the philosophical century now drawing to a close?

I am only too well aware that the "Kantianism" to which these Kantians subscribe really is the system I have just described and that it really does consist in just such a fantastic combination of the crudest sort of dogmatism (according to which the thing in itself is supposed to produce an impression within us) with the most resolute idealism (according to which all being is produced only by the thinking of the intellect and which knows nothing whatsoever of any other type of being). I wish to exempt the two   *484* worthy men to whom I have already referred [viz., Reinhold and Schulz] from what I am about to say concerning this type of Kantianism; for the former, demonstrating a mental strength and a love of truth that does the highest honor both to his head and to his heart, has renounced this system (though he still considers it to be Kant's, and thus my sole remaining disagreement with him is over this historical question), whereas the latter has remained silent concerning philosophy for some time now — more specifically, ever since the appearance of the more recent treatises — and thus one may fairly assume that he may have come to entertain some doubts concerning his own previous system. As a general rule, however, anyone who is sufficiently in control of his own inner sense to be able to distinguish thinking from being without mixing them up with each other must also be able to see that to take seriously a system of this sort, in which being and thinking are certainly jumbled together, is to do it altogether too much   *(238)* honor; though of course one would expect that only very few people will be able to overcome the natural propensity toward dogmatism and will suc-

38. This is an image that is ultimately derived from Locke (*An Essay Concerning Human Understanding*, II, xiii, § 19), though, as A. Philonenko has pointed out, Fichte presumably obtained it indirectly from his study of Salomon Maimon's *Versuch einer neuen Logik oder Theorie des Denkens* (1794). (See pp. 295 and 339 of the edition of Maimon's treatise republished as the third volume in a series of "Neudrucke seltener philosophischer Werke" sponsored by the *Kantgesellschaft* [Berlin: Reuther & Reichard, 1912].)

ceed in lifting themselves to the level of free speculative flight. How could anyone expect that something that proved impossible even for a man of overwhelming intellectual power such as Jacobi should be possible for certain others — whose names honor bids me refrain from mentioning here? One wishes such people had been content to be and to remain dogmatists forever. But that such incurable dogmatists should be able to imagine that Kant's *Critique* should have anything to say to them; that, since Kant's Critical writings were praised in a famous journal (by God knows what accident!), they should therefore think that they too could follow the current fashion and become Kantians themselves; that since then, in their delirium, they should have spent years and years filling ream after ream of expensive paper, without even once during this long period of time having come to their senses and without ever having understood a single sentence from their own pens; that, up until this very day, they should still remain unable to rub the sleep from their eyes now that they have felt themselves jolted, preferring instead to strike out with their hands and feet against the

485   unwelcome disturbers of their peace; and that the German public, in its thirst for instruction, should have enthusiastically purchased these scribbled pages and should have sought to imbibe the spirit of the same, copying and re-copying them, without noticing that these writings contain no meaning at all: all of this will forever remain recorded in the annals of philosophy as the scandal of our century, and our descendants will be unable to account for the events of these years except by postulating the outbreak and spread of some sort of mental epidemic during this period.

"But," someone might still say to me, "if we leave out of consideration the book of Jacobi's you have cited — which admittedly presents a difficulty for us, since it quotes Kant's own words — then your argument amounts to no more than this: 'This is absurd; therefore, Kant did not say it.' Even if we concede the major premise in this argument — as, unfortunately, we must — why could Kant not have asserted this absurdity just as well as we others, among whom there are some whose merits you yourself recognize and whose common sense you would not, one hopes, deny completely?" — To this I would reply: The originator of a system occupies a different situation from that of his interpreters and followers. The very same thing that would not count as evidence of an absolute lack of reason and common sense among the latter would indeed constitute such evidence in the former case. The reason for this is that the followers are not yet in possession of the Idea of the whole; for if they were, then they would have

(239)   no need to study the new system. What they have to do is to try to assemble the Idea of the whole from *the parts* its originator has laid before them; and in fact, so long as these parts do not yet fit together to form a natural whole

for them, then they are not yet completely determined, formed, and finished in their own minds. Perhaps it may require a certain amount of time for these followers to grasp these various parts, and during this time they may incorrectly determine some of the details concerning the individual parts. As a result of this, they may place some of these parts into contradiction with others — when considered, that is, *in relationship to the whole that they have to construct* though they have not yet done so. In contrast, the originator of this system begins with the Idea of the whole, within which all of the parts are united; and he presents these parts individually, because it is only through the parts that he is able to communicate the whole. The task of his followers is to synthesize something they themselves do not yet possess at all, but are only supposed to obtain as a result of this process of synthesis. The task of the originator is to analyze what he already has in his possession. It by no means follows from this that the followers are actually aware of the contradiction among the individual parts in relationship to the whole that is to be assembled from them. Though this contradiction may perhaps subsequently become apparent to some other person who assembles these same parts into a whole — for how could these followers become aware of this contradiction if they have not yet reached the point of combining these various parts into a single whole? But it certainly does follow that the person who proceeded from the actual combination of these parts would indeed have thought — or would have supposed that he had thought of — any contradiction between the various parts of his presentation, for *he* certainly once had all the parts together alongside one another. There is nothing absurd about thinking first of dogmatism and then of transcendental idealism. Anyone can do this; indeed, we must do so to the extent that we philosophize about both systems. It is, however, absurd to wish to think of these two systems *as one and the same*. An interpreter of the Kantian system is not necessarily guilty of doing this, but its originator certainly would have been guilty of just this absurdity if his system had, in fact, proceeded from such a unification of dogmatism and idealism.

486

For me, at least, it is impossible to impute this absurdity to any person who is still in control of his reason. How then could I impute it to Kant? Consequently, until such time as Kant himself explicitly declares, in so many words, that *he derives sensation from an impression produced by the thing in itself*, or, to employ his own terminology, that *sensations have to be accounted for within philosophy by appealing to a transcendental object that exists in itself outside of us*, I will continue to refuse to believe what these interpreters tell us about Kant. But if he does make such a declaration, then I would sooner take the *Critique of Pure Reason* to be the product of a most remarkable accident than the work of a human mind.

Nevertheless, my opponents will retort, Kant clearly and in so many words says (in § 1 of the *Critique of Pure Reason*) that "the object is given to
(240)   us," that "this is possible insofar as the mind is affected in a certain way,"
487   and that "we possess an ability to obtain representations through the mode in which we are affected by objects, and this is entitled 'sensibility.'"[39] He even asks (on p. 1 of the Introduction), "How should our power of cognition be awakened into exercise unless this occurred by means of objects that affect our senses and, on the one hand, produce representations by themselves while, on the other, they set in motion the activity of our understanding, which compares, combines, and separates these representations and thereby works up *the raw materials* of the sensible impressions into the kind of cognition which is called 'experience'?"[40] — This will fairly well exhaust the number of passages they will be able to cite in support of their interpretation. Merely to compare passages with passages, to compare words with other words in abstraction from the Idea of the whole (with which I do not suppose these interpreters are yet acquainted), let me begin with the following question: If it should turn out that the passages cited really cannot be reconciled with the countless number of later passages that repeat the assertion that there can be no question at all of any effect exercised upon us by a transcendental object existing in itself and apart from us, then why is it that these interpreters prefer the *few* passages that they believe teach a form of dogmatism to the *innumerable* passages that teach transcendental idealism? Why do they not choose instead to sacrifice the former to the latter? This is undoubtedly because they did not begin their study of Kant's writings in an unprejudiced manner, but also brought along, as their criterion for evaluating any explanation, their own dogmatism. This dogmatism, which they consider to be the only correct system, is so deeply woven into their innermost being that they believe an intelligent person like Kant must surely have subscribed to it. Consequently, they never sought any instruction from Kant on this topic, but only sought confirmation of their own dogmatism.

But is it really true that these apparently contradictory assertions cannot be reconciled with one another? In the passages quoted, Kant speaks of "objects." If we want to know what this term signifies for Kant, we certainly do not have to decide this for ourselves; we need only attend to Kant's own explanation of this point. He states (as quoted on p. 221 of
(241)   Jacobi's treatise) that "it is the understanding which adds the object to

39. KRV, A19/B33.

40. KRV, B1. (As usual, Fichte's quotation differs in minor ways from Kant's text.)

appearance,[41] and it does this insofar as it *connects* the manifold of appearances *within a single consciousness*. We say therefore that we cognize an *object* when we have *introduced* synthetic unity into the manifold of intuition, and the concept of this unity is the representation of the object = X. *This = X is, however, not the transcendental object* (i.e., the thing in itself), *for we do not know even this much about the latter*."[42] What then is the object? It is something the understanding *adds* to appearances; i.e., it is *a mere thought*. — The object exercises an effect: *Something merely thought of exercises an effect*. But what does this mean? If I possess even an ounce of logical ability, this can only mean the following: This object exercises an effect only insofar as it exists; therefore, *it is only thought of as exercising an effect*. "The ability to obtain representations through the mode in which we are affected by objects": What is this? Since this affection itself is only something we think of, then everything associated with this affection [including, therefore, our own ability to be affected] is, undoubtedly, also something that is only thought of, and thus, this too is nothing but a sheer thought. When you posit an object that is accompanied by the thought that it has exercised an effect upon you, then you also think of yourself as *affected in this case*. And when you think that this is what occurs in the case of *every* object you perceive, then you think of yourself as *generally affectable*.[43] In other words, it is *by means of this act of your own thinking* that you ascribe receptivity or sensibility to yourself. Thus the object, considered as something given, is *also something merely thought of*; and therefore the passage plucked from the Introduction to the *Critique of Pure Reason* merely characterizes the system of *necessary thinking* in terms borrowed from the

41. "welcher das Object (den Gegenstand) zur Erscheinung hinzu thut." Both Kant and Fichte use two different terms for "object" (viz., *Object* and *Gegenstand*). In this first sentence quoted by Jacobi, Kant employs the term *Object*, whereas in the remaining sentences in this assembled quotation he uses the term *Gegenstand*. It is Fichte, not Jacobi, who inserts the word *Gegenstand* in parenthetical apposition with *Object*.

42. As his source for this patchwork quotation, Jacobi, whose account relies exclusively on the first edition of the *Critique of Pure Reason*), cites KRV, A246, 253, 254, 115 [sic., actually 105], and 494. (Note that, with the exception of the last one, none of these passages are contained in the third edition, which is the edition customarily used and cited by Fichte. This may explain why, at this critical juncture of his argument, Fichte cites Jacobi's presentation rather than quoting Kant's own text directly.)

43. "als *afficirbar überhaupt*": i.e., as possessing a general power or capacity to be affected in various specific ways.

empirical viewpoint, a viewpoint that can be explained and derived only by means of the *Critique* that follows.

Can one therefore explain cognition without having to assume the occurrence of any *contact* or *affection* whatsoever? To summarize the difference in a few words: All of our cognition does indeed begin with *an affection*, but not with an affection *by an object*. This is Kant's view of the matter, and it is also the position of the *Wissenschaftslehre*. Since Herr Beck, *(242)* if I have understood him correctly, has overlooked this important fact, and *489* since Herr Reinhold* has not directed enough attention to that which conditions and makes possible the act of positing a Not-I, I consider it to be appropriate to take this opportunity to provide a brief discussion of this topic. In doing this, I will employ my own terminology rather than Kant's, since I naturally have a better mastery of the former than of the latter.

Just as certainly as I posit myself at all, I posit myself as limited, and this occurs as a consequence of my intuition of my own act of self-positing. I am finite in virtue of this intuition.

Since this limitation of mine conditions my positing of myself, it constitutes an original limitation. — One might still demand some further explanation of this; and thus one might try to account for my limitation as the object of reflection by referring to my necessary limitation as the reflecting subject — an explanation that would imply that the reason I am finite for myself is because I can think only of what is finite. Or, conversely, one might try to account for the limitation of the reflecting subject by referring to the limitation of the object of reflection — an explanation that would imply that the reason I think only of what is finite is because I myself am finite. But neither of these explanations would explain anything at all; for I am originally neither the reflecting subject nor the object of reflection, and neither of these is determined by the other. Instead, I am *both of these in their unity with each other*; though I am admittedly unable to think of this unity, because whenever I think, I must distinguish the object of reflection from the reflecting subject.

By virtue of its intuition and of its concept, every limitation is a *completely determinate* limitation; no limitation is, as it were, a limitation "as such" or "in general."

As we can see, the necessity *of some limitation of the I* has been derived

---

* In his discussion of the chief elements of the *Wissenschaftslehre* in his previously mentioned *Miscellaneous Writings*.[44]

44. See section 14 of Reinhold's *Auswahl vermischter Schriften*, vol. 2, "Der Anhänger der Wissenschaftslehre (spricht)," pp. 293 ff.

from the very possibility of the I. The *specific determinacy* of this limitation is, however, not something that can be derived in this way; because, as we can also see, such determinacy is itself what provides the condition for the very possibility of all I-hood. Consequently, we have arrived at the point at which all deduction comes to an end. The determinacy in question appears to be something absolutely contingent and furnishes us with the *merely empirical* element in our cognition. It is because of this determinacy, for example, that I am, of all possible rational beings, a *human being*, and that, of all human beings, I am this *specific* person, etc.

The determinate character of my limitation manifests itself as a limita-   *490*
tion of my practical power (this is the point where philosophy is driven
from the theoretical to the practical realm). This determinate limitation is   *(243)*
immediately perceived as a *feeling*: sweet, red, cold, etc. (I prefer the name "feeling" to Kant's "sensation," for it becomes a sensation only when it has been related to an object by means of an act of thinking.)

Forgetting to take into account the role of original feeling leads to an unfounded transcendent idealism and to an incomplete philosophy which is unable to account for the purely sensible predicates of objects. It seems to me that Beck has gone astray in this manner, whereas Reinhold seems to think it is the *Wissenschaftslehre* which has erred in this way.

The wish to provide a further explanation of this original feeling and to attribute it to the efficacy of "something" leads, as I have just shown, to the dogmatism of the Kantians — a dogmatism with which they would like to burden Kant himself. This "something" of theirs is necessarily identical with the wretched "thing in itself." For the reason already indicated, all *transcendental* explanation comes to an end with immediate feeling. But the *empirical* I we observe from the transcendental standpoint does indeed provide itself with an explanation of its own feelings, and it does this in accordance with the following law: There can be nothing limited unless there is also something that limits it. It creates for itself, by means of intuition, a realm of extended matter; and then, by means of thinking, it transfers its merely subjective feelings to this material realm, which it then considers to be the ground of these same feelings.[45] It is only by means of this synthesis that the empirical I is able to construct an object for itself. The empirical I obtains its universe by continuing to analyze and to explain its own state; the philosopher obtains his science by observing the laws in accordance with which this process of explanation proceeds. This

45. "es erschafft sich durch die Anschauung eine ausgedehnte Materie, auf welche es jenes bloß Subjective des Gefühls durch Denken überträgt, als auf seinen Grund."

constitutes Kant's *empirical realism*, which, however, is also a *transcendental idealism*.

The entire determinacy of the I, and hence the sum of all the feelings that become possible thereby, is to be viewed as *a priori*, i.e., as absolute and as determined without any effort on our part. This is what Kant calls "receptivity"; and he calls any particular determinacy included within this whole an "affection." Without this, consciousness would certainly be inexplicable.

491   It is undoubtedly an immediate fact of consciousness that I feel *myself* to be determined in a particular way. If certain widely celebrated philosophers now wish to *explain* this feeling, then how can they fail to see that they thereby wish to ascribe to feeling something not immediately included within the fact in question? And how can they do this except by means of thinking, and indeed, by thinking in accordance with a category, which, in the case we are here considering, is the principle of a "real ground"?[46] Assuming they do not possess, as it were, an immediate intuition of the

(244)   thing in itself and its relationships, then what more do they know about this principle than this: that *they* are required to think in accordance with it? It follows that they are asserting no more than this: that they are required to supply the thought of a thing as a ground or foundation [of the immediately felt determinations of their consciousness]. We are quite prepared to concede this claim and even to join them in affirming it, insofar as it pertains to the standpoint they occupy. Their thing is a product of their own thinking. But then they immediately turn around and repeat the claim that this thing is a "thing in itself," i.e, something that is not a product of thinking. I honestly do not understand them. I can neither entertain this thought myself nor can I imagine how anyone else could do so; and with this declaration I wish to have done with these philosophers once and for all.[47]

7.

(245)   Following this digression, let us now return to our original plan of describing the path followed by the *Wissenschaftslehre* and defending it against the

46. "hier nach dem Satze des RealGrundes"; i.e., in accordance with the category of causality.

47. With the remark "(To be continued in a future issue)," the second published installment of *An Attempt at a New Presentation of the Wissenschaftslehre* comes to an end at this point.

objections of certain philosophers.[48] We said above (in section 5) that the philosopher observes himself while engaged in the act of constructing for himself a concept of himself. I would now like to add something else to this: viz., that *he thinks of this acting in which he is engaged.* — The philosopher undoubtedly knows what it is he is talking about. Yet a mere intuition yields no consciousness; one possesses knowledge only of what one actually thinks about and grasps conceptually. This act of comprehending his own acting is, as was also mentioned above, an act that it is quite possible for the philosopher to accomplish; for he already possesses some experience, and thus he already possesses a *general* concept of *acting as such* — in contrast with *being*, with which he is also already familiar. Furthermore, he also possesses a concept of the *specific* kind of acting we are here discussing, inasmuch as it is, on the one hand, an acting of the *intellect* as such, and thus, a purely ideal activity and by no means a real exercise of our practical power in the narrower sense of the term. On the other hand, of all the possible actions in which this intellect can engage as such, the particular acting in question is nothing but *the self-reverting acting of the intellect*; it is not a type of acting which is directed outward toward any object.

   Yet we must not lose sight of the fact that here too, as in every other case, intuition is and remains what underlies and is comprehended within every concept. In an absolute sense, we are unable to "think up" or to create for ourselves anything simply by means of an act of thinking.[49] We

---

48. Though the various objections to which Fichte addresses himself in this third installment are of quite general interest, he is, in fact, replying to a quite specific set of published objections to the *Wissenschaftslehre*, some of which are identified explicitly in the text and some of which are not. The objections discussed in section 7 were all raised by F. K. Forberg in an essay entitled "Briefe über die neueste Philosophie" which appeared on pp. 44–88 of the same issue of the *Philosophisches Journal* as this installment of Fichte's "Second Introduction" (viz., vol. VI, no. 1) and was subsequently continued in a later issue (VII, 4, pp. 259–72). Forberg's "Briefe" have recently been reprinted in *Aus der Frühzeit des deutschen Idealismus: Texte zur Wissenschaftslehre Fichtes 1794–1804*, ed. Martin Oesch (Würzburg: Königshausen + Neumann, 1987), pp. 153–78.

   Fichte was, of course, acquainted with Forberg's objections prior to their publication because he himself was co-editor of the *Philosophisches Journal* at this point. The specific passages from Forberg's essay to which Fichte's replies are addressed have been identified by the editors of GA, I,4 and are reprinted in the notes to their text of the "Second Introduction." They are also furnished by Peter Baumanns in his edition of *Versuch einer neuen Darstellung der Wissenschaftslehre* (Hamburg: Meiner, 1975).

49. "Wir können uns nichts absolut ERdenken, oder durch Denken erschaffen."

can think only of what we have immediately intuited. An act of thinking not based upon any intuition, i.e., one that does not grasp a simultaneously *(246)* present act of intuiting, is empty; indeed, it is not really an act of thinking at all. At most, it may be considered to be the thought of a mere sign for a concept, and if, as one would expect, the sign in question is a word, then nothing more may be involved in such an act than the thoughtless utterance of this word. I determine my intuition for myself by thinking of something posited in opposition to it. This, and only this, is the meaning of the expression, "I comprehend the intuition."

As a consequence of this act of thinking, the acting that is thought of within this act of thinking becomes, for the philosopher himself, something *objective*, that is to say, something that — insofar as he thinks of it — hovers before him as something that limits the freedom (i.e., the indeterminacy) of his thinking.[50] This is the true and original meaning of the term "objectivity." Just as surely as I think at all, I think of something determinate; for otherwise I would not have been engaged in an act of thinking and would have thought of nothing. In other words, my freedom of thinking, which I posit as capable of having been directed at an infinite number of objects, is now directed only upon this limited sphere, viz., the sphere that is involved in thinking about my present object. My freedom of thinking is restricted to this sphere. When I turn my attention upon myself, I freely confine myself to this particular sphere. On the other hand, when what I am attending to is simply some object, then *I find myself to be confined* *493* *within* and restricted by a certain sphere; and when I think about this object, I forget about my own act of thinking — which is what always happens when one is occupying the standpoint of ordinary thinking.

What has just been said may serve to remove the following objections and to correct the misunderstandings involved.

Some people contend that every act of thinking must necessarily be directed at some being. Consequently, if no being pertains to the I with which the *Wissenschaftslehre* begins, then this I is unthinkable, and the entire science constructed upon the basis of something so thoroughly self-contradictory is empty and nugatory.

If I may, I should like to begin with a general remark concerning the spirit that animates this objection. Insofar as the philosophers who make this objection are able to assimilate to their own logic the concept of the I postulated by the *Wissenschaftslehre* and are able to examine this concept in

---

50. "d.h. ihm vorschwebend, als etwas, inwiefern er es denkt, die Freiheit (die Unbestimmtheit) seines Denkens Hemmendes."

accordance with the rules of their logic, they undoubtedly do think of this concept. For otherwise, how would they be able to compare it with and to relate it to other concepts? If they were really unable to think of this concept of the I, then they would also be unable to say the least thing about it. *(247)* It would remain simply unknown to them in every respect. But, as we can see, they have actually succeeded in generating the thought of the I, from which it of course follows that they must be able to do this. Nevertheless, according to their own rules, which they previously learned by heart and misunderstood, they should not have been able to do this; thus they would rather directly deny the possibility of accomplishing the very action they themselves have just accomplished than renounce these rules. They place more faith in some old book than they do in their own innermost consciousness. How little inner awareness must such people have of what they themselves do! Their own philosophical specimens must have been produced quite mechanically, unaccompanied by even the slightest inner attentiveness and spirit. Even though it came as a surprise to him, Monsieur Jourdan at least believed he had been speaking prose all of his life without realizing it.[51] If, however, these philosophers had been in his place, then they would have proven — in the most beautiful prose! — that they were unable to speak in prose, since they were unacquainted with the rules of the same, and since the conditions for the possibility of something must certainly precede its actuality. Should Critical idealism continue to trouble *494* these thinkers, one may expect them to turn to Aristotle for advice about whether they are really alive or are already dead and buried.[52] Indeed, they already harbor some secret doubts concerning this point, inasmuch as they doubt the possibility of becoming conscious of their own freedom and I-hood.

It would thus appear to be quite appropriate to dismiss their objection without any further ado, since it contradicts and therefore negates itself. Instead, however, let us see if we can determine where the basis for this misunderstanding really lies. — What can it mean to say that every act of thinking must necessarily commence with some being? Are we to understand this claim as identical to the principle we ourselves have just postu- *(248)*

51. See Molière, *Le bourgeois gentilhomme*, Act II, Scene iv.

52. This is an allusion to Forberg's attempted *reductio ad absurdum* of the claim that one cannot abstract from the thinking subject, a claim which, in Forberg's view, is based on the following inference: From the fact that I *can* think of myself as not thinking, it follows that I *cannot* think of myself as not thinking. "But," asks Forberg rhetorically, "by the shade of Aristotle!, does this follow?" ("Briefe," *Philosophisches Journal*, VI, 1, p. 84.)

lated and developed: viz., the principle that every act of thinking includes something that is thought of, i.e., an object of thinking, to which this determinate act of thinking confines itself and which appears to limit it? If this is all these philosophers mean to say, then we must undoubtedly grant them this premise, which the *Wissenschaftslehre* has no wish to deny. The I with which the *Wissenschaftslehre* begins undoubtedly also possesses this sort of objectivity, viz., objectivity for mere thinking. Or, to express exactly the same thing in a different way: the act by means of which the I constructs itself for itself possesses this sort of objectivity. It obtains this objectivity only through thinking, and it is only for thinking that it possesses such objectivity; i.e., it possesses only an *ideal* being. — If, however, the being that our critics are talking about is not to be understood as a sheerly *ideal* being, but is, instead, supposed to be a *real* being; if, that is to say, it is to be understood as something that limits not merely the ideal activity but also the genuinely efficacious and truly practical activity[53] of the I; if it is supposed to be something that endures within time and subsists (i.e., offers resistance) within space: if this is what they are talking about, and if they seriously wish to maintain that we are able to think only about things of this type, then they are advancing an entirely new and unprecedented claim, for which they surely should have furnished a careful proof. If they were right about this, then of course no metaphysics would be possible at all, for the concept of the I would be unthinkable; it would, however, also be true that no self-consciousness — and therefore no consciousness whatsoever — would be possible either. In this case, we would certainly have to cease to philosophize. But our opponents would have achieved nothing thereby, for they would have to stop trying to refute us as well. But do they really, even in their own case, view this matter in the way they pretend? Do they not instead, at every moment of their lives, think of themselves as free and active? Do they not, for example, think of themselves as the freely active originators of those oh-so-penetrating and highly original objections they from time to time bring against our system? Is this "they themselves" something that resists their own efficacy? Or is it not, instead, the exact opposite of what offers such resistance; i.e., isn't this the efficaciously acting subject itself? Concerning this point, I must refer them to what was said above (in section 5). If one were to ascribe this type of being to the I, then the I would cease to be an I at all; it would become a thing, and the very concept of the I would be destroyed. To be sure, this type of being will subsequently (not subsequently in time, but rather in the

495

53. "die reell wirkende, eigentlich praktische Thätigkeit."

series of deductions[54]) be ascribed to the I as well, though, even then, it will continue and must continue to remain an I in our sense of the term. On the one hand, spatial extension and subsistence will be ascribed to it, and in this respect it becomes a determinate body; on the other hand, temporal identity and duration will be ascribed to it, and in this respect it becomes a soul. It is, however, the task of philosophy to demonstrate this and to provide a genetic account of how the I comes to think of itself in these ways. Accordingly, this is not something philosophy has to presuppose, but rather is part of what has to be derived. — What it comes down to is this: The I is, to begin with, nothing but a "doing." Whenever one thinks of the I, however, even if one thinks of it only as active, one already possesses an empirical concept of the I — a concept that must first be derived.*

(249)

Our opponents, however, do not wish to advance the principle in question without any proof at all. On the contrary, they wish to prove it from logic, and indeed, from the principle of contradiction — God willing!

496

If there is anything that clearly reveals the deplorable state of contemporary philosophy (insofar as philosophy is considered to be a science) it is developments of this sort. Were anyone to make similar statements about mathematics, natural science, or any of the other sciences — statements that demonstrate one's absolute ignorance concerning the first and most elementary principles of the science in question — he would, without any further ado, be sent back to the classroom from which he departed too soon. Is it only within philosophy that we are not allowed to respond in this way? When someone demonstrates a similar ignorance within philosophy,

---

54. "nicht hinterher in der Zeitreihe, sondern in der Reihe der Abhängigkeit des Denkens" (literally: "but rather, in the series of the dependence of thinking"). That is to say, the concept of the "being" of the I is derived later in the series of systematically interrelated deductions (or acts of philosophical thinking) of which the *Wissenschaftslehre* consists.

* I can briefly summarize the main point here as follows: *All being* signifies *a limitation of free activity. On the one hand*, the activity in question can be viewed as an activity *of the mere intellect* (as the subject of consciousness). Anything posited as limiting only this activity possesses nothing but *ideal being*; i.e., it possesses *objectivity merely in relation to consciousness*. This type of objectivity is present in every representation, including our representations of the I, of virtue, of the ethical law, etc., as well as in such utter fictions as a square circle, a sphinx, and the like: [These are all] *objects of mere representation*.

On the other hand, this free activity can be viewed as *acting efficaciously* or *possessing causality*. In this case, what limits this activity obtains *real existence*. The *actual world*.

must we, instead, courteously praise his perspicacity and, without batting
an eye or displaying any annoyance or cracking a smile, provide him in
public with the private instruction he so sorely needs? Have philosophers
been unable in two thousand years to arrive at agreement on even a single
principle, one they can now assume all of their professional colleagues will
accept without the need of any further proof? If there is such a principle,
surely it is the principle that recognizes the difference between logic, which
is a strictly formal science, and real philosophy,[55] or metaphysics. — What
then is asserted by this fearsome logical principle of contradiction, by
means of which our entire system is supposed to be laid low with a single
blow? To the best of my knowledge, this principle states no more than this:
If a concept is already determined by a certain attribute, then it must not be
determined by any other attribute that is the opposite of the former. This
principle, however, has nothing whatsoever to say concerning *which* attribute should originally determine a particular concept; nor can it, by its
very nature, say anything about this. For this is a principle that presupposes that the original determination of the concepts involved has already
been accomplished, and only on this assumption does the principle of contradiction have any applicability at all. For information concerning the
nature of this original determination we have to turn to some other science.

These same philosophers tell us that it is *contradictory* for any concept
not to be determined by the predicate of real being. But how could this be
contradictory, unless they themselves had already determined the concept
in question by the predicate of real being and then subsequently wished to
remove this predicate without changing the nature of the concept itself?
But who asked them to determine the concept in this way? Have these
logical virtuosi failed to notice that it is they themselves who have postulated this principle and that they are, therefore, here proceeding in a pal-
pable circle? Whether or not there actually is any concept that originally —

55. "von der reellen Philosophie." The distinction between "real" and "formal"
philosophy is explained as follows in the introduction to the *Grundlage des
Naturrechts* (GA, I,3: 313–17 = SW, III, pp. 1–6): Whereas a merely formal philosophy concerns itself merely with concepts in isolation from their objects, a
"genuine" or "real" (*reelle*) philosophy always deals simultaneously with concepts
and objects and grasps and establishes the underlying identity of the same. That is,
a purely formal philosophical science (such as formal logic) concerns itself with
possible thinking, whereas a real philosophical science (such as metaphysics) confines itself to the domain of *necessary* thinking. According to Fichte, "the goal of
Kant's writings was to inaugurate such a real philospohy and to destroy all merely
formal philosophizing" (GA, I,3: 317 = SW, III, p. 6).

in accordance, that is, with the laws of synthetic (and not merely of analytic) reason — *is not determined by the predicate of real being* is something
they can discover for themselves only through intuition. All logic can do
for them is to warn them against subsequently assigning the predicate of
being to this same concept, which of course means that logic can only warn
them against assigning the predicate "being" to this concept in the same
sense in which they have previously denied that it is determinable by this
predicate. But even if they have not yet personally *become conscious* of an
intuition of this sort, one in which no "being" is present, they nevertheless
possess such an intuition. This is guaranteed by the very nature of reason.
But if they have not yet obtained consciousness of this intuition, then *all of
their* concepts, which can only have stemmed from sensory intuition, will
indeed be determined by the predicate of real being; and if they think logic
is the source of their knowledge of this fact (whereas, in truth, it is based
simply upon the intuition of their own miserable, empirical self), then they
are guilty of nothing but a terminological confusion. Hence, so far as they
personally are concerned, they would indeed be contradicting themselves
if they were subsequently to think of any *of their* concepts unaccompanied
by the predicate of being. Let them therefore restrict their rule to themselves, for it is indeed universally valid within their sphere of possible
thinking; and let them always keep a watchful eye on this rule so they can
be sure they never violate it. But so far as it concerns us personally, we
cannot make any use of this rule; for we possess a few concepts in addition
to theirs, and their rule does not apply to the realm in which these latter
concepts are to be found. Nor can they deliver any judgment concerning
this realm, for it simply does not exist for them. Let them tend to their own *(251)*
business and let us tend to ours. Even to the extent that we grant them the *498*
principle that states that some object of thought must be present within
every act of thinking, this is by no means a logical principle; instead, it is a
principle presupposed by logic and one through which logic itself first ʈₕᵢₙₖᵢₙ𝓰
becomes possible. "To think" and "to determine an object" (in the previously indicated sense of "object"): these are one and the same act. The two ᵈᵉᵗᵉʳᵐⁱⁿⁱⁿᵍ
concepts are identical. Logic furnishes us with the *rules* that govern the act ᶜᵃⁿ
of determining an object; therefore, I should think, logic presupposes, as a ᵒᵇʲᶜᵗ
fact of consciousness, this act of determining as such. That every act of
thinking has an object is something that can be shown only within intuition. Think, and while you are thinking, pay attention to how you do this.
You will undoubtedly discover in this case that you also posit an object of
this act, which you posit over against or in opposition to this same act of
thinking.

[margin handwritten: How can you conclude from nothing?]

Another objection, which is related to the one we have just examined, goes as follows: If you do not begin with some being, then how, without being inconsistent, can you ever succeed in deriving a being? So long as you pursue your labors honestly and do not resort to sleight of hand, you will never be able to produce from what you are working on anything other than what is already contained therein.

To this I reply: We will certainly never be able to derive any "being" in the sense in which you are accustomed to using this term, that is, any *being in itself*. What the philosopher concerns himself with is an acting subject, and one that acts in accordance with certain laws; what he then establishes is the series of necessary actions that must be engaged in by this acting subject. Among these actions, there is one that appears to the acting subject itself as a being, and — in conformity with certain laws, which themselves have to be shown — necessarily must appear to this subject in this way. But for the philosopher, who views this same thing from a higher standpoint, it is and remains a mode of acting. A being exists only for the I the philosopher is observing, for this observed I thinks in a realistic manner. What exists for the philosopher is acting, and acting is all that exists for him; for, as a philosopher, he thinks in an idealistic manner.

[margin handwritten: essence of transc. ideal.]

[margin: 499 (252)]

[margin handwritten: Being is derivative & negative concept]

Let me take this opportunity to state this point quite clearly and simply: The essence of transcendental idealism as such, and, more specifically, the essence of transcendental idealism as presented in the *Wissenschaftslehre*, is that the concept of being is by no means considered to be a *primary* and *original* concept, but is treated purely as a *derivative* one, indeed, as a concept derived through its opposition to activity, and hence, as a merely *negative* concept. For the idealist, nothing is positive but freedom, and, for him, being is nothing but a negation of freedom. It is only on this condition that idealism possesses a solid foundation and remains consistent with itself. In contrast, the dogmatist believes that his system possesses a secure foundation in being, which he considers to be something that cannot be further examined and that requires no further ground or foundation; hence he finds the idealist's claim to be a folly and a horror,[56] for it — and it alone — threatens his very existence. For, whatever afflictions may have beset him from time to time, he has always sought refuge in an appeal to some sort of original being, even if this was nothing but a completely crude and formless matter. But idealism does away with this completely and leaves the dogmatist standing there naked and alone. To defend himself against such an attack, the dogmatist possesses no weapons beyond the attestation

56. "eine Thorheit, und ein Greuel." See I Corinthians 1:23.

of his sincere displeasure, coupled with his assurance that he simply does not understand what he is expected to do and that he neither wishes nor is able to think of what is requested [by the idealist]. We are quite happy to believe him when he assures us of this, and in turn we ask simply that he should also believe us when we insist that we, for our part, are quite able to think of our own system. If the dogmatist finds this to be too difficult as well, then we can refrain from making even this demand and can let him think whatever he pleases about this matter. For we have solemnly confessed on many occasions that we cannot force anyone to accept our system, since the acceptance of this system is something that depends upon freedom. — As I have said, the sole recourse left to the dogmatist is simply to assure us of his own sheer incapacity, which is a purely subjective matter. The idea, however, of seeking shelter behind the protection of general logic and swearing by the shade of the Stagarite whenever one is totally bewildered is quite a novel strategy, albeit one that, even in a time of universal despair, will not find many imitators, for one requires only the barest classroom acquaintance with what logic actually is in order to scorn such protection.   *500*

One should not allow oneself to be deceived when opponents of this sort parrot the language of idealism and pay it lip service by assuring us that they know that the only type of being with which we can be concerned is a *being for us*. They remain dogmatists. For anyone who maintains that all thinking and all consciousness must proceed from some being thereby makes being into something original, and dogmatism consists in doing just this. Such a confusion of terminology only serves to display all the more clearly the utter confusion that prevails among their concepts. A *being merely for us*, which is nevertheless supposed to be an *original* being that   *(253)* cannot be derived from anything else: What can this mean? Who is this "we" for whom alone this being is supposed to exist? Is it "*intellects* as such"? If so, then the proposition "it is something for the intellect" surely means the same as "it is represented by the intellect," and the sentence "it exists *only* for the intellect" means the same as "it is *only* represented." Accordingly, the concept of a being that, when viewed from a certain standpoint, is supposed to occur independently of representation must nevertheless be derived from representation, since it is only through representation that this concept is supposed to exist at all. If this is what our opponents mean to say, then they are in much closer agreement with the *Wissenschaftslehre* than they themselves would ever have imagined. Or they might maintain that the "we," for whom alone being is supposed to exist, are themselves things, original things, and therefore things in themselves.

How, in this case, is anything supposed to exist *for* these things, and how are they supposed to exist for themselves? For it is implicit in the concept of a thing merely that it should exist, not, however, that anything else should exist *for it*. What can this little word "for" mean to people who defend this view? Is it perhaps nothing more than a harmless ornament they have adopted for the sake of fashion?

8.

[margin handwriting: One can't abstract from I]

The *Wissenschaftslehre* asserts that one cannot abstract from the I. This claim can be viewed in two different ways. *Either* one can view it from the standpoint of ordinary consciousness, in which case what is asserted is that

501

we never entertain any representation but that of ourselves. Throughout every moment of our entire lives we are constantly thinking "I," "I," "I," and never anything except "I." *Or* it may be viewed from the philosopher's standpoint, in which case it means the following: Whatever we may think of as occurring within consciousness, we must also think of the I as well. In explaining the various determinations of our mind, we may never abstract from the I. Or as Kant puts it: All of my representations must be capable of being accompanied by the "I think" and must be thought of as accompanied thereby.[57] How absurd it would be for anyone to advance this claim in the first sense and how simple it would be to refute it. If it is taken in the second sense, however, then no one who is able to understand it at all will have any objection to raise against it. Indeed, if this thought had only been clearly grasped sooner, then the thought of the thing in itself could have

(254)

been dispensed with long ago; for one would then have realized that we are the subject who thinks whatever it is we may be thinking, and therefore that we can never encounter anything independent of us, since everything is necessarily related to our thinking.

9.

[margin handwriting: I as specific person]

Other opponents of the *Wissenschaftslehre* make the following confession: "For our part, when we think of the concept of the I we are unable to think of anything except our own precious person, as distinct from all others. The word 'I' signifies my own specific person, the person who is called Caius or Sempronius, in contrast with all of the other people who have different names. Thus, if I do what the *Wissenschaftslehre* asks and abstract

57. See KRV, B131–32.

from this individual personality, nothing whatsoever remains that could be characterized as 'I.' What remains left over is something I might just as well call 'it.'"[58]

What is actually asserted in the objection so boldly advanced here? Is it concerned with the original, real synthesis of the concept of the individual (i.e., the concept of one's own precious person and of other persons as well), and do those who offer this objection wish to maintain that the concept of the I is nothing more than a synthesis of the concept of an object as such (i.e., the concept of an "it") with the distinction between this "it" and *502* others like it, which are therefore also "its" and nothing more? Or is this an objection based simply upon linguistic usage, and do those who make this objection wish to say no more than this: that within our language the word "I" designates nothing more than individuality? So far as the first sort of objection is concerned, anyone who still has his wits about him must certainly be able to see that the distinction between one object and others like it (i.e., between one object and other objects) yields nothing but [the concept of] a *specific object*, and by no means [that of] a specific *person*. The concept of a person is synthesized in a quite different manner. *I-hood* (i.e., *(255)* self-reverting activity or subject-objectivity — call it what you will) is originally opposed to the *it*, to mere objectivity; and the act of positing these concepts is an absolute act of positing, one not conditioned by any other act of positing — not synthetic, but thetic. The concept of I-hood that arises within ourselves is then transferred to and synthetically united with something which, in this first act of positing, was posited as an "it," a mere object, something outside of us. It is by means of this conditioned synthesis that a "you" first arises for us. The concept of the "you" arises from the union of the "it" and the "I." The concept of the I within this opposition (i.e., the concept of the I as an individual) is the synthesis of the I with itself. I am the subject that posits itself — not simply as such, but *as I* — in the act just described; and you are what is posited within this same act as an I, not *by yourself*, but *by me*. One is undoubtedly able to abstract from this product of a yet to be described act of synthesis, for one should certainly be able to turn around and analyze something one has synthesized oneself. All that remains after one has performed such an act of abstraction is [the concept of] the I as such, i.e, the non–object. Consequently,

58. Though this is a paraphrase of an objection raised in Forberg's "Briefe" (*Philosophisches Journal*, VI,1, p. 60), a similar objection had been raised a year earlier by J. B. Erhard in his hostile review of Schelling's *Vom Ich als Princip der Philosophie*.

if this is how the objection in question is supposed to be construed, it is quite absurd.

    Is it then linguistic usage upon which our opponents base their objection? Suppose that they were right about this, and that the word "I" has hitherto been employed only to designate the individual: even if it were true that people had hitherto failed to take note of a difference that can be exhibited within the original synthesis and had failed to assign it any name

503   in their language, would it therefore follow that they must never take note of this distinction or give it a name? But are our opponents, in fact, right about this? To what linguistic usage can they be referring? Could it be philosophical usage to which they refer? I have already shown that Kant employs the concept of the pure I in the same sense in which it is employed by the *Wissenschaftslehre*. When I assert that I am the thinking subject in some act of thinking, do I thereby oppose myself merely to other persons outside of myself? Or do I not, instead, posit myself in opposition to *all objects of thought*? Kant says that "the principle of the necessary unity of apperception is itself an identical, and thus an analytic, proposition" (*Critique of Pure Reason*, p. 135).[59] This sentence has the same meaning as what was just said: viz., that the I does not come into being by means of any act of synthesis, the various elements of which one might subsequently be able to disassemble; instead, the I originates through an absolute thesis. The I

(256)   we are talking about here, however, is I-hood as such or in general; for the concept of individuality obviously does arise through synthesis, as I have just shown, and the first principle of the latter is a synthetic principle. — Reinhold, in formulating his principle of consciousness,[60] speaks about "the subject" (in plain language: "the I") and refers to it only as the "representing subject." But this is irrelevant to the point at issue; for when I distinguish myself, as the representing subject, from the object represented, do I thereby distinguish myself merely from other persons? Or do I, instead, distinguish myself from the entire realm of everything that is represented? Even in the case of those philosophers whose praises we have previously sung, namely, those who, unlike Kant and the *Wissenschaftslehre*, do not presuppose that the I is prior to the manifold of representation, but instead,

59. KRV, B135. Again, Fichte's quotation differs in minor ways from Kant's text.

60. The "principle of consciousness" is the first principle of Reinhold's Elementary Philosophy; that is to say, it is the allegedly self-evident principle from which he proposed to derive his entire system. Reinhold formulated it as follows: "In consciousness, the subject distinguishes the representation from the subject and the object and relates it to them both" (*Beyträge*, I, p. 167).

cobble it together from the latter: Is the unified thinking subject they discover within the manifold of thinking merely the individual? Or is it not instead the intellect as such? In short, has even a single reputable philosopher prior to our opponents made the discovery that the word "I" signifies only the individual and maintained that if one were to abstract from individuality nothing would remain but an object as such?

Is it then ordinary usage they are talking about? In order to provide evidence on this point, I will have to introduce some examples from everyday life. — Suppose you call out to someone in the dark, "Who is there?" *504* And suppose too that, acting on the assumption that you will recognize his voice, he replies, "It is I." In this case it is clear that he is referring to himself as this specific person and that this is the manner in which what he says is meant to be understood: "I am the person who goes by such and such a name, and I am not some other person with a different name." He replied in this way because when you asked *"Who* is there?" you already assumed the presence of some rational being or another and merely wished to know which, of all the rational beings that might possibly be present, was actually there. But let us imagine (if you will forgive me for using this example, which I find to be particularly apt) that you are sewing or altering someone's garment while she is still wearing it and that you accidentally manage to cut her. In this case she will cry out, "Stop, that is *I*! You are cutting *me*!" What is she trying to say in this case? She is not announcing to you that she is this or that specific person and no other, for this is something you already know quite well. Instead, what she wishes to tell you is that what you have just cut is not her dead and insensate garment, but her living and feeling self — which is something you did not know. In this case, she employs the word "I" in order to distinguish herself, not from other people, but rather from things. Throughout the course of our lives, we *(257)* never cease for a moment to make this distinction; indeed, if we were to fail to make this distinction we would find ourselves unable to take a single step upon the ground or to move our hand through the air.

In short, I-hood and individuality are very different concepts, and it is quite obvious that some assemblage is involved in the latter. Through the former concept we oppose to ourselves everything outside of us, not merely persons other than ourselves; the concept of I-hood comprises not merely our own specific personality, but our entire mental or spiritual nature. We have now seen that the word "I" is employed in this manner in both philosophical and ordinary usage, and thus the objection we are considering not only demonstrates an extraordinary thoughtlessness; it also betrays a great ignorance of and lack of familiarity with the usual philosophical literature.

Yet our opponents continue to insist that they are unable to think of the concept they have been asked to think of, and we must take them at their word on this. To be sure, insofar as they are rational, spiritual beings at all, they simply cannot dispense with the general concept of the pure I as such,[61] for in that case they would also have to refrain from raising any objections against us — just as a block of wood would have to do. What they do lack, however, and are unable to elevate themselves to the level of, is *the concept of this concept*. They certainly possess this concept within themselves; they simply do not realize that they possess it. The reason for this incapacity does not lie in any particular weakness of their intellectual power, but rather in a weakness of their entire character. The final goal of their acting is their own I (in the sense in which they understand this word, i.e., their own individual person), which thus also constitutes the limit of their ability to think clearly. For them, their own individual I is the only true substance, and reason is merely an accident of this substance. Their own person does not present itself to them as a particular expression of reason; instead, reason is present simply in order to assist this person in making his way in the world, and if he were able to manage equally well without reason then we could dispense with it, and it would not exist at all. This attitude manifests itself throughout the entire system of their concepts and in everything they say. Indeed, many of them are sufficiently candid to make no secret of this. Insofar as they alone are concerned, they are quite right to insist upon this incapacity; but they must not pretend that something possessing merely subjective validity is also objectively true. The relationship between reason and individuality presented in the *Wissenschaftslehre* is just the reverse. Here, the only thing that exists in itself is reason, and individuality is something merely accidental. Reason is the end and personality is the means; the latter is merely a particular expression of reason, one that must increasingly be absorbed into the universal form of the same. For the *Wissenschaftslehre*, reason alone is eternal, whereas individuality must ceaselessly die off. Anyone who will not first accommodate his will to this order of things will never obtain a true understanding of the *Wissenschaftslehre*.

10.

We have frequently said to our opponents that one can succeed in understanding the *Wissenschaftslehre* only if one has first satisfied certain condi-

61. "Nicht, daß sie des Begriffs überhaupt vom reinen Ich, nach der bloßen Vernünftigkeit, und Geistigkeit entbehrten."

tions. They do not want to hear any more about this, and our frank admo- *506* nition only provides them with an occasion for issuing a fresh complaint against us. Every conviction, they maintain, must be communicable through concepts; moreover, not only must conviction be communicable through concepts, but it must also be possible to force one's conviction upon anyone else purely by means of concepts. Thus they claim that it sets a bad example, is an instance of deplorable fanaticism, etc., for us to pre- tend that our science is accessible only to certain privileged spirits and to assert that no one else will be able to see anything in it nor understand anything concerning it.

Let us first of all see what the *Wissenschaftslehre* has actually had to say on this point. We have not maintained that there exists any sort of original and innate difference between human beings which makes some people capable of thinking of or of learning something that others, because of their very nature, are simply unable to think. Reason is the common possession of everyone and is entirely the same in every rational being. The same talent possessed by any one rational being is also possessed by every other rational being. Indeed, as we have often stated, and as we have repeated in the present treatise, the concepts with which the *Wissenschaftslehre* is con- cerned are concepts that are actually operative in every rational being, where they operate with the necessity of reason; for the very possibility of any consciousness whatsoever is based upon the efficacy of these same concepts. The pure *I*, of which our opponents profess to be unable to think, underlies all of their thinking and is present in their every act of thinking, for otherwise no act of thinking could occur at all. Everything proceeds quite mechanically up to this point. But to understand the neces- sity just asserted, to think, in turn, of this act of thinking: this is not some- thing that occurs mechanically. In order for this to occur, we must, through freedom, elevate ourselves to an entirely different sphere, a sphere to which we do not obtain immediate entry simply by virtue of the fact that we exist. If this power of freedom is not already in place and being exer- *(259)* cised, then one can neither understand nor benefit from the *Wissen- schaftslehre*.[62] It is this power alone that furnishes the premises upon which one can then proceed to construct anything further. — Surely our oppo- nents will not wish to deny that every science and every art presupposes a certain amount of prior knowledge which one must possess before one can *507* begin to cultivate the science or art in question. — Yet they might still

62. "Wenn dieses Vermögen der Freiheit [that is, this capacity to act freely] nicht schon da ist, und geübt ist, kann die WissenschaftsLehre nichts mit dem Menschen anfangen."

reply as follows: If such prior knowledge is all we lack, then provide us with it. Simply present it to us in a definite and systematic way. Is it not your own fault that you proceed directly to the matter itself without any further ado and expect the public to understand you before you have shared with them these preliminary cognitions that nobody except you possesses? To this we would reply: The explanation for this is that the cognitions in question are not the sort that can be furnished to anyone in a systematic manner. They do not force themselves upon anyone, nor can they be forced upon anyone; in a word, this is a kind of acquaintance one can derive only from oneself and only if one has previously acquired a certain facility. Everything depends upon one's having already become ardently aware of one's own freedom and prizing it above all else; and this is something that can be achieved only by the constant — *and clearly conscious* — exercise of one's own freedom. The *Wissenschaftslehre* will become universally comprehensible and easy to understand just as soon as it becomes the main goal and deliberate aim of all education, from the earliest age, only to develop the pupil's inner energy and not to channel it in any particular direction, i.e., just as soon as we begin to educate human beings for their own purposes and as instruments of their own will and not as soulless instruments for the use of others. Education of the whole person from earliest youth: This is the only way to propagate philosophy. At first, such an education must resign itself to being more negative than positive; i.e., it must consist only of interaction *with* the pupil and must not seek to exercise any influence *upon* him. It must strive, so far as possible, to be the former; that is to say, this should at least be its constant goal, and it should resort to influencing the pupil only when interaction with him proves impossible. So long as education — whether consciously or unconsciously — pursues the opposite goal and only tries to produce people who are useful to others, without considering that the principle of utilization also has its foundation within the individual, then it will continue to extirpate the root of self-activity in earliest youth and to accustom people to never initiating anything on their own, but always to expect the first stimulus to come from outside. So long as this situation continues to prevail, it will always remain an extraordinary gift of nature — an aptitude that cannot be further explained and can thus be designated by the vague term "philosophical genius" — if, in the midst of this universal enervation, some people should nevertheless succeed in elevating themselves to the level of this great thought.

It may well be that the chief reason for all of the errors committed by these opponents is that they are not clear in their own minds about what it

508
(260)

means to "prove" something, and hence they fail to appreciate that every demonstration must be based upon something simply indemonstrable. Here, too, they might have learned something from Jacobi, who has made this point quite clearly, along with many others of which they are equally ignorant.[63] — By means of demonstration, one can never obtain anything more than a conditioned, mediated certainty; something becomes certain in consequence of a demonstration only if something else is certain. If there is any doubt concerning the certainty of the latter, then its certainty must be connected with the certainty of some third thing, and so on, over and over again. Does this process of being referred backwards continue without end, or is there somewhere a final member of this series? I realize that some people are of the former opinion, but they have not reflected upon the fact that, if they were right about this, then it would also follow that they would not even be capable of entertaining the Idea of certainty, nor could they ever seek certainty. For it is only insofar as they themselves are certain of something that they are in any position to know what it means to "be certain." But if all certainty is merely conditional, then nothing whatsoever is certain — not even conditionally. If, however, there is a final member of this series, something whose certainty is simply not open to any further inquiry, then there is also something indemonstrable lying at the basis of all demonstration.

Nor do our opponents seem to have considered what it means to "prove something *to someone*." We do this by showing another person that a particular act of assenting to something or considering it to be true is, according to the laws of thinking that he also concedes to us, already contained in

63. See Jacobi's remarks on this topic in his first (1785) edition of his *Ueber die Lehre des Spinoza*, pp. 162–63: "We are all born into belief and must remain in belief, just as we are all born into society and must remain in society. *Totum parte prius esse necesse est* ["the whole is necessarily prior to the part," Aristotle, *Politics*, 1.2, 1253a20. —How could we ever strive for certainty unless we were already acquainted with certainty; and how could we be acquainted with it except through something we already cognize with certainty? This leads to the concept of an immediate certainty, which not only requires no proof, but which absolutely excludes the possibility of any proof and which, entirely by itself, is itself *a representation that agrees with the thing represented*. The kind of conviction obtained by proofs is a second-hand certainty, based upon comparison, and can never be genuinely certain and complete. If, therefore, every *act of considering something to be true* which is not derived from rational grounds is called 'belief,' then the kind of conviction that is based upon rational grounds must itself spring from belief and must obtain its force from belief alone."

another particular act of assenting that he himself acknowledges. Accordingly, since he assures us that he accepts the latter, he must necessarily
509   accept the former as well. Thus any communication of conviction by means
of proof presupposes that both parties agree upon at least something. How
then could the *Wissenschaftslehre* communicate itself to a dogmatist, since
it *simply does not agree with him upon a single point* concerning the *material*
of cognition,* and thus there exists no common ground from which they
could jointly proceed?

(261)   Finally, these opponents also do not seem to realize that, even when two
parties share some point in common, no one can think himself into the soul
of another person without being that other person. Instead, one has to
count upon the self-activity of the other; one cannot provide another person with a specific set of thoughts, but can do no more than offer him the
guidance that will help him to think these specific thoughts on his own.
The relationship between free beings is one of free interaction; it is by no
means a relationship of mere causality operating through mechanical
forces. Thus, like all of the disputes between us and them, this one too
comes back to the central point in dispute: They presuppose that the relationship of causality prevails everywhere, because they are, in fact, acquainted with no higher form of relationship. And this is also the reason
why they demand of us that we should implant this conviction within their

---

* I have already repeated this point several times. I have stated that I have nothing
whatsoever in common with certain other philosophers and that they do not now
occupy and never will be able to occupy the standpoint from which I write.[64] People
appear to have treated this declaration more as an indignantly expressed hyperbole
than as something I am completely serious about, for they have not ceased to reiterate their demand that I should prove my theory to them. I must therefore solemnly declare that I intend this claim to be taken in the most literal sense, that I am
completely serious about it, and that it expresses my deepest conviction. Dogmatism starts with a being, which it considers to be something absolute; consequently,
this is a system that can never go beyond being. Idealism is not in the least acquainted with any sort of being, considered as something that subsists for itself. In
other words, dogmatism begins with necessity, and idealism begins with freedom.
Hence they find themselves in two completely different worlds.

64. See, e.g., "A Comparison between Prof. Schmid's System and the *Wissenschaftslehre*," where Fichte declares that Schmid "is unable to enter the realm I
embrace; he cannot even put a foot across its border. Where I am, he never is. We
do not have a single point in common, on the basis of which we might be able to
reach mutual agreement" (GA, I,3: 265 = SW, II, p. 456; English trans., EPW,
p. 334).

souls — even though they are not prepared for this and will not make the least effort of their own to facilitate it. We begin with freedom, and, as is only fair, we assume that they are free as well. — To be sure, in presupposing the thoroughgoing validity of the mechanism of cause and effect, they directly contradict themselves. What they say stands in contradiction with what they do; for, to the extent that they *presuppose* mechanism, they at the same time elevate themselves above it. Their own act of thinking of this relationship is an act that lies outside the realm of mechanical determinism. Mechanism cannot grasp itself, precisely because it is mechanism. Only a free consciousness is able to grasp itself. Thus it might appear that we have here discovered a means for convincing our opponents on the spot. This, however, is just where the difficulty arises, because this is an observation that lies completely outside of their field of vision, and because they do not possess enough mental agility and dexterity to be able, when thinking of an object, to think not merely of the object in question, but also and at the same time of their own act of thinking about this object. By the same token, this entire remark must necessarily be incomprehensible to them, and is not intended for them at all, but is meant for others who can see and who stand watch.[65]

We will, therefore, repeat what we have said so many times before: We do not wish to convince these opponents, because one cannot will to do something impossible. We do not wish to refute their system for them, because we are unable to do this. We certainly can refute their system *for us*; indeed, it must be refuted, and this is something that can be accomplished quite easily. A single breath from a free human being is enough to blow their system away. But we cannot refute it *for them*. We do not write, speak, or teach *for* them, for there is simply no way we could accommodate them. If we nevertheless continue to talk *about* them, we do this, not for their sake, but for that of others, in order to warn them against the errors of the former and to divert them from such hollow and meaningless babble. Our opponents should not feel themselves demeaned by this declaration. If they do feel themselves to be somehow belittled by our comments, they merely reveal their own bad consciousness and place themselves publicly beneath us. Indeed, from their point of view, they occupy the same position in relation to us; for they are equally unable to refute or to convince us, nor can they have anything to say against us that will have the least effect.

510

(262)

---

65. "für Andere, die da sehen, und wachen." This would appear to be an allusion to Christ's words to his disciples in the garden of Gethsemane (Matthew 26: 40–41; Mark 14: 34–38).

We ourselves say this, and we would not be in the least upset if they were to say the same thing to us. It is not with any malicious intention of annoying them that we say what we say to them, but only to save them and us from wasted effort. It would quite honestly please us if they would not allow themselves to become annoyed by this. — There is, moreover, nothing demeaning about this situation *per se*. Anyone who today accuses his brother of this sort of incapacity was necessarily once in this same condition himself; for this is the condition into which we were all born, and it takes time to raise oneself above this condition. When our opponents have finally reached the point where this remark which they now find to be so hateful no longer incites them to anger, but instead stimulates them to reflect upon whether or not it might contain some truth after all, then it is also probable that they will, at the same time, have succeeded in overcoming the very incapacity with which we have here reproached them. From that moment on, they will be like us, and every reproach will fall away. We would thus be able to live in the most peaceful tranquility with them, if only they would permit us to do so, and it is not our fault if, from time to time, we become embroiled in bitter conflicts with them.

In passing, I should like to add the following remark, which I consider to be very pertinent at this point: From what has been said so far it also follows that a philosophy does not have to be *universally recognized to be valid* in order to be granted the status of a science — as seems to be assumed by certain philosophers whose own meritorious work is aimed, above all else, at bringing enlightenment to everyone.[66] Such philosophers demand the impossible. What does it mean to say that a philosophy really possesses universal validity? Who is the "everyone" who is supposed to recognize its validity? This can certainly not be everyone who bears a human face. For in this case, the validity of the philosophy in question would also have to be acknowledged by the common man, for whom thinking is never an end but merely a means for pursuing whatever business lies closest at hand; indeed, its validity would have to be recognized even by children. Perhaps then it is only philosophers who are supposed to recognize its validity? But who is to count as a philosopher? Certainly not everyone who has received a doctorate from a philosophical faculty nor everyone who has had something printed that he calls "philosophical" — indeed,

66. This appears to be an allusion to Reinhold, who claimed that a genuinely scientific philosophy would, in the long run, certainly be accepted by everyone (*allgemeingeltend* = "universally accepted or recognized to be valid"; *allgemeingültig* = "universally valid"). See, for example, *Versuch einer neuen Theorie des menschlichen Vorstellungsvermögens*, pp. 71 ff.

does this even include everyone who is a member of a philosophical faculty? Let someone attempt to provide us with a definite concept of a phi- *(263)*
losopher without first providing us with a definite concept of philosophy,
i.e., with a definite philosophy! Everyone can surely see in advance that *512*
those who believe themselves to be in possession of a scientific philosophy
will completely deny the title "philosopher" to anyone who fails to recognize their philosophy; thus they will make willingness to admit the validity
of their own philosophy a criterion for being counted a philosopher at all.
And indeed, they must proceed in just this way if they are to proceed
consistently, for there is but one philosophy. The author of the *Wissenschaftslehre*, for example, has long since asserted that this is his personal
opinion concerning the *Wissenschaftslehre* — considered, that is, as the one
system of *transcendental idealism*, and not merely as *one of the individual
presentations* of the same, which, as such, can always be improved — and he
does not hesitate for a moment to reaffirm this opinion explicitly on the
present occasion. In saying this, however, we become caught up in a pal-
pable circle. Anyone who is himself convinced will then assert, "My philosophy really is universally recognized by everyone who is a philosopher."
And he will be perfectly entitled to say this, even if not a single other
mortal soul accepts the principles of his philosophy — "for," he will add,
"anyone for whom my philosophy is not valid is not a philosopher."

My own opinion on this subject is as follows: If even a single person is
completely convinced of his own philosophy, if he remains equally convinced of it at every moment, if he is entirely at one with himself in this
philosophy, and if the free judgment he exercises when he philosophizes is
in complete harmony with those judgments forced upon him in the course
of his life: if this is really the case, then philosophy has achieved its goal and
run its full course in this one person, for it has set him down again at the
precise point where he, along with all other human beings, began. Should
this ever happen, then philosophy as a science will actually be present in
the world, even if no one beyond this one single person comprehends and
adopts it, and even if it should happen that this person has no idea how to
expound this philosophy to anyone else. One should not here make the
trivial rejoinder that every systematic thinker has always been convinced
of the truth of his own system. This claim is fundamentally false and is
based solely upon an ignorance of the true nature of conviction. In order to
know what conviction is, one must have experienced the fullness of con- *513*
viction within oneself. The systematic thinkers of the past were actually *(264)*
convinced of nothing more than one or another obscure point contained
within their systems (and perhaps were not clearly conscious of these systems at all); they were not convinced of the truth of their system as a whole.

Convictions = mind itself

Or, if they were, this was only when they were in a certain frame of mind. But this does not constitute conviction. Conviction can only be something that does not depend upon any particular time nor upon any particular alteration in one's condition. It is not something that can be present to the mind as something merely accidental; instead, it is identical with the mind itself. One can be convinced only of what is unalterably and eternally true. It is simply not possible to be convinced of an error. There have probably been very few people in the history of philosophy who have possessed this type of conviction; perhaps such conviction has been attained by hardly anyone, and perhaps by no one at all. I am not speaking here of the ancients. It is even doubtful whether they ever consciously posed for themselves the real question that philosophy has to answer. I here wish to take into account only the greatest thinkers of the modern age. — *Spinoza* could not have been convinced of his own philosophy. He could only have *thought* of it; he could not have *believed* it. For this is a philosophy that directly contradicts those convictions that Spinoza must necessarily have adopted in his everyday life, by virtue of which he had to consider himself to be free and self-sufficient. He could have been convinced of his own philosophy only to the extent that it contains some element of truth, i.e., only insofar as it includes within itself a portion of philosophy as a science. He was convinced that a purely objective mode of reasoning must necessarily lead to his system, and he was right about this. But in the course of his thoughts it never occurred to him to reflect upon his own act of thinking; this is where he went astray, and this is how he came to place his speculations in contradiction with his life. *Kant* might have been convinced; but, if I understand him correctly, he was not convinced at the time he was writing his [first] *Critique*. He refers in this work *to a deception that continually recurs, despite the fact that one knows that it is a deception.*[67] How can Kant know that this deception will always recur, particularly since he himself was the first person to bring this alleged deception to light? And for whom — except for Kant himself — could it have recurred while he was writing his *Critique*? This is something he could only have experienced at first hand. To know that one is deceived and yet to remain deceived: This is not a state of conviction and harmony with oneself; instead, it is a state of serious inner conflict. In my experience, no deception recurs; for no deception whatsoever is present within reason. What then is the deception that is supposed to recur? Is it not this: that things in themselves exist outside of and independently of us? But who makes this assertion? This is certainly not

514

67. See KRV, A293/B349–A298/B355.

anything asserted by ordinary consciousness, which speaks only *of itself* and thus can only declare that things are present for ordinary consciousness itself (that is to say, for us, insofar as we occupy the standpoint of ordinary consciousness). And this is no delusion that could or should be prevented by philosophy; it is our commonly shared truth.[68] Ordinary consciousness knows nothing about any "thing in itself," precisely because it is ordinary consciousness, which, it is certainly to be hoped, will not overstep its own proper bounds. It is a false philosophy that attributes to ordinary consciousness this concept [viz., that of a thing in itself] it has invented within its own philosophical domain. The deception in question here, which is quite avoidable and which can be completely extirpated by true philosophy, is, therefore, one you have created all by yourself; and as soon as you obtain a clear understanding of your philosophy, this delusion will fall away — like scales from your eyes — never to recur again. You will then cease to suppose that in everyday life you know anything more than this: that you are finite, and that you are finite in *this determinate* manner, which you have to explain to yourself by referring to the presence of a *world of this particular sort* outside of yourself; and it will no more occur to you to transgress this boundary than it would occur to you to cease being yourself. *Leibniz* might also have been convinced [of his philosophy]. For if he is understood correctly — and why should he not have understood himself correctly? — he is right. If supreme facility and freedom of spirit are evidence of conviction; if skill in accommodating one's own way of thinking to every form, in applying it in an unforced way to every part of human knowledge, in easily dispersing any doubts that might arise, and, in general, in employing one's system more as an instrument than as an object [is evidence of conviction]; and if open-mindedness, cheerfulness, and a good-natured approach to life provide evidence that a person is at one with himself: then perhaps Leibniz was convinced, the only convinced person in the history of philosophy.*

(265)

515

68. "unsre einige Wahrheit." Since Fichte often employs *einige* as a synonym for *einzige*, this same phrase might also be rendered "our sole truth."

* A brilliant sketch of the essence of Leibniz's philosophy, as compared with Spinoza's, may be found in Schelling's most recent work, *Ideas for a Philosophy of Nature* (Leipzig bei Breitkopf, 1797). See the introduction, pp. xxxv ff. and pp. xli ff.[69]

69. F. W. J. Schelling, *Ideen zu einer Philosophie der Natur*. (*Sämmtliche Werke*, II, pp. 20 ff. and 37 ff.; English translation by Errol E. Harris and Peter Heath [New York: Cambridge University Press, 1988].) For an illuminating discussion of the

11.

I would now like to add a few words concerning a most remarkable confusion, namely, the confusion between the I as an intellectual intuition, with which the *Wissenschaftslehre* commences, and the I as an Idea, with which *(266)* it concludes.[70] As an intellectual intuition, the I contains nothing but the form of I-hood, self-reverting acting, which, to be sure, also becomes the content of the I. This intuition has been sufficiently described above. The I exists in this form only *for the philosopher*; and insofar as one grasps it in this form, one thereby raises oneself to the level of philosophy. But the I is present as an Idea *for the I* itself, i.e., for the I the philosopher is observing. The philosopher does not portray this as his own I, but rather as the Idea of the natural, albeit completely cultivated, human being — just as no "being," in the proper sense of the word, is present for the philosopher himself, but only for the I he is investigating. Hence the latter I lies within an entirely different series of thinking than does the former.

The I as an Idea is identical with a rational being.[71] On the one hand, it is the latter insofar as this being has completely succeeded in exhibiting universal reason within itself, has actually become rational through and through, and is nothing but rational. As such, it has ceased to be an indi-516 vidual, which it was only because of the limitations of sensibility. On the other hand, the I as an Idea is the rational being insofar as this being has also succeeded in completely realizing reason outside of itself in the world, which thus also remains posited within this Idea. The world remains in this Idea as a world as such, i.e., the substrate along with these particular mechanical and organic laws; but these laws are here geared completely

---

quite interesting similarities between the systems of Leibniz and Fichte, see the remarks on this subject by Robert Latta in his introduction to his translation of Leibniz, *The Monadology and Other Philosophical Writings* (Oxford: Oxford University Press, 1898), pp. 178–82. See too Jean Grondin, "Leibniz and Fichte," in *Fichte: Historical Contexts/Contemporary Controversies*, ed. Daniel Breazeale and Tom Rockmore (Atlantic Highlands, N.J.: Humanities Press, 1994), pp. 181–90.

70. Once again, it was Forberg who sought to identify the (unintuitable) Idea of the absolute I with which the *Foundations of the Entire Wissenschaftslehre* concludes with the I as an "intellectual intuition," with which, according to Schelling's interpretation, it must begin. (See *Philosophisches Journal*, VI,1, p. 71.)

71. "Das Ich, als Idee, ist das VernunftWesen." The term *Wesen* combines the meanings of the English words "being," "essence," and "creature." Hence *das Vernunftwesen* = "the essence of reason" as well as "the rational creature."

toward exhibiting the final goal of reason.[72] All that the Idea of the I has in common with the I as an intuition is this: in neither case is the I considered to be an individual. In the latter case, it is not thought of as an individual because I-hood has not yet been determined as individuality; in the former case, on the other hand, it is not thought of as an individual because individuality has vanished as a result of a process of cultivation in accordance with universal laws. But these two I's are also opposed to one another, inasmuch as the I, considered as an intuition, contains nothing but the form of the I, and does not include any reference at all to the proper content of the I, which becomes thinkable only when the I thinks of a world. In contrast, the entire content of I-hood is included in the thought of the I as an Idea. Philosophy in its entirety proceeds from the former, which is thus its basic concept. From this, it proceeds to the latter,[73] to the I as an Idea, which can be exhibited only within the practical portion of philosophy, where it is shown to be the ultimate aim of reason's striving. As we have said, the former is an original intuition, which becomes a concept in the manner sufficiently described above. The latter is nothing but an Idea. It cannot be thought of in any determinate manner, and it will never become anything real; instead, it is only something to which we ought to draw infinitely nearer.

12.

To the best of my knowledge, this exhausts the various misunderstandings that have to be taken into account and that one may legitimately hope to help correct by means of a clear explanation. But there are also certain other ways of attacking this system, and against attacks of this sort one can take no measures at all, nor are any such measures needed.

What, for example, can one do when a system whose entire essence, *(267)* from start to finish, is aimed at overlooking individuality within the theo- *517* retical realm and disavowing it within the realm of practice is characterized as "egoism" by people who cannot have raised themselves to the point where they might obtain any insight into this system — precisely because they themselves are theoretical egoists in secret and practical egoists in

72. Reading, with the original text and GA, "durchaus geleitet, den Endzweck der Vernunft darzustellen," for SW's "durchaus geeignet [. . .]" ("completely suited for [. . .]").
73. Reading, with the original text and GA, "geht sie hin" for SW's "geht sie nicht hin" ("it does not proceed to the latter").

public — and when one goes on to infer from this system that its originator possesses an evil heart* and therefore that his system must be false? One simply cannot make any rational reply to objections of this sort, for those who make these charges know only too well that they are untrue, and they do not say these things because they believe them to be true, but for an entirely different reason. Indeed, this system itself is the last thing they are concerned with. Its author may, however, perhaps elsewhere have said something that offended them, and he may in some way — God knows how or where! — be an obstacle to them. As far as they themselves are concerned, such people behave in a manner entirely in keeping with their own way of thinking as well as with their own interests, and it would be foolish to attempt to alter their nature by engaging in discussion with them. But when thousands and thousands of people who are unfamiliar with a single word of the *Wissenschaftslehre* and whose profession does not require them to know anything about it, people who are neither Jews nor their confederates,[75] neither aristocrats nor democrats, neither Kantians of the old school nor Kantians of any of the more recent schools, and who are not

(268)

---

* A well-meaning person unacquainted with recent literary events might well ask: "Has this style of argumentation still not been abandoned?" No, I would reply, it is now more common than ever, and it is particularly employed against me. Though such attacks are, for the moment, still conducted orally, from lecterns and the like, they will soon find their way into print as well. Preparation for such an attack may be found in the reply that the person who reviewed Schelling's *On the I* in the *Allgemeine Literatur-Zeitung* has made to Herr Schelling's "Anti-Critique" — though, admittedly, there was little he could say by way of reply to this "Anti-Critique," beyond impugning the reputation of its author and of his system.[74]

74. J. B. Erhard was the author of a highly critical review of Schelling's *Vom Ich as Princip der Philosophie* which appeared in the October 11, 1796 issue of the *Allgemeine Literatur-Zeitung*. Schelling's reply, entitled "Antikritik. Einiges aus Gelegenheit der Rec. meiner Schrift: Vom Ich als Princip der Philosophie etc.," appeared in the December 10, 1796 "Intelligenzblatt" of the same journal, which also included Erhard's "Reply" to Schelling's "Anti-Critique." It is Erhard's intemperate reply to which Fichte refers in the above note.

75. As the draft of this paragraph (see GA, II,4: 363–64) makes clear, this is a concealed allusion to the Berlin bookseller and publisher Christoph Friedrich Nicolai (1733–1811), who was also editor of the influential *Allgemeine deutsche Bibliothek*. Nicolai himself was a member of the inner circle of Berlin illuminati and boasted of his close relations with Lessing and Moses Mendelssohn. A zealous exponent of "popular philosophy" and bitter opponent of every variety of Kantianism, Nicolai publicly attacked Fichte and Schelling in 1796, in vol. 11 of his *Beschreibung einer Reise durch Deutschland und die Schweiz* (quoted in Erich

even original thinkers who were just on the verge of making public some
important discovery when the author of the *Wissenschaftslehre* stole it from   *518*
them or distracted them from it: when people like this, whose only apparent interest in this subject is their desire to make others think that they too
are well educated and well versed in the mysteries of the most recent literature, eagerly take up this claim and repeat it again and again, then one may
surely hope that, for their own sakes, they will pay some heed to our request that they think more carefully about what they are saying and why
they are saying it!*

Fuchs, ed., *Fichte im Gespräch*, vol. 1 [Stuttgart-Bad Cannstatt: Frommann-
Holzboog, 1978], pp. 320–29). After Fichte's move to Berlin, his public dispute
with Nicolai, who did his best to prevent Fichte from obtaining any sort of academic employment, intensified and finally drove Fichte to publish a bitter polemic
of his own entitled *Fr. Nicolai's Leben und sonderbare Meinungen* (1801). (In GA,
I,7: 365–463.)

* This thoughtless parrotry on the part of young people, their willingness to pick
up and to pass along the first juicy scandal that falls into their hands, simply so that
people will believe that they too are well informed: this is a sign of the times. Thus,
for example, the Eudämonists[76] announce that their journal is actually still continuing to find readers and supporters (as reported, anyway, in the Hamburg
Zeitung, for one cannot obtain their journal itself in the area where I live). Of course,
one cannot base any conclusions on the assertions of these well-known and publicly
exposed liars; nevertheless, if one could obtain reliable information about this from
another source, this would be a significant piece of information for any description
of the present age.

Given the conflict prevailing among the most extraordinary publications in the
literary and political world, it is no wonder that in Germany a half dozen sheer
morons, out of despair at being unable to attract attention to themselves in any
other way, should have lost what little good sense they may once have had and,
taking advantage of the fact that the police in their area were not sufficiently vigi-
lant to lock them up in time, should have spewed forth their nonsense in scurrilous
publications. The only trace of good sense they have shown so far was their decision not to publish their names. But from a city in Westphalia, where one can still
obtain copies of *Eudämonia*, I hear that the authors of this journal have promised to
make their names public at the first opportunity. Their madness will then have
reached its zenith.

It is no wonder that all of this has happened. The same thing could have occurred   *(269)*
in any age and in any nation. But could it really be true that there are many people
in Germany who are either tasteless enough to be able to listen for more than an
hour to these babbling madmen (whom one might indeed listen to once, simply out
of curiosity, in the same way one might visit a madhouse while on a journey) or

who, despite the fact that they have learned how to read, are obtuse and stupid enough not to notice, in their naiveté, that their popular orators are poor fools? If this is true, it would be a phenomenon whose basis could only lie in some strange mental epidemic from which our age is suffering, the discovery and cure of which would have to be left to the physicians. And if this were the case, it would be very desirable to know exactly which places and persons were particularly afflicted by this epidemic.

In its madness, this gang even brags that it enjoys the co-operation, approval, and support of certain German princes. This crude slander must have gone unnoticed, for otherwise they would not have been allowed to go unpunished. Which German prince would let it be said of himself that he had in his pay public pasquillants who attack his own subjects and those of other rulers, and who even go so far as to attack both the persons and the institutions of other princes and heirs to the throne? What German prince would want it said of himself that he had bestowed his favor upon fools? Have things come to such a pass in Germany? Even if a German patriot were to be forced to conclude that this is true, he would at least have the comfort of knowing that no one in the entire nation — at least no one still in control of his reason — had been found who was miserable and base enough to permit himself to be employed for this purpose.

P.S. Habent sua fata libelli.[77] After I had already written this note I happened by chance to come across Rebmann's *Heather Blossoms*[78] (Hamburg, bei Mutzenbecher), which I would have read earlier if it had not already been the subject of several rather indifferent reviews. In the fourth essay, which is written with a precision, clarity, force, and liveliness quite rare among our popular authors, one will find more detailed information concerning the gang discussed above. This essay can certainly be recommended to anyone who is interested in the truth.[79]

76. *Eudämonia, oder Deutsches Volksglück* was the name of a fugitive journal that appeared intermittently during the 1790's and circulated somewhat surreptitiously in various German states. According to its anonymous editors, *Eudämonia* was founded in order to combat instigators of disorder and enemies of throne and altar. Defenders of the French Revolution and exponents of Enlightenment were subjected to especially harsh and often libelous criticism in the pages of this journal. (For a discussion of the place of *Eudämonia* within German conservatism of the 1790s, see Frederick C. Beiser, *Enlightenment, Revolution, and Romanticism: The Genesis of Modern German Political Thought 1790 – 1800* ([Cambridge, Mass. and London: Harvard University Press, 1992], pp. 326–34.)

In an article published in *Eudämonia* in 1796 ("Verunglückter Versuch im christlichen Deutschlande eine Art von öffentlicher Vernunft-Religionsübung einzuführen") Fichte was accused of attempting to turn his lecture hall into a "temple of reason." In the following years, this same journal continued its campaign against Fichte, constantly reiterating the charges of atheism and Jacobinism and thereby helping to prepare the climate for the "Atheism Controversy" of 1798/

99. Fichte replied publicly to these attacks in the April 16, 1796 "Intelligenzblatt" of the *Allgemeine Literatur-Zeitung* ("Erklärung gegen den Aufsatz: Verunglückter Versuch im chistlichen Deutschlande eine Art von öffentlicher Vernunft-Religionsübung einzuführen," in GA, I,3: 279–88).

77. "Books have fates of their own."

78. G. F. Rebmann (1768–1824) published his *Haydeblümchen* in 1796. Chapter Four of this book, entitled "Die Wächter der Burg Zion," contains a critical discussion of *Eudämonia*.

79. The third installment of *An Attempt at a New Presentation of the Wissenschafts-lehre* ends at this point, with the preceding long footnote (which, for some reason, is not included in the text printed in SW, but is printed in GA, I,4: 268–69).

Chapter One

All consciousness is conditioned by our immediate consciousness of ourselves.

I.

With the permission of the reader, with whom it is our task to reach agreement, I will address him informally in the second person.

(1) You are undoubtedly able to think "I"; and insofar as you do this you will discover that your consciousness is internally *determined* in a specific manner and that you are thinking of *only* one thing: viz., precisely what you comprehend under the concept "I." It is this of which you are conscious, and when you think "I" you are not thinking of any of the other things of which you could otherwise well be thinking and of which you may have previously been thinking. — For the moment, I am unconcerned with whether you may have included more or less in the concept "I" than I have. Your concept certainly includes what I am concerned with, and this is enough for me.

(2) Instead of thinking of this particular, determinate [concept], you could also have thought of something else: of your table, for example, or of your walls or your window; moreover, you actually do think of these objects if I summon you to do so. You do this in response to a summons and in accordance with a concept of what you are supposed to think of (which, as you suppose, might just as easily have been some other object, or so I submit). Accordingly, while engaged in this act of thinking, in this movement of transition from thinking of the I to thinking of the table, the walls, etc., you take note of the activity and freedom that are involved therein. Your thinking is, for you, an *acting*. Have no fear that by admitting this you may be conceding to me anything you may later come to regret. I am speaking of nothing but the activity of which you become immediately conscious when you are in this state — and only insofar as you are conscious of this activity. If, however, you should find yourself to be conscious of no activity at all in this case (and many celebrated philosophers of our own day find them-

selves in just this situation), then let us part from each other in peace at this point, for you will be unable to understand anything I say from now on.

I am addressing myself to those of you who understand what I am saying concerning this point. Your thinking is an acting; and hence, when you are thinking of some specific thing, you are acting in some specific manner. In other words, the reason you are thinking of precisely this is because, in thinking, you have acted in precisely this way; and if, in engaging in this act *(272)* of thinking, you had acted differently (if you had thought *differently*), then what you are thinking of would be something different (you would be thinking of *something different*).

(3) You should now be thinking of something quite specific: namely, "I." This is a particular thought, and thus, according to the principle just enunciated, you must necessarily think in a particular manner in order to produce this thought. My task for you, intelligent reader, is this: You must now become truly and most sincerely conscious of *how* you proceed when you think "I." Since our concepts of the "I" may not be exactly the same, I must assist you in doing this.

While you were thinking of your table or your wall, you were, for yourself, the *thinking subject* engaged in this act of thinking, since you, as an intelligent reader, are of course aware of the activity involved in your own act of thinking. On the other hand, what *was thought of* in this act of thinking was, for you, not you yourself, but rather something that has to be distinguished from you. In short, in every concept of this type [i.e., in every concept of an object], the thinking subject and what is thought of are two distinct things, as you will certainly discover within your own consciousness. In contrast, when you think of *yourself*, then you are, for yourself, not only the thinking subject; you are also at the same time that of which you are thinking. In this case the subject and the object of thinking are supposed to be one and the same. The sort of acting in which you are engaged when you are thinking of yourself is supposed to turn back upon or "revert into" yourself, the thinking subject.[1]

It follows from this that *the concept of the I or the act of thinking of the I* *523* *consists in the I's acting upon itself*, and conversely, *such an acting upon itself yields an act of thinking of the I and no other thinking whatsoever*. You have just discovered within yourself the truth of the first of these claims and have conceded this to me. If you balk at the second claim and have any doubts about whether we are warranted in affirming the converse of our

---

1. "dein Handeln im Denken soll auf dich selbst, das Denkende, zurückgehen."

first assertion, then I will leave it up to you to make the following experiment: When your thinking turns back upon yourself, as the thinking subject, does this ever produce any concept other than that of yourself? Can you even think the possibility that some other concept could be produced in this way? — The concept of a self-reverting act of thinking and the concept of the I thus have exactly the same content.[2] The I is what posits itself,[3] and it is nothing more than this. What posits itself is the I and nothing more. Nothing else but the I is produced by the act we have just described; and the I can be produced by no other possible act except the one described.

You can also now appreciate the sense in which you were asked to think of the I. Linguistic signs have passed through the hands of thoughtlessness and have acquired some of its indeterminacy; one is therefore unable to make oneself sufficiently well understood simply by employing such signs. The only way in which a concept can be completely specified or determined is by indicating the act through which it comes into being: If you do *(273)* what I say then you will think what I am thinking. This is the method that, without exception, we will be following in the course of our inquiry. — Though you may have included many things in your concept of the I which I have not (e.g., the concept of your own individuality, for this too is signified by the word "I"), you may henceforth put all of this aside. The only "I" that I am concerned with here is the one that comes into being through the sheer self-reverting act of your own thinking.

(4) The propositions that have been advanced *are the immediate expression of the observation we have just made*, and these propositions could arouse

2. "erschöpfen sich gegenseitig." Literally: "mutually exhaust one another."

3. "Das Ich ist das sich selbst Setzende." The verb *setzen* ("to posit") is a basic term in Fichte's technical vocabulary. It is the most general term one can employ to refer to the *act of consciousness* itself. Any object of consciousness — whether real or imaginary, whether an external object or the I itself — is therefore "posited by the I." Taken by itself, the verb *setzen* does not necessarily imply any "constitution" or "creation" of the object of consciousness; it simply signifies that the conscious subject — whether freely or under compulsion — "puts" or "places" something within its field of awareness. "To posit" something is thus an essential condition for "being conscious" at all (though it does not follow that we are, in fact, always explicitly aware of all of the acts of positing involved in, for example, our everyday consciousness of objects; on the contrary, Fichte contends that we are typically unaware of many of these acts of positing — which can thus be described as occurring "unconsciously" — and become aware of them only through philosophical reflection).

doubts only if one were to consider them to be anything more than the immediate expression of the same. I maintain that the I comes into being only through a self-reverting act of thinking, and when I say this I am not talking about anything except what can come into being purely by means of an act of thinking. All I am talking about here is what immediately appears within my consciousness whenever I think in the manner indicated, and if you too think in this manner, then this will immediately appear within your consciousness as well. In short, I am talking only about the concept of the I. Here I am not yet in the least concerned with any "being" the I may have apart from this concept. At the appropriate time we will see whether and to what extent one can talk about any being of this sort at all. In order to shield the reader against any possible doubts that might arise, and in order to protect him against the danger of seeing, in the course of this inquiry, a previously conceded proposition subsequently employed in some sense that he did not wish to concede, I will amend the propositions just established (viz., "the I is an act of self-positing" and other similar propositions) by adding the phrase "for the I."

524

At the same time I can also explain the reason for the reader's concern about perhaps having conceded too much. But I will do so only if the reader will promise not to allow himself to become distracted thereby, for this entire remark is a merely incidental one which really does not belong here, and I add it merely in order to avoid leaving any point obscure, even for a moment. — It was asserted that your I comes into being only through the reversion of your own act of thinking back upon itself. You probably harbor in some small corner of your soul the following objection to this claim: Either, "I am supposed *to think*, but before I can think I have *to exist*"; or, "I am supposed to think *of myself*, to direct my thinking back upon myself, but whatever I am supposed to think of or to turn my attention back upon must first exist before it can be thought of or become the object of an act of reverting." In both of these cases, you postulate an *existence* of yourself that is independent of and presupposed by the thinking and being-thought-of of yourself.[4] In the former case, you postulate the independent existence of yourself as the *thinking subject*; in the latter, the independent existence of yourself as *what is to be thought of*. In connection with this objection, first simply answer for me the following question: Who is it that claims that you must have existed prior to your own act of thinking? It is undoubtedly you yourself who make this claim, and when you make such a claim you are undoubtedly engaging in an act of thinking. Furthermore, as you will also

(274)

4. "postulirst du ein von dem Denken und Gedachtseyn deiner selbst unabhängiges, und demselben vorauszusetzendes, *Daseyn* deiner selbst."

525   claim, and as I am only too ready to concede, this is a necessary act of
thinking, one that forces itself upon you in this context. One nevertheless
trusts that it is only insofar as and only inasmuch as you think about this
existence that has to be presupposed that you possess any knowledge of it.
It follows that this existence of the I is also nothing more than a posited
being of yourself, that is, a being that you yourself have posited. If we
examine it closely enough, therefore, we will find that the fact with which
you have confronted us amounts to no more than this: *In addition to the act
of self-positing which you have at present raised to clear consciousness, you must
also think of this act as preceded by another act of self-positing, one that is not
accompanied by any clear consciousness, but to which the former act refers and
by means of which it is conditioned.* Until such time as I have had a chance to
explain to you the fecund law in accordance with which this occurs, you can
avoid becoming misled by the fact to which you have called attention if you
will keep in mind that it asserts no more than what has just been stated.

II.

Let us now shift to a higher speculative standpoint.

(1) "Think of yourself, and pay attention to how you do this": This was my
first request. You had to attend to yourself in order to understand what I
was saying (since I was discussing something that could exist only within
yourself) and in order to discover within your own experience the truth of
what I said to you. This *attentiveness* to ourselves in this act was the *subjective* element common to us both. *What* you paid attention *to* was the manner in which you went about thinking of yourself, which did not differ
from the manner I went about thinking of myself; and this was the object
of our investigation, the *objective* element common to us both.

    Now, however, I say to you: pay attention to *your own act of attending to*
your act of self-positing. Attend to what you yourself did in the inquiry
you have just completed and note how you managed to pay attention to
yourself. What constituted the subjective element in the previous inquiry
must be made into the object of the new inquiry we are now beginning.[5]

526   (2) The point that concerns me here is not all that easy to grasp. Yet if one
fails to grasp it, then one will fail to grasp anything, since my entire theory
is based upon this. Perhaps, therefore, the reader will allow me to guide

    5. As a comparison with § 1 of Fichte's lectures on "Foundations of Transcen-
dental Philosophy (*Wissenschaftslehre*) *nova methodo*" reveals, Fichte is here simply

him through the entrance and to place him just as close as possible to what he is supposed to observe.

When you are conscious of any object whatsoever — of the wall over there, let us say — then, as you just conceded, what you are really conscious of is your own act of thinking of this wall, and only insofar as you are conscious of this act of thinking is any consciousness of this wall possible. In order for you to be conscious of your own thinking, however, you must be conscious of yourself. — You say that *you* are conscious of *yourself*; in saying this, you necessarily distinguish your *thinking* I from the I that is *thought of* in the act of thinking the I. In order for you to be able to do this, however, the thinking subject within this act of thinking must, in turn, be the *object* of a higher act of thinking, for otherwise it could not be an object of consciousness. At the same time, you also obtain thereby a new *subject*, one that is conscious of what was previously the *being* of self- *(275)*

---

repeating the classroom instructions he was accustomed to give to his own students. Hendrik Steffens, who was present as a student for some of Fichte's lectures during the winter semester of 1798/99, included in his memoirs the following account of the listeners' puzzled reaction to these same instructions:

"I cannot deny that I was awed by my first glimpse of this short, stocky man with a sharp, commanding tongue. Even his manner of speaking was sharp and cutting. Well aware of his listeners' weaknesses, he tried in every way to make himself understood by them. He made every effort to provide proofs for everything he said; but his speech still seemed commanding, as if he wanted to dispel any possible doubts by means of an unconditional order. 'Gentlemen,' he would say, 'collect your thoughts and enter into yourselves. We are not at all concerned now with anything external, but only with ourselves.' And, just as he requested, his listeners really seemed to be concentrating upon themselves. Some of them shifted their position and sat up straight, while others slumped with downcast eyes. But it was obvious that they were all waiting with great suspense for what was supposed to come next. Then Fichte would continue: 'Gentlemen, think about the wall.' And as I saw, they really did think about the wall, and everyone seemed able to do so with success. 'Have you thought about the wall?' Fichte would ask. 'Now, gentlemen, think about whoever it was that thought about the wall.' The obvious confusion and embarrassment provoked by this request was extraordinary. In fact, many of the listeners seemed quite unable to discover anywhere whoever it was that had thought about the wall. I now understood how young men who had stumbled in such a memorable manner over their first attempt at speculation might have fallen into a very dangerous frame of mind as a result of their further efforts in this direction. Fichte's delivery was excellent: precise and clear. I was completely swept away by the topic, and I had to admit that I had never before heard a lecture like that one." Quoted in Erich Fuchs, ed., *Fichte im Gespräch*, vol. 2 (Stuttgart–Bad Cannstatt: Frommann-Holzboog, 1980), p. 8.

consciousness.[6] I now repeat this same argument over and over again, as before, and once we have embarked upon such a series of inferences you will never be able to point to a place where we should stop. Accordingly, we will always require, for every consciousness, another consciousness, one that takes the former as its object, and so on, forever. In this way, therefore, we will never arrive at a point where we will be able to assume the existence of any actual consciousness. — You are conscious of yourself as an object of consciousness only insofar as you are conscious of yourself as the conscious subject; but then this conscious subject becomes, in turn, an object of consciousness, and you must then, once again, become conscious of yourself as the subject who is conscious of this object of consciousness — and so on, *ad infinitum*. How could you ever arrive at any original consciousness in this way?

In short, consciousness simply cannot be accounted for in this way. Once again, what was the gist of the line of reasoning we just pursued, and what is the real reason why the nature of consciousness could not be grasped in this way? The gist of the argument was as follows: I can be conscious of any *527* object only on the condition that I am also conscious of myself, that is, of the conscious subject. This proposition is incontrovertible. — It was, however, further claimed that, within my self-consciousness, I am an object for myself and that what held true in the previous case also holds true of the subject that is conscious of this object: this subject too becomes an object, and thus a new subject is required, and so on *ad infinitum*. In every consciousness, therefore, the subject and the object were separated from each other and each was treated as distinct. This is why it proved impossible for us to comprehend consciousness in the above manner.

Yet consciousness does exist. Hence, what was just claimed concerning it must be false, and this means that the opposite of this claim is true; that is to say, there is a type of consciousness in which what is subjective and what is objective cannot be separated from each other at all, but are absolutely one and the same. This, accordingly, would be the type of consciousness that is required in order to explain consciousness at all. Let us *(276)* now, without any further elaboration of this point, return straightaway to our inquiry.

(3) When you did as we asked and thought, first of objects that are supposed to lie outside of you, and then of yourself, you undoubtedly knew

6. "das vorhin das Selbstbewusst*seyn* war." I.e., one's previous self-consciousness now becomes the object of a new higher-level act of reflection, which thus requires the positing of a new subject.

that you were thinking, what you were thinking, and how you were think-ing. You must have known these things, for we were able to discuss this with one another, as indeed we have just done.

How then did you manage to obtain this consciousness of your own thinking? "I knew it immediately," you will reply. "My consciousness of my own thinking is not, as it were, an accidental feature of my thinking, an additional something that is posited only afterwards and subsequently con-nected with my thinking; instead, such consciousness is inseparable from thinking." — You will and must answer my question in this way, since you are quite unable to think of your thinking without having any conscious-ness of it.

Thus, from the very start, we could have discovered the type of con-sciousness we were just seeking, a consciousness in which what is subjec-tive and what is objective are immediately united. The consciousness in question is our consciousness of our own thinking. — Hence you are im-mediately conscious of your own thinking. But how do you represent this   *528* to yourself? Evidently, you can do this only in the following way: Your inner activity, which is directed at something outside of you (viz., at the object you are thinking about), is, at the same time, directed within and at itself. According to what was said above, however, self-reverting activity is what generates the I. Accordingly, you were conscious of yourself in your own act of thinking, and this self-consciousness was precisely the same as your immediate consciousness of your own thinking; and this is true whether you were thinking of some object or were thinking of yourself. — Self-consciousness is therefore immediate; what is subjective and what is objective are inseparably united within self-consciousness and are abso-lutely one and the same.

The scientific name for such an immediate consciousness is "intu-ition,"[7] which is the name by which we wish to designate it as well. The intuition we are now discussing is an *act of self-positing as* positing (that is, as positing anything "objective" whatsoever, which can also be I myself, considered as a mere object); by no means, however, is it a mere *act of positing*, for then we would find ourselves once again entangled in the pre-viously indicated impossibility of explaining consciousness. As far as I am concerned, everything depends upon one's understanding and being con-vinced of this point, which constitutes the very foundation of the entire system to be presented here.

---

7. See Kant's definition of "intuition" as the mode of cognition [*Erkenntnis*] in which "a cognition is immediately related to its object" (KRV, A19/B33).

All possible consciousness, as something objective for a subject, presupposes an immediate consciousness in which what is subjective and what
is objective are simply one and the same. Otherwise, consciousness is simply incomprehensible. Unless one has grasped the subject and the object in
(277) their unity right from the start, one will forever seek in vain to discover any
bond between them. For this reason, any philosophy that does not begin at
the point where the subject and the object are united will necessarily be
superficial and incomplete; it will be unable to explain what it is supposed
to explain, and hence it will be no philosophy at all.

This immediate consciousness is the intuition of the I just described.
The I necessarily posits itself within this intuition and is thus at once what
is subjective and what is objective. All other consciousness is connected to
529 and mediated by this immediate consciousness, and only through this connection with immediate consciousness does it become consciousness at all.
Immediate consciousness alone is unmediated and unconditioned by anything else. It is absolutely possible and is quite simply necessary if any
other consciousness is to occur. — The I should not be considered as a
mere subject, which is how it has nearly always been considered until now;
instead, it should be considered as a subject-object in the sense indicated.

The sole type of being of the I with which we are here concerned is the
being it possesses within the self-intuition we have now described; or, more
rigorously expressed, the being of the I with which we are concerned is the
being of this intuition itself. I am this intuition and nothing more whatsoever, and this intuition itself is I. This act of self-positing is not supposed to
produce an I that, so to speak, exists as a thing in itself and continues to exist
independently of consciousness: Such a claim would undoubtedly be the
greatest of all absurdities. Nor does this intuition presuppose an existence
of the I as an (intuiting) thing, independent of consciousness. Indeed, in my
opinion, such a claim would be no less absurd than the previous one;
though, of course, one should not say this, since the most famous philosophers of our philosophical century subscribe to this opinion. The reason I
maintain that no such existence [of the I] has to be presupposed is as follows: If you cannot talk about anything *of which you are not conscious*, and if,
however, everything of which you are conscious *is conditioned by the self-
consciousness here indicated*, then *you cannot turn around and allow this self-
consciousness to be conditioned by some determinate object* of which you are
conscious: viz., the alleged existence of the I apart from all intuiting and
thinking. Either you must admit that you are here speaking of something
without knowing anything about it (which you are hardly likely to do), or
else you must deny that all other consciousness is conditioned by the self-

consciousness in question (which, if you have understood me at all, you will be quite unable to do). — At this point, therefore, it also becomes obvious that, through our very first proposition, one has unavoidably adopted the standpoint of transcendental idealism — not just for the case in question, but for all possible cases — and that understanding this proposition is exactly the same as being convinced of the truth of transcendental idealism. *530*

The intellect thus intuits itself only as an intellect, or as a pure intellect; and it is precisely this self-intuition that constitutes its essential nature. *(278)* Accordingly, in the event that there might turn out to be some other type of intuition as well, we are entitled to designate the type of intuition we have been discussing here "*intellectual* intuition," in order to distinguish it from any other type of intuition. — Instead of "intellect," I prefer to use the term "I-hood," because, for anyone capable of the least bit of attentiveness, this term indicates, in the most direct way, the self-reverting of activity.*

* The word "self" has frequently been employed of late to designate this same concept.[8] If my derivation is correct, all the words in the family to which the word "self" belongs (e.g., "self-same," "the same," etc.[9]) signify a relationship to something that has already been posited, though only insofar as it has been posited *through its mere concept*. If what has been posited is I, then the word "self" is formed. Hence the word "self" presupposes the concept of the I, and everything that is thought to be absolute within the former is borrowed from the concept of the latter. Perhaps in a popular exposition the term "self" is more convenient, because it adds a special emphasis to the concept of the I as such, which — after all — is always obscurely thought of along with the word "self." Such an emphasis may well be required by the ordinary reader, but it seems to me that in a scientific exposition one should employ the term that designates this concept in the most immediate and proper way. — In a recently published work intended for the public at large, however, the concept of the self is distinguished from and opposed to that of the I, and a sublime theory is derived from the former and a detestable one is derived from the latter, even though the author of the work in question must know, at least as a historical fact, that the word "I" has also been taken in a quite different sense and that a system in which there is no place at all for the detestable theory in question is currently being erected upon the concept to which the word "I" (taken in this latter sense) refers. It is simply incomprehensible what purpose is supposed to be served by this — so long, that is, as one neither wishes nor is able to assume any hostile intent on the part of the author in question.

8. This appears to be a specific allusion to a comment by Johann Christian Gottlieb Schaumman (1768–1821), professor of philosophy at Gießen, that the word *self* "seems to me to be *purer* and *more precise* than '*I*.'" See Schaumman's *Versuch eines neuen Systems des natürlichen Rechts* (1796), p. 133.

9. "Z.B. Selbiger, u.s.w. derselbe, u.s.w." ("self" = *Selbst*.)

III.

Let us now direct our attention to yet another circumstance involved in observing the activity we have been asked to perform. What follows, however, should be treated as no more than a provisional remark from which nothing will be immediately inferred and the implications of which will become apparent only later. Nevertheless, we cannot let this opportunity pass without adding the following remark.

(279)   You discovered yourself to be active both in the act of representing an object and in the act of representing yourself. Now look again very carefully at what occurred within you when you entertained the representation of this activity. Activity is "agility" or inner movement; the mind here tears itself away from something absolutely opposed [to activity] — a description that is by no means intended, as it were, to make comprehensible what is incomprehensible,[10] but is instead designed to call attention more forcibly to an intuition that is necessarily present within everyone. — This agility is intuited as a *process by means of which the active force wrenches itself away from a state of repose*, and it can be intuited in no other way. And if you actually accomplished what we asked you to do, this is in fact how you intuited this agility.

In compliance with my summons, you thought of your table, your wall, etc.; and after you had succeeded in actively producing within yourself the thoughts of these objects, you then remained caught up in a state of peaceful and unchanging contemplation of them (*obtutu haerebas fixus in illo*,[11] as the poet says). Next I asked you to think of yourself and to take special note of the fact that this act of thinking is a kind of doing. In order to do this, you had to tear yourself away from your state of contemplative repose; that is to say, you had to tear yourself away from that determinacy of your thinking and determine your thinking differently. Moreover, you were able to notice that you were active only insofar as you took note of this act of wrenching yourself away and this act of altering the determinacy in question. I can do no more here than appeal to your own inner intuition; I cannot exter-

10. "Thätigkeit ist Agilität, innere Bewegung; der Geist reisst sich selbst über absolut entgegengesetzte hinweg; — durch welche Beschreibung keinesweges etwa das unbegreifliche begreiflich gemacht." (Note: *unbegreifliche* = "incomprehensible," in the sense of "incapable of being discursively grasped by means of concepts.")

11. "You were clinging transfixed in that gaze." Freely quoted from Virgil, *Aeneid*, I, 495.

nally demonstrate to you something that can exist only within you.

The result of attending to oneself in the requested manner would be 532 this: One discovers oneself to be active only insofar as one opposes to this activity a state of repose (in which the inner force is arrested and becomes fixed). (We should mention in passing that the converse of this proposition is true as well: One cannot become conscious of a state of repose unless one posits an activity. Activity is nothing apart from repose, and vice versa. Indeed, this proposition is universally true and will later be established in its universal validity: viz., that no matter what is being determined, all determination occurs by means of opposition. Here, however, we are concerned only with the individual case before us.)

What then was the particular determinacy of your thinking which, as a state of repose, immediately preceded that activity by virtue of which you thought of yourself? Or, more precisely, what determinacy was immediately united with that activity, in such a way that you could not perceive the one without perceiving the other? — In order to indicate the action you were supposed to perform, I asked you to think of *yourself*, and you were able to understand me without any further ado. Accordingly, you knew the (280) meaning of the term "I." But you did not have to know, and I assume that you did not know, that the thought of the I is a thought that comes into being by means of a reversion of activity upon itself. This is something you first had to learn. Yet, according to what we have already said, the I is nothing but a self-reverting acting, and a self-reverting acting is the I. How then could you have been acquainted with the I without also being acquainted with the activity by means of which the I arises? This is possible only as follows: When you understood the word "I," you discovered *yourself* (*i.e., your acting as an intellect*) to be determined in a particular manner, yet you did not explicitly recognize what was determinate in this case *as an acting*. Instead, you recognized it only as a *determinacy* or a *state of repose*, without actually knowing or even inquiring into the origin of this determinacy of your consciousness. In short, when you understood me, this determinacy was immediately present. This is why you understood me and were able to give an appropriate direction to the activity that I summoned you to perform. The determinacy of your thinking produced through thinking of yourself[12] therefore was and necessarily had to be that 533 state of repose from which you wrenched yourself into activity.

This may be expressed more clearly as follows: I asked you to "think of

12. "Die Bestimmtheit deines Denkens durch das Denken deiner selbst."

yourself," and when you understood this last word you also engaged — *in the very act of understanding it* — in that self-reverting activity that produces the thought of the I. But you accomplished this without realizing what you were doing, for you were not paying any special attention to this. And this was the origin of what you discovered within your own consciousness. I then asked you to pay attention to how you were able to accomplish this. You then engaged once again in the same activity in which you had engaged previously, but this time you did so with attentiveness and consciousness.

Inner activity, grasped in its state of repose, is generally called a "concept." Consequently, what was necessarily united with the intuition of the I was the concept of the I; and without this concept any consciousness of the I would have remained impossible, for it is this concept that first completes and comprises consciousness.

A concept is never anything other than the very activity of intuiting — simply grasped, not as agility, but as a state of repose and determinacy. This is true of the concept of the I as well. The concept of the I is the self-reverting activity, grasped as something stable and enduring; thus it is in this way that the I as active and the I as the object of my activity coincide.

(281)

Nothing is present within ordinary consciousness but concepts; by no means are intuitions as such ever encountered there, despite the fact that concepts arise only by means of intuitions (though this occurs without any consciousness on our part). Only through freedom can one lift oneself to a consciousness of intuition, as has just been done in the case of the I. Every conscious intuition, moreover, is related to a concept, which indicates the particular direction freedom has to take. This explains how, in every case, as in the particular case we have been examining, the object of intuition can be said to exist prior to the intuition itself. The object in question is precisely the concept. From this discussion, one can see that the concept is nothing but the intuition itself, grasped as a state of repose and not as such, i.e., not as an activity.[13]

534

13. With the (unfulfilled) promise "(To be continued in future issues)," the fourth and final published installment of *An Attempt at a New Presentation of the Wissenschaftslehre* concludes at this point.

Review of the Journal for Truth

Published in the *Philosophisches Journal* 1797.

[*Review of*] *the* Journal for Truth, *no.2*

(Hamburg: Bachmann und Gundermann)

The author of this work, Prof. Werner from Gießen,[1] has challenged us to come to terms with the philosophical system he has already presented in his *Aetiology*, a system he briefly expounds on pp. 14-44 of the second issue of his journal. For a variety of reasons we consider it our duty to satisfy this request.

Herr Werner's system quite correctly begins (see § 1 of the article just cited) with immediate consciousness, which he "wishes to be understood as signifying nothing more than those alterations that occur in the I whenever it acts or is passively affected."[2] (How does he become acquainted with this distinction between "acting" and "being passively affected"?) "Consciousness itself must be completely separated from whatever it is that might have *aroused* it, as well as from whatever it is that it would like

This review was published in vol. VI, no. 1 of the *Philosophisches Journal* (which appeared in early November of 1797), pp. 107–17 (in GA, I, 4: 431–37, the pagination of which is provided within parentheses in the margins of the English translation; not in SW).

1. Georg Friedrich Werner (1754–98) was a professor of military science at Gießen and was apparently the founder of and principal (or even sole) contributor to the extremely obscure *Journal für Wahrheit*. The editors of GA, I,4 report that "despite intensive research in German and in many foreign libraries," they were unable to locate a single copy of the issue here "reviewed" by Fichte. In fact, Fichte's essay is not so much a review of the *Journal for Truth* as it is a reply to a specific challenge contained in an unnamed article published by Werner in the second issue of the same. The philosophical position summarized and defended in Werner's article appears to have been the same as the one he had previously propounded in his universally ignored *Erster Versuch einer allgemeinen Aetiologie*, vol. I (1792), a work that Fichte later described, in his review of Bardili's *Grundriß der ersten Logik*, as one of the most absurd works ever published in the entire field of philosophy (SW, II, pp. 499–500 = GA, I,6: 445).

2. "bei'm Handeln oder bei'm Leiden." *Leiden* normally means "suffering," but the sense of "suffering" intended here is not psychological pain, but includes all of those *passive* states of consciousness in which the I finds itself to *be affected* by something. Accordingly, *ein Leiden* is usually rendered here as "a passive state of being affected" or "a state of being passively affected."

to *refer* to. — Consciousness is what occurs in a willing and sensing being immediately prior to its acting and immediately following its being passively affected." — First of all, this last sentence is not intended to provide a real explanation[3] of consciousness. Even in his previously published work, Herr Werner has quite correctly noted that consciousness itself does not permit of any further explanation, but must be immediately given to everyone through his own experience. Therefore, Herr Werner's quoted words do no more than supplement his earlier account of the nature of consciousness, and thus no objection can be raised against the form of what he says. This, however, simply means that one has to object all the more strongly to the content of the same, for the unfounded assumptions that underlie his system are already contained within this assertion. Herr Werner states several times (e.g., on p. 91) that the superiority of his philosophy consists in the fact that it takes as its sole foundation nothing but consciousness itself, understood in a simple and invariant sense. How is it then that here, at the very entrance to his system, he is able to talk about a "passive state of being affected" which precedes consciousness and is thus not itself consciousness? And how can he at this point speak of an "acting" that follows upon consciousness and is therefore also not supposed to be the same as consciousness? Perhaps we do Herr Werner an injustice when we infer that what follows upon and what precedes something must be distinguished from and be different from what lies in the middle between   *(432)* them, for perhaps he himself has not made this inference and has consequently failed to notice it. It becomes clear later on, however, that it is also his own view that the "acting" he speaks of is something entirely different from the inner activity of mere consciousness; instead, the acting in question is an action directed at external objects. Similarly, his "passive state of being affected" also must be something different from consciousness itself, since consciousness of a mere passive state of being affected is simply impossible. Thus, once again we must ask, How does Herr Werner become aware of this acting and of this passive state of being affected? Since they themselves are not supposed to be identical to consciousness, and since everything in his philosophy is supposed to be based upon consciousness and to begin with consciousness, this acting and this state of being passively affected must be *immediate objects* of consciousness. To be sure, if this is indeed the case, then it would have been desirable if Herr Werner had begun by asking the following questions: What does it mean for something to be an "object of consciousness"? *How* is such an *object* possible?

3. "eine RealErklärung."

And, given this account of how an object of consciousness is possible, is an *immediate* object of consciousness possible at all, and are the indicated states of acting and being passively affected immediate objects of this sort? Pre-Critical philosophy owed all of its errors precisely to the fact that it neglected to ask this very question concerning the possibility of any object of consciousness at all; and if Herr Werner is permitted to assume that an external acting and a state of being passively affected are immediate objects of consciousness, then — since there cannot be any consciousness of an instance of acting apart from some consciousness of an object at which this action is directed, and since there can be no consciousness of a state of being passively affected without some consciousness of the ground of such passivity — Herr Werner's system is already off to a very good start, and it surely has no need whatsoever to employ those means it later employs in order to proceed beyond immediate consciousness.

We do not, however, need to raise such objections against Herr Werner's system, and we will gladly drop them, since, quite apart from them, we find that this system contains something else that is absolutely incomprehensible — something that is probably incomprehensible to Herr Werner himself and is certainly incomprehensible to the greater portion of our readers. With this, we enter upon a domain where we may hope to make something more clearly visible to the eyes of some observers.

"By means of *passive* consciousness," writes Herr Werner (§ 5). We do not desire to challenge him any further concerning this expression, but will let it count as valid for whatever it can validly designate: viz., our consciousness of our own limitation, of our inability. "By means of passive consciousness we become convinced of the existence of an *other* — which, here in any case, is not yet supposed to be anything more than *not I*: something that is not *my* will, not *my* energy." (Quite right!) "The *cause* of this passive consciousness is called 'substance.' Of course, we cannot perceive this cause in itself. What we perceive or sense is *our own* consciousness." (This is quite correct, and if Herr Werner had only pursued this train of thought consistently, this would certainly have kept him from embracing (433) his own system.) "However, we know the following things about this cause: (a) It is *not* I; (b) it is located in a certain place outside of us; (c) and what it produces within us is an effect of impenetrability."[4]

This knowledge of a cause, even though we do not immediately per-

---

4. "sie bringt in uns die Wirkung Undurchdringlichkeit hervor." I.e., as a result of being "passively affected" we attribute the property of "impenetrability" to the external ground that supposedly "affects" us.

ceive the cause in question, is the foundation-stone of the entire *Aetiology*, which takes its very name from this inference from the effect to the cause. It is through this inference that our cognition subsequently proves to be a cognition of the *thing in itself*. (To be sure, the *I* is the only *thing in itself* with which we are supposed to be acquainted, but this is only one inconsistency more [in Herr Werner's system].) This inference also leads to the following conclusions: that the world is determined "so that a physical body does not consist of an infinite number of elements, but of a finite number" (since matter is not infinitely divisible); "that the geometer's assertion that every line is *infinitely divisible* is an absurdity that dishonors his science, which is otherwise so certain and useful; that the I, construed in the narrowest sense, is not a complex substance, but is a simple substance or an element and is, *precisely for this reason*, indestructible, i.e., immortal; that we must assign a will to every thing; that all of the elements in nature belong to a *single* class, even though the distance from the I of man to the element of stone or earth may be very great; that anyone who denies that he thinks *in his head* could just as well deny that he thinks and senses at all"; etc., etc.

We will not examine these inferences, but will, instead, leave it to our readers to figure out for themselves how, beginning with those premises he shares in common with every variety of dogmatism, Herr Werner can arrive at precisely these results. All that we have to do in order to justify our own behavior and that of other independent thinkers toward his system[5] is to say a few words concerning these premises themselves. If the foundation is overturned, then whatever is constructed upon this foundation must certainly collapse on its own.

The *Aetiology* is not only written *after* Kant, it is written in specific opposition to the Kantian system, which it is meant to refute. In evaluating the *Aetiology*, therefore, one may assume an acquaintance with those propositions that Kant has proven and may employ Kant's system as a criterion of evaluation.

As we have seen, Herr Werner makes the following inference: I discover myself to be passively affected; this is an immediate fact of consciousness. *First of all, this state of being passively affected must have some cause; secondly, this cause must be a quite specific or determinate one, namely, the cause that explains this determinate state of being passively affected. Therefore*, there *are* such causes: namely, things in the world. — Herr Werner's   *(434)*

5. I.e., in order to justify the complete neglect of Werner's system by Fichte and other professional philosophers.

entire philosophical system consists in the systematic inventory of these causes.

Kant would object to this line of argument in the following way: Before we discuss this system of causes, let us first examine the validity of the inference by means of which you transport us into this new world. — In the minor premise of your syllogism you assert that your state of being passively affected must have a cause, one that can be recognized and determined on the basis of its effect. First of all, tell me how you know this. If you reply "This is simply how it *is*" in the same sense in which you speak of a necessary connection *between things* — that is, as if your state of being passively affected were one thing and the cause thereof were another — then you must either have an *immediate* cognition of the thing in itself, in which case you do not need — here or anywhere else — to employ the principle of causality in order to infer that things exist; or else this relationship between things [that is, between the state of being passively affected and the thing in itself] is also something with which you have become acquainted only indirectly, i.e., by means of an inference. If so, then first show us the inference in question — in which case, of course, we will be entitled to inquire once again concerning the foundation of your premises. You will thus have no recourse but to contend that one must *necessarily think of* a cause in addition to one's own state of being passively affected — a cause that is determinable by this effect. Moreover, the necessity of thinking in this way is something you are cognizant of quite *immediately*, since it is indeed a determination of your own self-consciousness — a point we will be only too willing to concede to you.

After this, you may (as would be quite reasonable) wish to assert no more in the minor premise of your syllogism than you actually know, in which case you may wish to express yourself as follows: "I am required to think of a determinate cause in addition to this state of being passively affected." If, however, this is what you wish to assert, then you can assert nothing more in your conclusion than this: "*Therefore*, I really *do think* of such a cause, which, for me, is a world determined in such and such a way." This too is something we will be only too willing to grant you. In asserting this, however, you remain within the sphere of your own consciousness and never escape from it, and your entire "system of the world" is nothing more whatsoever than the system of your necessary thinking.

Herr Werner has but two ways to avoid this conclusion: Either he can reject this Kantian argument and refute it, or else he can accept it and interpret his system in such a way that it can co-exist with this argument.

If he wishes to pursue the first course of action, then he must demonstrate how he himself is able to talk about something and can hope to make others understand what he has to say on this subject *without this same something being present within his own consciousness.* If, instead, this is something that is supposed to be present within consciousness, yet is not an object of immediate perception (which Herr Werner himself admits in the case of *(435)* the things themselves), then he must explain how something of this sort could ever occur within consciousness except by means of the free, productive action of thinking and of the power of imagination. Indeed, since he is writing after and in opposition to Kant, he really should have explained this in advance — if, that is, he wanted anyone who comes after Kant to take even the least notice of his writings. For, as things now stand, he bases his argument upon the very principles his opponents reject, without doing anything whatsoever to establish these same principles or to secure them against the attacks of his opponents. — We confess that we by no means expect that Herr Werner (or any other mortal) will be able to accomplish what we have demanded; nor do we expect that he will be able to utter an intelligible word to this end, since the fundamental principle of Criticism — namely, that we are unable to escape from the sphere of our own consciousness — seems to us to be so evident that anyone who understands it at all must necessarily affirm it.

Should Herr Werner elect to pursue the second course, then he might claim that he certainly does not interpret his own system in any sense other than the only sense that remains possible following Kant's investigations, and he might maintain that he considers his own system to be nothing more than an account of *what we necessarily have to think*, and by no means an account of a *system of things in themselves which is supposed to exist independently of the intellect.* In this case, he might maintain that, considered from the empirical standpoint, the world certainly does appear to be something that is external to us and is present without any assistance from us; and he might assert that his own system occupies merely this latter standpoint and is meant to apply only to the empirical standpoint, and that he simply considered it to be superfluous to make explicit mention of something which, since Kant, has gone without saying for everyone who has understood Kant. To be sure, we do not expect that he will actually say this; but if he does, then he will have simply placed his confidence in those necessary laws of thinking beyond which he cannot go, and he will have recognized that his world is determined by these laws and not by the concept of the existence of this world in itself. In fact, however, it is the latter that Herr Werner assumes throughout, and a single example should suffice to convince our readers of this: According to the laws of reason, we simply must think of matter as infinitely divisible. A philosophy that was determined by nothing but the laws of reason and did not wish to go beyond these laws would posit matter accordingly, and would contend that this is the way matter must appear from the empirical viewpoint and the way it must be treated within all of the sciences, which necessarily adopt this viewpoint. The *Aetiology*'s assertion that there are ultimate, indivisible elements of matter is based upon the assumption that matter is a thing in itself, which, to be sure, cannot be infinitely divisible, since the reality of matter would be completely destroyed thereby. For this reason, all dogmatists must either take refuge in indivisible *atoms* (such as Herr Werner's "elements"), or, if they understand the contradiction involved in this assumption, must replace these elements with *monads*, which are not supposed to be material and which are not supposed to occupy space, but which, as soon as one tries to think of them in a determinate manner, become both material and spatial.

(436)

Everyone who tries to contribute to the advance of science deserves respect and merits some reply — all the more so if he does this with such visible enthusiasm and such a warm love of truth as the author of the *Aetiology*. By passing this judgment [on Herr Werner's system], we have attempted to pay him the respect he deserves. Given the present, lamentable state of philosophical literature, the fact that he either is unfamiliar with or else simply ignores the present state of the science about which he is writing, and that he either does not understand or else does not pay any attention to current work in this field, is not, by itself, a sufficient reason to deprive him of the right to demand some reply; for, if this were the case, then we would have to suspend almost all judgment of philosophical writings. He possesses at least one advantage over the most celebrated philosophers (especially those among the Kantians), who know just as little as he does about what is going on in philosophy: He knows what he himself wants to do, which is more than they know.

We cannot believe that, by saying this, we will have succeeded in convincing him, for he himself (on pp. 93 ff.) quotes from *Aenesidemus*[6] approximately the same objection we have here briefly directed against the foundation of his philosophy, and he believes that he has refuted this objection in his *Aetiology*. The insight required in this case is indeed some-

6. *Aenesidemus oder über die Fundamente der von dem Herrn Professor Reinhold in Jena gelieferten Elementar-Philosophie* (1792). For more on this anonymously published defense of skepticism, see the note to § 6 of the "Second Introduction" to *An Attempt at a New Presentation of the Wissenschaftslehre* (above, pp. 52–53n.).

thing that cannot be demonstrated to anyone, but is something one must generate from oneself, like a bolt of lightning that suddenly illuminates a long, thick darkness.

We must, however, make the following declaration: So long as Herr Werner's system remains at its present standpoint, and so long as he fails to pursue either of the courses we have indicated, we will simply have nothing further to do with his system nor with anything he may have to say in reply to our judgment of it; for, in this case, he can do nothing more than repeat what we already know very well and attempt to clarify something we already understand quite clearly. — For the sake of others, we will also add the following remark: The purpose of publicly treating a science in books is to advance this science. For apprentices, there are courses offered in the universities. A person who is unfamiliar with the present state of a science should not wish to write anything about it before he has studied the available books on the subject and until he has understood them. To repeat the same objections and refutations over and over again and publicly to pro- *(437)* vide every individual with the private instruction he requires is simply a waste of time and paper and is, in the long run, unfeasible.

The Editors[7]

---

7. Though Niethammer and Fichte signed many of their individual contributions to the *Philosophisches Journal* in this way, the foregoing review is unmistakably a product of Fichte's pen. Notice, for example, how the last sentence echoes a very similar passage in the "Second Introduction" to *An Attempt at a New Presentation of the Wissenschaftslehre* (SW, I, p. 496 = GA, I,4: 249; see above, pp. 81–82).

Note to "Fichte and Kant, or an Attempted Comparison between the Fichtean and the Kantian Philosophy"

Published in the *Philosophisches Journal* 1798.

(487)   Such objections,[1] taken simply by themselves, would be enough to make
clear to me something I know only too well in any case: namely, that the
"Kantians" never know what they themselves are talking about, that they
have never understood Kant, and that they will never grasp the *Wissenschaftslehre*. Charging that the *Wissenschaftslehre* is a transcendent system,
they wish to instruct us concerning the subjective nature of the forms of
our acts of representing. With the passage of time, however, the real source
of the illness that afflicts the *Wissenschaftslehre* has become more evident to
everyone: What it suffers from, dear fellow countrymen, is idealism —
pure, unadulterated idealism!

"But," [they object,] "the *Wissenschaftslehre* bases its inferences and
demonstrations upon concepts, and Kant has explicitly rejected such a
procedure."[2] So? This is a severe criticism indeed! Perhaps Kant and his
followers possess the skill to speak without thinking or to think without

This note was appended by Fichte, acting in his capacity as co-editor of the
Philosophisches Journal, to an anonymously published essay titled "Fichte und
Kant, oder Versuch einer Ausgleichung der Fichteschen und Kantischen
Philosophie," in vol. VII, no. 3 of the *Philosophisches Journal* (which appeared in
May of 1798), pp. 208–10 (in GA, I,4: 487–88, the pagination of which is supplied
within parentheses in the margins of the English translation; not in SW). The
unnamed author of the essay in question was Johann Christian August Grohmann
(1769–1847), an enthusiastic Fichtean who attempted to show that the *Wissenschaftslehre* not only is true to the spirit of Kant's Critical philosophy, but also
marks an important advance upon the latter. Though this note was originally published with no indication that it was by Fichte, it was subsequently identified in a
later issue of the *Philosophisches Journal* as the work of "the author of the
Wissenschaftslehre."

1. Fichte's note is appended to the following passage in Grohmann's essay: "'By
all the gods and goddesses!' cry our opponents, the opponents of the *Wissenschaftslehre*, the *so-called strict Kantians*: 'Who can fail to recognize the
empty circularity contained in the syntheses and antitheses that make up the *Wissenschaftslehre*? And who can fail to recognize the *transcendent* manner in which it
proceeds when it dogmatically bases its demonstrations and inferences upon concepts — whereas Kant destroyed dogmatism by making us aware of the subjective
forms of our representing and thinking!'"

2. See, for example, Kant's 1790 essay, "Ueber eine Entdeckung nach der alle
neue Kritik der reinen Vernunft durch eine ältere entbehrlich gemacht werden
soll" ("On a Discovery According to which Any New Critique of Pure Reason Has
Been Made Superfluous by an Earlier One," trans. in Allison, *The Kant-Eberhard
Controversy*, pp. 107–60), in which he explicitly responds to J. G. Eberhard's rationalistic critique of transcendental philosophy.

employing concepts. (But what am I saying? No honest Kantian will shrink from making this latter claim, for very few of them yet realize that their thinking is identical to their concept.) Perhaps they possess the skill to connect their thoughts with one another in a systematic fashion without also connecting their concepts and without deriving the one from the other. Kant may well have meant to say that one should not base one's inferences upon *arbitrarily fabricated* concepts, which is something that also was said several times before Kant. The *Wissenschaftslehre* establishes the reality of its concepts[3] within intellectual intuition, and it employs these concepts in no wider sense whatsoever than that which they have acquired within intellectual intuition. "But why do we need to present any additional evidence against you? You yourself admit that you are caught up in a circle."[4] — Yes indeed, just think of it: the *Wissenschaftslehre* derives the laws of reason by thinking in accordance with the laws of reason! Is it then supposed to accomplish its derivations by thinking in a manner contrary to the laws of reason? — Granted, Kant himself is not guilty of this circularity; instead, he is guilty of the unpardonable circularity of deriving the laws of reason from logic. The Kantians themselves have not acquired any grey hairs from worrying about how such logic is itself supposed to have come into being. Anything that lies beyond the *Critique* is for them an unknown world. — The mistake committed by the *Wissenschaftslehre* is merely this: It knows what it is doing, and it affirms the same. If only its author had   *(488)* been prudent enough to keep silent on this point, then these "Critical philosophers" would have been able to go on "criticizing" to the end of their days without ever discovering this circle in his work.

3. "Die Wissenschaftslehre realisirt ihre Begriffe."

4. See, e.g., § 7 of BWL, where Fichte admits and calls explicit attention to the circular relationship between the laws of reflection (or "the intellect's necessary manner of acting") and the transcendental deduction of the same, an admission reaffirmed in § 1 of GWL. The precise implications of Fichte's recognition that certain types of circularity are simply unavoidable in philosophy have been vigorously debated in the recent literature on Fichte. See, for example, the essays on this subject by Daniel Breazeale, Alain Perrinjaquet, and Tom Rockmore in *Fichte: Historical Contexts/Contemporary Controversies* (Atlantic Highlands, N.J.: Humanities Press, 1994).

Postscript to the Preceding Article and Preface to the Following One

Published in the *Philosophisches Journal* 1798.

Postscript to the Preceding Article and Preface to the Following One

(463) Clouds of dust truly billow from the battlefield occupied by the author of the preceding "Letters," and the witness to this battle must indeed take measures to protect his eyes.[1] Yet we are reluctant to believe that the author has raised this dust on purpose, just so he can throw it into the spectators' eyes. We can well understand how he might have raised this dust cloud quite inadvertently, simply as a result of a few false steps or an unfortunate choice of words, or because of a few too-sweeping charges.

We are engulfed in a cloud with the very first charge, and the true point of contention vanishes from view. The author of these "Letters" describes himself as having previously maintained that the combination — note that I say "the *combination*"[2] — of the concept of the I and the concept of the

---

This long note was inserted by Fichte, acting in his capacity as co-editor of the *Philosophisches Journal einer Gesellschaft Teutscher Gelehrten*, between two articles published by Friedrich Karl Forberg in vol. VII, no. 4 of the *Philosophisches Journal* (which appeared in May of 1798), pp. 259–72 (in GA, I,4: 463–69, the pagination of which is provided within parentheses in the margins of the English translation; not in SW). The first of Forberg's two articles in vol. VII, no. 4 of the *Philosophisches Journal* is the second and concluding installment of his "Briefe über die neueste Philosophie," the first installment of which appeared in the same issue of the *Philosophisches Journal* as the second half of Fichte's Second Introduction to *An Attempt at a New Presentation of the Wissenschaftslehre*. (The complete text of Forberg's "Briefe" is reprinted in Oesch, *Aus der Frühzeit des deutschen Idealismus*, pp. 153–81.) The second of Forberg's articles, the one that follows Fichte's "Postscript and Preface," is "Versuch einer Deduction der Kategorieen" (pp. 282–314).

1. Forberg's "Letters on the Most Recent Philosophy" were primarily devoted to a furious attack upon the philosophy of Fichte (and Schelling). In § 7 of his "Second Introduction to the *Wissenschaftslehre*" Fichte replied in some detail to each of the charges contained in the first published installment of Forberg's "Briefe" (though without ever mentioning Forberg by name). Forberg's attack upon Fichte's philosophy continues in the second installment of his "Briefe," and thus the primary purpose of this "Postscript" was to continue Fichte's reply to Forberg's criticisms, exposing in the process a number of widespread misunderstandings of the *Wissenschaftslehre*.

2. "die *Zusammensetzung*": literally, "the positing together."

absolute is an impossible and contradictory combination. He furthermore claims that his alleged opponents[3] have replied that the combination in question must nevertheless certainly be possible, even for this author of these "Letters," and therefore cannot be contradictory; for, to the extent that he criticizes this combination of concepts, he must combine them himself, since otherwise he would not be able to talk about this combination at all.[4]

With the author's permission, let me say that what we were referring to *(464)* was, to our knowledge, something completely different. The opponents of the author of these "Letters" did not begin with a concept constructed by any act of combination (A determined by B). Indeed, to proceed in this way would invalidate their entire system and would, in their view, be the greatest contradiction. Instead, they proceeded from something entirely simple (= A), something that, according to them, is not immediately a concept at all, but is an intuition. To our knowledge, the author of these "Letters" did indeed claim that nothing of this sort is present for him at all nor present within his world. It is not merely that he is unable to think of this [that is, of the absolute I] as characterized in some particular way; he claims to be unable to think of it at all. In reply to this claim his opponents may very well have remarked that he simply cannot be completely unable to think about the absolute I, since he does talk about it; moreover, I still fail to see what could be said against this point.

Tell me, honorable and intelligent reader, when someone says, "I cannot think of A at all," or "I can certainly think of A and also think of B, but I cannot think of A and B as one and the same," are these simply two different ways of saying the same thing, or are two different things being asserted in these two cases? You will undoubtedly reply that these two sentences assert two different things. Now re-examine the evidence and see whether, in what we have said so far, we were talking about the former or about the latter and whether the preceding "Letters" are not obviously

3. Viz., Fichte and Schelling. Throughout the following text, Fichte continues to refer to himself and Schelling collectively as "the opponents of the author of these 'Letters,'" or, more simply, as "we."

4. This "reply," cited by Forberg in the "Continuation" of his "Letters," was made by Fichte himself near the beginning of § 7 of the Second Introduction to his *Attempt at a New Presentation of the Wissenschaftslehre* (see above, pp. 78–79). However (as Fichte now proceeds to remind his critic), what Fichte had claimed that Forberg himself "must surely possess" was not any "combination of concepts," but rather the single concept of the absolute I.

(465)   concerned with the latter. You will then observe, to your amusement, how bravely our author engages in battle with a phantom of his own creation.

The opponents named by this author are quite well aware that one can certainly, through one's power of imagination, hold together contradictory attributes and can try to unite them in one's understanding as well; and thus, though one cannot actually think a contradiction, one can certainly imagine one. Indeed, the very essay to which the preceding series of polemical "Letters" seems to be directed refers to just this point in order to provide a detailed explanation of how it is possible for the absolutely contradictory system of the "Kantians" to be entertained by an otherwise rational mind.[5]

As soon as Herr Forberg succeeds in comprehending the I at all, he will then be able — entirely on his own — to appreciate the sense in which the I can certainly be called "absolute." He has now[6] succeeded in comprehending the I very well, and thus he has undoubtedly also succeeded in appreciating the sense in which it can be called absolute. It does not matter in the least whether he now or ever employs the same terms to designate this. Anyone who does not like the expressions "I," "absolute," and the like can, without giving any further thought to the matter, dispense with these terms entirely. Our system does not engage in disputes over words, and we quite readily admit that someone can apprehend the spirit of this system without thereby having to clothe it in its previous uniform.

*   *

*

As we have already said, we have no desire to investigate whether the author of these "letters" was himself conscious of the confusion with which we have just reproached him. The confusion that permeates the tenth and

5. See § 6 of Fichte's Second Introduction to the *Wissenschaftslehre* (above, pp. 70–71).

6. I.e., on the evidence of Forberg's second article, the "Attempt at a Deduction of the Categories." In his second contribution to the *Philosophisches Journal* vol. VII, no. 4, Forberg appears to have made a complete about-face and to have abandoned his main criticisms of Fichte, whose system he now seems to adopt as his own. Hence, the second, "prefatory," function of Fichte's note: to bring his public controversy with Forberg to an amicable end and to welcome this erstwhile critic into the fold of the *Wissenschaftslehre*.

eleventh Letters, however,[7] is plainly not his fault. What prevents him from seeing the true point of contention in this case is not the dust he himself has raised, but the old dogmatic scales that cover his eyes.

He had previously asked whether the disputed A [viz., the absolute I] *is* or *is not*; and he seemed to have been quite sure that our system would be impaled on the horns of this dilemma. In the preceding "Letters" he provides a very inaccurate account of the reply he received to this objection.[8] The answer that he received was not, as *he* reports, that some sort of being does indeed apply to this A — albeit an ideal and not a real type of being. *(466)* Instead, the reply he received was as follows: The entire presupposition that underlies this question, that is, the assumption that everything that we can talk about must either be or not be, is completely inadmissible and dogmatic. Our philosophy is acquainted with something that is even higher than any being. In short, we replied that our A neither *is* nor *is not*; in no possible sense is "being" a predicate of this A. — We did say that A, whenever it is thought of, is of course the object of an act of thinking; but this was no more than a passing remark, one added merely in order to forestall certain possible future objections.

To be sure, the author now denies ever having made this dogmatic assumption, and he asks his readers not to believe a word of this and not to believe that he ever claimed that it was contradictory *not to determine any concept through the predicate of real being*. Let the well-disposed reader relate this claim as best he may to what this same author has written in the past. The worst charge that could be brought against our author would be *that he is once again, at the very moment when he denies ever having made such an assumption, guilty of making it once again*. And this is precisely the charge which has been brought against him.

The predicate "*real*" being" means the same thing to him as "*actual* being,"[9] and he assures us that he is "of course able to think of something beyond what is actual: for example, of *what is possible*." — Isn't it amazing *(467)* what one sometimes discovers quite by accident!

---

7. In fact, Forberg's published "Letters" contain only ten letters. Presumably Forberg himself decided to suppress the last letter sometime after Fichte had written this "Postscript."

8. The "reply" to which Fichte refers is contained in § 7 of the Second Introduction (above, pp. 77–86).

9. "Das Prädikat des *realen* Seyns ist ihm gleichgeltend mit dem des *wirklichen* Seyns."

I would like to know what the term "possible" means. Does this concept signify anything other than a relationship to a *real* being, and is it not therefore *merely a further determination* of the concept of real being as such? I would like to know what the expressions "possible," "actual," and "necessary" could mean if some being were not always thought of as well — a being that is, in each case, either possible, actual, or necessary. Anyone, therefore, who wishes to determine A by the concept "possible"[10] certainly wishes to determine it by the predicate "real being." If this same person then discovers that A is contradictory because it cannot be determined by the predicate "real being," then the premise of his inferences is surely this: It is contradictory not to allow any concept to be determined by the predicate "real being." — Incidentally, it has not escaped my attention that several other conceptual confusions are also present here, further discussion of which would serve, on the one hand, to exonerate the author of these letters, and, on the other hand, to incriminate him even further. However, it is not my duty to untangle these confusions for him on this occasion.

From what has already been said, the author of these letters will also be able to see why we ourselves cannot be satisfied with the customary formula which allows the term "real" to be replaced by "actual" — though at the risk of his finding our use of the former term to be somewhat mysterious.

We will not even allow the predicate "possibility" to be bestowed upon our system's pure I, though the author of these "Letters" has tried to do just this. Nor will we accept any other gifts of this sort. The categories are, one and all, nothing more than ways of determining sensory intuition — which itself, along with all of its determinations, exists only by means of the I. The I is the intelligible ground of all appearances, and no predicate of the sensory world pertains to it. The pure I is neither actual nor possible nor necessary; for it *is* not at all, and if it *were*, and if it were to exist in any

---

10. Forberg had suggested precisely this in his tenth "Letter": namely, that "if the concept of the absolute I were only the concept of something possible, then we would at least not have made the objection that it is not encountered within the series of what is actual." Nevertheless, he goes on to argue that "for us, the concept of the absolute I is not a possible concept, but an impossible one; furthermore, we believe that we can also understand, with the greatest degree of self-evidence, that this is all that it can be for any possible understanding and that some deception must necessarily be involved if anyone considers it to be anything else" ("Briefe," *Philosophisches Journal*, VII,4, p. 266).

of the ways indicated, then, for just this reason, it would not be *the pure I*. The *actual* I of the author of these "Letters" is his own person, and this author's *possible* I was, at the time he was writing these letters, the I that was supposed to obtain a grasp of transcendental idealism.

*   *

*

To be sure, there is no need for me to explain this point any further to Herr Forberg, for he himself has provided a brilliant presentation of it in the trenchant essay that immediately follows.[11] I would particularly like to refer the reader to the passage that (with the kind permission of the author) I have had printed in italics and that begins: "A theory such as ours, there-   *(468)* fore, will also not begin with being, as what is highest in the series." — Starting at precisely this point, the author was able to gain entry into our philosophy, and he could not have laid hold of it at any more appropriate point nor at any point more worthy of his mind, which I have always valued very highly. — I may perhaps allow myself these few words of praise on his behalf, because some people, including this author himself, have taken certain replies I have made to objections similar to his to be directed specifically against him personally.

   Any conflict between us is completely suspended by the following article, which faithfully presents the innermost spirit of my system. It has never been my intention to say anything other than what he says in this article. In this context, all of the reproaches he has brought upon himself cancel themselves, since they no longer apply to him. If he wishes to maintain that they did not apply to him earlier either, I personally will not object. His opponents, for their part, are not so disinclined to confess their own sins once they have become aware of them nor so intent upon forcing others who succeed in improving themselves to confess their previous sins as the author of these "Letters" seems to assume. I know very well that Herr Forberg did not previously understand my system; nor could he have understood it, for he was a dogmatist. I do not believe that he will soon — if ever — be able to attach the correct meaning to those expressions he once interpreted so falsely. I will not, however, engage in a dispute over terminology. Accordingly, if it will help him to make further progress, let Herr Forberg continue to believe that I once propounded a contradictory and absurd system and that I have only now begun, gradually and surrepti-

11. Forberg's "Versuch einer Deduction der Kategorieen."

tiously, to redefine, to qualify, and to retract my former crass assertions.[12]
May he discover more and more of these tacit retractions in my future
writings! I know very well that it will only be he himself who will be uncon-
(469) sciously retracting his own crass interpretations of my previous expressions; and, as for myself personally, I know that, from the very beginning,
I have understood myself quite well — and I have understood myself precisely in the way that others, including Herr Forberg, are now also beginning to understand me. Let this dispute between us remain undecided,
however, for I utterly disavow everything that concerns nothing but my
own person.

Perhaps Herr Forberg will now gradually cease to be as angry with me
as he may have been while he was writing the preceding "Letters." I am not
angry with him. In order to win over to the side of truth a new adherent of
such brilliance I would gladly allow myself to be chided ten times more
harshly.

Fichte

12. This sentence is almost an exact quote from Forberg's characterization of his
"sly opponents" near the end of his tenth "Letter." (Fichte's use of the vocabulary
of "confession" and "sin" in the previous passage is also derived directly from
Forberg.)

On the Basis of Our Belief in a Divine
Governance of the World

Published in the *Philosophisches Journal* 1798.

On the Basis of Our Belief in a Divine Governance of the World

177
(347)

The author of this essay has long recognized that it is his duty to submit to the larger philosophical public, for examination and joint discussion, the results of his philosophical reflections on the topic announced in the above title, a topic with which he has previously dealt in his classroom lectures.[1] Moreover, he wished to treat this topic with the clarity and precision that is required of every author by the holiness this subject possesses in the eyes of so many worthy people. In the meantime, however, his time was occupied by other projects, and the fulfillment of his resolution was postponed time and again.

In his role as co-editor of this journal, it is the responsibility of the present author to publish the following essay by an excellent philosopher.[2]

"Ueber den Grund unsers Glaubens an eine göttliche Weltregierung" was published by Fichte in vol. VIII, no. 1 of the *Philosophisches Journal einer Gesellschaft Teutscher Gelehrter* (which appeared in November of 1798), pp. 1–20 (in SW, V, pp. 177–89, the pagination of which appears in the margins of the English translation; and GA, I,5: 347–57, the pagination of which is provided within parentheses in the margins of the English translation). At the time of this publication Fichte was co-editor of this journal, along with his colleague Friedrich Immanuel Niethammer.

1. Though he had first announced a course of lectures on the philosophy of religion for the summer semester of 1795, Fichte did not teach that semester and hence the announced course was cancelled. Ironically, at the time this essay appeared, Fichte had once again announced lectures on this topic for the summer semester of 1799 — by which time he had been discharged from his position at Jena. However, he regularly dealt with such topics as God and immortality in his introductory course on Logic and Metaphysics (first offered in the winter semester of 1795/96 and repeated every semester thereafter). See Fichte, "Nachgelassene Schriften zu Platners *Philosophischen Aphorismen*, 1794–1812" (GA, II,4: 37–353), as well as the two student transcripts of lectures from the same course, "Ideen über Gott und Unsterblichkeit" and "Vorlesungen über Logik und Metaphysik" (GA, IV,1: 157–67 and 173–450).

2. An allusion to Friedrich Karl Forberg's "Entwickelung des Begriffs der Religion," which immediately followed Fichte's essay in vol. VIII, no. 1 of the *Philosophisches Journal*, pp. 21–46.

On the one hand, this facilitates the author's task, inasmuch as the article in question is, in many respects, in agreement with his own convictions on this subject. Hence he can simply refer to the essay that follows and allow the author of the latter to speak for him as well. On the other hand, the present author also feels a pressing urgency to explain his own thoughts on this subject, inasmuch as there are many other respects in which the same *178* essay not so much conflicts with his convictions as simply fails to arrive at them. It nevertheless seems important to the present author that the way of thinking about this subject which does indeed follow from his own philosophical views should be laid before the public right at the beginning and in a complete fashion. For the moment, however, he must content himself with merely conveying the outlines of his thoughts on this topic and must *(348)* reserve any fuller discussion for some future time.

Until now, almost every view of this topic has been confused, and will perhaps continue to be confused for a long time to come, by treating the so-called moral proof of a divine governance of the world (or indeed, any philosophical proof of the same) as if it constituted a *proof* in the proper sense of the term. The confusion lies in the apparent assumption that belief in God is supposed to be first inculcated in and demonstrated to humanity by means of such demonstrations. Poor philosophy! Were such a belief not already present within human beings, then from where, I would like to know, did philosophy's representatives (who, after all, are also nothing but human beings) themselves obtain what they wish to convey to us through the force of their proofs? Or, if these representatives are, in fact, superior beings of some sort, then how can they expect to obtain a hearing from the rest of us, and how can they expect to be understood by us unless they presuppose that we possess a belief analogous to their own? — This is not the actual state of affairs, however. Philosophy can do no more than *explain* facts; by no means can it produce any facts — beyond, that is, the fact of philosophy itself. Just as it would never occur to a philosopher to try to persuade men that, from now on, they are entitled to think of objects as matter in space and that they may also think of the alterations of these objects as following each other in time, so too would it never occur to him to try to persuade men that they do indeed believe in a divine governance of the world. Both surely occur without any help whatsoever from the philosopher, who presupposes this as a fact, and whose sole task is simply to derive such facts, as such, from the necessary manner in which every rational being must operate. Consequently, we by no means wish our argument to be viewed as a means for convincing the unbeliever; instead, we wish it to be considered as a derivation of the believer's conviction. Our

179   sole concern is to answer the causal question, "How does a human being arrive at this belief?"

The decisive point, upon which the answer to this question depends, is the following: In our answer, this belief should not be represented as, so to speak, an arbitrary assumption one may adopt or not adopt as one pleases, that is, as a free decision to consider true whatever the heart wishes and to do so because this is what it wishes. Nor should this belief be represented as a hope that supplements or takes the place of sufficient (or insufficient?)[3] grounds of conviction. What is grounded in reason is purely and simply necessary, and what is not necessary is — precisely for this reason — contrary to reason. To hold something of this latter sort to be true is an illusion and a dream, no matter how pious the dream may be.

(349)   Granted that the philosopher presupposes this belief [in a divine governance of the world], where shall he look in order to find what he is supposed to uncover, that is, the necessary ground or basis of this belief? Perhaps this is to be sought in some alleged necessity of inferring from the existence or structure of the sensible world to a rational creator of the same.[4] Certainly not, for the philosopher knows very well that only a misguided philosophy, one that finds itself in the predicament of wishing to explain something whose existence it cannot dispute but whose true ground is hidden from it, is capable of such an inference — an inference that can never be drawn by the original understanding, which stands under the tutelage of reason and is guided by its operation. Either one views the sensible world from the standpoint of ordinary consciousness, which one can also call the standpoint of natural science, or else one views it from the transcendental standpoint. In the first case, reason is required to stick with the being of the world itself, a being that is treated as something absolute: The world is, simply because it is; and it is the way it is, simply because that is the way it is. Within this standpoint, one begins with an absolute being, and this absolute being is precisely the world: these two concepts are identical. The world becomes a self-grounding whole, complete within itself; and, precisely for this reason, it becomes an organized and organizing *180*   whole which possesses within itself and within its own immanent laws the ground of all the phenomena that occur within it. Insofar as it is our task to

----

3. The original version, as published in the *Philosophisches Journal*, has "der zureichenden Ueberzeugungsgründe." The text in vol. 5 of SW, however, includes a note to this passage, which supplies the reading "unzureichenden(?)."

4. An allusion to the so-called cosmological and teleological proofs of God's existence.

provide an actual explanation of *the world and its forms*, and thus to the extent that we find ourselves within the realm of pure — note that I said *pure* — natural science, it is complete nonsense to offer an explanation of the world and of its forms in terms of the goals or purposes of any intellect. Furthermore, to assert that an intellect is the creator of the sensible world provides us with no assistance whatsoever and does not advance our inquiries in the least, for such an assertion possesses not the least intelligibility and furnishes us with nothing but a few empty words rather than with an answer to a question that should never have been raised in the first place. The determinations of an intellect are undoubtedly concepts. But the first intelligible word still remains to be uttered in explanation of how such concepts either manage to transform themselves into matter (which is what must occur within the monstrous system of creation from nothing) or else are able to modify whatever matter is already present (which is what must occur within the scarcely more rational system that posits the mere operation of concepts upon an independent, eternal matter).

To be sure, all of these difficulties vanish when one views the sensible world from the transcendental standpoint. In this case, there is no world that subsists on its own. Wherever we look, we see nothing but the reflection of our own inner activity. However, one cannot inquire concerning the ground of something that does not exist; nor can one, in order to explain it, presuppose something lying outside it.*   (350)

---

* One would then have to inquire concerning the ground of the I itself. Among the undeniably original questions that have been addressed to the *Wissenschaftslehre*, this one alone remained for the latest Göttingen metaphysician, who actually did raise just this question [concerning the ground of the I itself] in his review of the *Wissenschaftslehre* in the *Göttingische Gelehrten Anzeigen*.[5] The sorts of people one has to deal with when one engages in philosophy in our philosophical century! Can the I explain itself, or even wish to explain itself, without thereby proceeding outside of itself and thus ceasing to be an I? Anything that one can even ask for an explanation of is certainly not the pure (absolutely free and independent) I, for *all explanation produces dependency*.

A similar type of objection, and one that proceeds from the same spirit, is the following objection made by the same reviewer: viz., that the *Wissenschaftslehre* has failed to *demonstrate* its own *first principle* — yes, he really did say that it failed to demonstrate its first principle! But if the principle with which it begins could be proven, then it would — precisely for this reason — not be the first principle. Instead, the highest principle from which the principle in question were demonstrated would be the first principle, which would then be the starting point. Every proof presupposes something that simply cannot be proven. — That from which the *Wissenschaftslehre* proceeds can neither be grasped through concepts nor

181
(351)

Consequently, there is no possible path leading from the sensible world to the assumption of a moral world order — so long, that is, as one confines one's thoughts purely to the sensible world alone and does not, like the philosophers in question, tacitly presuppose a moral order of the same.

Hence this belief [in a moral world order; that is, in a divine governance of the world] must be grounded upon our concept of a supersensible world. There is such a concept. I discover myself to be free of any influence

communicated thereby; it can only be directly intuited. For anyone who lacks this intuition, the *Wissenschaftslehre* must necessarily remain groundless and something purely formal, and this system simply has nothing to say to such a person. This is not the first time I have made such a frank admission, but it now appears to be the custom that, even after one has publicly made a general announcement of this sort, one must still communicate it separately to each new individual opponent; moreover, one is not supposed to display the least annoyance at having to do this. With this remark, I hope, in all friendliness, to have discharged my duty toward this opponent. His πρῶτον ψευδος[6] is this: it has not yet become sufficiently clear to him that, if there is to be any truth at all, and especially if there is to be any indirect or mediated truth (that is to say, any truth that is mediated through inference), then there must also be something that is *immediately* true. Once he has understood this, then let him search for such an immediate truth until he finds it. Only then will he be capable of passing judgment on the system of the *Wissenschaftslehre*, for only then will he understand it — which, his repeated assurances notwithstanding, is not yet the case. Perhaps, once he has coolly deliberated on the above remarks, this may even seem probable to him as well.

5. Fichte's reference is to the highly critical remarks concerning the *Wissenschaftslehre* that appeared in a review of K. L. Reinhold's *Vermischte Schriften* that was published in the December 7, 1797 issue of the *Göttingische Anzeigen von gelehrten Sachen*, no. 194, pp. 1929–34. The University of Göttingen was during this period the center of orthodox (or, in Fichte's terminology, "dogmatic") Kantianism, and the *Göttingische Anzeigen von gelehrten Sachen* was long a forum for critics of Fichte's philosophy and published many critical, indeed abusive, reviews of his works. The review in question was written by Friedrich Bouterwek (1766–1828), Professor of Philosophy at Göttingen. Bouterwek's hostile review, which obviously wounded Fichte very deeply, is frequently mentioned by Fichte himself in his letters of this period. (See, for example, his letters to Kant, January 1, 1798 and to Johann Jakob Wagner, January 3, 1798.) During the Atheism Controversy, however, Bouterwek came forward in defense of Fichte. See Bouterwek's February 3, 1799 letter to Fichte in which he assured Fichte that he found nothing "atheistic" about his system and graciously offered his permission for Fichte to use his letter in any way he deemed appropriate.

6. "first mistake."

from the sensible world, absolutely active in and through myself, and thus I discover myself to be a power elevated above everything sensible. This freedom, however, is not indeterminate; it possesses a goal of its own. Yet it does not obtain this goal from without; instead, it posits it through itself. I myself, along with my necessary goal, constitute what is supersensible.

I am unable to doubt this freedom and this determination thereof without, at the same time, renouncing myself.

I claim that this is something I cannot doubt; indeed, I maintain that I cannot even entertain the possibility that it is not so, the possibility that this inner voice deceives me and must first be authorized and established by something lying outside it. At this point, therefore, my reason is quite unable to take me any further; I have reached the limit of all interpretation and explanation. This pronouncement is what is absolutely positive and categorical.[7]

182

I can go no further — so long, that is, as I do not wish to destroy my own inner self. Therefore, the sole reason why I cannot go any further is because I cannot *will* to go any further. Here lies that which sets a limit to the otherwise unbridled flight of argumentation, that which binds the mind because it binds the heart. Here is the point where thinking and willing are united, where they become one and bring me into harmony with myself. To be sure, I could, in principle at least, proceed further — if, that is, I wanted to place myself in contradiction with myself; for argumentation possesses no immanent limit within itself. It freely proceeds into infinity; and it must be able to do so, for I am free in all of my expressions, and only I myself am able to set a limit for myself through willing. Hence our conviction concerning our own moral determination or vocation is itself already the result of a moral disposition and is a matter of *belief* or of *faith*.[8] To this extent, it is quite correct to say that belief or faith is the element of all certainty. — So must it be, since morality, as surely as it is morality at all, can certainly be constituted only through itself and surely not by means of any sort of logically coercive thought.

I could indeed go further — if, that is, I were willing, even in a purely

---

7. "ich kann sonach hierüber gar nicht weiter vernünfteln, deuten, und erklären. Jener Ausspruch ist das absolut positive, und kategorische." (SW erroneously prints "Ausdruck" for "Ausspruch.")

8. "und ist *Glaube*." The reader is reminded that there is but a single German word (*Glaube*) for the two English terms "belief" and "faith." Though the former translation is usually preferred in this volume, occasionally the context calls for the latter.

theoretical sense, to plunge into the realm of what is unbounded and ungrounded, and if I were willing to dispense absolutely with any firm standpoint whatsoever and were content to find inexplicable even that certainty that accompanies all of my thinking and without a deep feeling of which I could not even embark upon speculation. For there is no firm standpoint except the one just indicated, and it is based not upon logic, but upon one's moral disposition or sentiment; and so long as our argument either fails to progress to this point or else proceeds beyond it, we remain upon a boundless ocean where every wave is propelled forward by yet another.

To the extent that I adopt this goal that is posited for me by my own nature and make it into the goal of my real acting, I at the same time posit that it is possible to accomplish this goal through real acting. These two propositions are identical, since "I propose a goal for myself" means "I posit it as actual at some future time." But possibility is necessarily posited along with actuality. Unless I want to disown my own essence, I must propose for myself the former, that is, the accomplishment of this goal. Accordingly, I must also assume the latter, namely, that this goal can be accomplished. Indeed, this is not actually a case of what comes first and what comes second, but rather of an absolute unity. In fact, here we have not two acts, but one and the same indivisible act of the mind.

With this, one can observe, first of all, the absolute necessity of the conclusion we have just reached[9] (if I may be permitted for a moment longer to treat the accomplishability of the ethical goal as if it were the conclusion of an argument). What is involved here is not a wish, nor a hope, nor an act of reflecting upon and evaluating reasons pro and con, nor a free decision to make a certain assumption whose opposite one still considers to be possible. Once one has resolved to obey the [ethical] law within oneself, then the assumption that this goal can be accomplished is utterly necessary. It is immediately contained within this very resolve. It is identical to it.

Secondly, one should also note the order of this sequence of thoughts. Here one does not infer actuality from possibility, but just the reverse: not "I ought because I can," but rather, "I can because I ought." What comes first and is most immediate is that I ought to do something and what it is that I ought to do. This requires no additional explanation, justification, or authorization; it is recognized all by itself and is true on its own. It is neither grounded in nor determined by any other truth; on the contrary, it is

---

9. "die absolute Nothwendigkeit des Vermittelten." More literally, "the absolute necessity of what has been mediated."

much more the case that all other truths are determined by it. — This sequence of thoughts has very frequently been overlooked. A person who says "Before I can judge whether I ought to do something, I first have to know whether I can do it" either annuls the primacy of the ethical law, and thereby annuls the ethical law itself (if, that is, this represents a practical judgment on his part), or else (if this is a purely speculative judgment) he totally misunderstands the original progression of reason.   *184*

I simply must propose for myself the goal of morality. The accomplishment of this goal is possible; it is possible through me. This means, as is revealed by simple analysis, that all of the actions that I ought to accomplish, as well as my own states, which are a condition for accomplishing such actions, are related to the goal I have set for myself as a means to the same. My entire existence, the existence of all moral beings, and the sensible world, as the common theater of our actions, thereby obtain a relation to morality. There thus opens before us an entirely new order, of which the sensible world, with all of its immanent laws, is merely the passive foundation. The sensible world proceeds peacefully along its own path, in accordance with its own eternal laws, in order to constitute a sphere for freedom. But it exercises not the least influence upon morality or immorality, and it has no power at all over a free being. Autonomous and independent, the latter soars above all nature. The goal of reason can be actualized only through the efficacious acting of a free being; moreover, in accordance with a higher law, this goal will quite surely be achieved through such acting. It is possible to do what is right, and thanks to this higher law, every situation is arranged for this purpose. In consequence of this same arrangement, an ethical act infallibly succeeds and an unethical one infallibly fails. The entire world has thus become transfigured for us.   *(353)*

This alteration in the way things appear will become even clearer if we raise ourselves to the transcendental viewpoint. The world is nothing more than our own inner acting (*qua* pure intellect), made visible to the senses in accordance with comprehensible laws of reason and limited by incomprehensible boundaries within which we simply find ourselves to be confined:[10] This is what is asserted by transcendental theory, and no one should be blamed for being made uneasy by this complete disappearance of the ground beneath one's feet. Granted, the origin of these boundaries is incomprehensible; but, replies practical philosophy, what is it that bothers   *185*

10. "Die Welt ist nichts weiter, als die nach begreiflichen VernunftGesetzen versinnlichte Ansicht unsers eignen innern Handelns, als bloßer Intelligenz, innerhalb unbegreiflicher Schranken, in die wir nun einmal eingeschlossen sind."

you about this? Nothing is clearer or more certain than the *meaning* of these boundaries: They constitute your determinate place in the moral order of things. Whatever you perceive as a consequence of these boundaries possesses reality, the only kind of reality that pertains to you or exists for you. It is the ongoing interpretation of what your duty commands, the living expression of *what* you ought to do, just because you ought to do it. Our world is the material of our duty made sensible. This is the truly real element in things, the true, basic stuff of all appearance. The compulsion with which belief in the reality of the world forces itself upon us is a moral compulsion — the only kind of compulsion that is possible for a free being. Short of self-destruction, no one can surrender his moral calling so completely that it does not, even within these boundaries, at least continue to preserve him for future improvement. — Thus, when our belief in the *(354)* reality of the sensible world is viewed as the result of a moral world order, the principle of such belief can appropriately be described as "revelation." What reveals itself therein is our duty.

This is the true faith. This moral order is what we take to be *divine*. It is constituted by right action. This is the only possible confession of faith: joyfully and innocently to accomplish whatever duty commands in every circumstance, without doubting and without pettifogging over the consequences. In this way, what is divine becomes living and actual for us. Every one of our actions is accomplished under this presupposition, and all of the consequences of our acts are preserved only within the divine.

True atheism, genuine unbelief and godlessness, consists in pettifogging over the consequences of one's actions, in refusing to hearken to the voice of one's own conscience until one believes that one has first foreseen the success of the same. One thereby elevates one's own judgment above that of God, and makes oneself into God. Anyone willing to do what is evil in order to obtain good results is a godless person. In a morally governed world, good can never come from evil; and, as surely as you believe in such a moral governance of the world, it is impossible for you to think that it could. — You are not permitted to lie, even if the world should fall into *186* ruin as a consequence of your refusal to do so. This, however, is no more than a figure of speech, for if you were able to believe, in all seriousness, that the world would crumble [as a consequence of your refusal to lie], then, at the very least, your own nature would be utterly self-contradictory and self-destroying. But this is precisely what you do not believe; nor can you believe it, nor are you permitted to do so. You know that a lie is certainly not included within the plan of the world's preservation.

Faith of the sort we have just derived is, however, faith in its entirety.

This living and efficaciously acting moral order is itself God. We require no other God, nor can we grasp any other. There is no ground within reason itself for going beyond this moral world order and, by means of an inference from what is grounded to the ground thereof, assuming another particular being as the cause thereof. Therefore, original understanding certainly does not make such an inference and has no knowledge of any such particular being. Only a philosophy that misunderstands itself makes such an inference. Is this moral world order then simply an accidental one? Is it an order that could equally well be or not be, and that could be the *specific* order that it is, but could also be otherwise, so that you would then first have to explain its existence and character with reference to a ground and could legitimate your faith in this order only by indicating the ground in question? When you cease to listen to the demands of a nugatory system, but rather inquire of your own inner self, you will find that this moral world order is the absolute starting point[11] of all objective cognition, just as your freedom and moral calling constitute the absolute starting point of all *(355)* subjective cognition. And you will also discover that all other objective cognition must be grounded and determined through it, whereas it simply cannot be determined by anything else, since there is nothing beyond it. You cannot even seek to discover an explanation of this order without thereby damaging the status of this assumption in your own eyes and thus shaking it. Its status is such that it is certain absolutely through itself and permits of no sophistry. Yet you would make it dependent upon sophistry.

But how can such sophistry ever succeed? Once you have shaken immediate conviction, how will you make it secure? Your faith is indeed in jeopardy if you can affirm it only by affirming it along with this ground that you *187* yourself construct — and at the collapse of which your faith too must be allowed to collapse.

Even if one wished to permit you to make this inference and to assume the existence of a particular being as the cause of this moral world order, what is it that you would actually have assumed in this case? This being is supposed to be distinct from both you and the world. It is supposed to act efficaciously within the world, and it is supposed to do so in accordance with concepts. Accordingly, it must be capable of entertaining concepts; it must possess personality and consciousness. But what do you mean by "personality" and "consciousness" in this case? Are you talking about what you have discovered within yourself, about those aspects of yourself with which you have become familiar and have called "personality" and "con-

11. "das absolut erste."

sciousness"? By paying the least attention to how you construct such concepts, however, you could learn that you simply do not and cannot think of personality and consciousness apart from limitation and finitude. Hence, by ascribing these predicates to it, you make this being into a finite being similar to yourself, and thus you have not succeeded in thinking of God at all — which is what you wished to do — but simply of a magnified version of yourself. You can no more explain the moral world order by referring to such a being than you can explain it by referring to yourself. It remains, as before, unexplained and absolute; and in fact, so long as you use words like "personality" and "consciousness," you have not succeeded in thinking of anything at all, but have merely set the air to vibrating with an empty sound. Indeed, you could easily have foreseen that this would occur. You are finite: How could what is finite ever grasp and comprehend infinity?

Faith thus clings to what is immediately given, and it remains unshakably firm. If, however, it were made dependent upon the concept [of a separate, supreme being], then it would become unstable, since the concept in question is impossible and is full of contradictions.

It is, accordingly, a misunderstanding to claim that it is doubtful whether a God exists or does not exist. What is by no means doubtful but is, rather, the most certain thing of all, and indeed, the ground of all other certainty and the sole absolutely valid objective [truth], is this: that there is a moral world order; that every rational individual is assigned his own specific place in this order and has a contribution to make to it through his own labor; that the fate of such an individual, to the extent that it is not, as it were, the product of his own endeavors, is the result of this plan, and without this plan no hair falls from his head nor, within his sphere of activity, does any sparrow fall from a roof; that every genuinely good action will succeed and every evil one will surely fail; and that, for him who really loves the good, all things must serve the best.[12] On the other hand, anyone who reflects upon this, even for a moment, and who is willing to admit honestly to himself the results of his reflections, will have no doubt whatsoever that the concept of God as a particular substance is impossible and contradictory; and it is permissible to say this quite openly and to put an end to the idle prattle of the schools, so that the true religion of joyful right action can make its appearance.

Two outstanding poets have given inimical expression to this confession of faith which characterizes the reasonable, good man. In the poem

188
(356)

---

12. See Matthew 10:29–30 and Romans 8:28.

"Who May Say?" one of these poets[13] allows one of his characters to speak
as follows:

> Who may say,
> "I believe in God"? [. . .]
> Him — who may *name*? (i.e., seek a concept and word for him)
> And who *proclaim*,
> "I believe in him"?
> Who may feel,
> Who dare reveal
> In words, "I do not believe in him"?
> The All-Embracing (after, that is, one has first apprehended   *(357)*
>   him through the moral sense and not, as it were, by means
>   of theoretical speculation, and after one has already come to
>   view the world as a theater for the action of moral beings),
> The All-Sustaining,
> Does he not embrace and sustain   *189*
> You and me, as well as himself?
> Do not the heavens vault above?
> Is the earth not firmly fixed below?
> Do eternal, twinkling stars not rise?
> Do we not stare into each other's eyes?
> Does not everything impinge
> Upon your head and heart,
> And weave in timeless mystery,
> Invisibly visible, and not apart?
> Let it fill your heart, it is so great.
> And when your rapture in this feeling is complete,
> Then you may call it what you will:
> Call it "bliss!" or "heart!" or "love!" or "God!"
> I do not have a name
> For this. Feeling is all!
> Names are nothing but sound and smoke,
> Befogging the glory of heaven.

13. Johann Wolfgang von Goethe. The following passage is from *Faust* I (1790),
lines 3427–58. Note that the passages in parentheses are comments on the text,
interpolations added by Fichte. Fichte also omits a few lines near the beginning of
the poem, indicated by ellipses in square brackets.

The other poet[14] sings:

> A holy *will* lives,
> As the human will falters and comes to naught.
> High over time and space, there weaves
> And breathes the highest *thought*.
> Though change is eternal and will never cease,
> The spirit therein remains at peace.

14. Friedrich Schiller, "Die Worte des Glaubens," originally published in Schiller's own *Musen-Almanach für das Jahr 1798*, pp. 221–22. In this celebrated poem ("Words of Faith") Schiller expresses his own Kantian faith in freedom, virtue, and God. Fichte quotes from the fourth stanza, though he omits the opening clause ("And a God exists") and adds emphasis to two words not emphasized by Schiller himself: *Wille* ("will") and *Gedanke* ("thought").

From a Private Letter

Published in the *Philosophisches Journal* 1800.

From a Private Letter
(January 1800)

You ask me why I so peacefully witness the truly unprecedented manner in which my theory of religion has been distorted. My reply is that powerful parties have declared that my theory amounts to atheism. The words of such powerful people must be confirmed, and those who explicate my theory of religion must demonstrate both their own zeal for orthodoxy and their unlimited devotion to the powerful. For this reason, *they* — that is, the very same people before whom my essay[1] lay for half a year without their having detected the least hint of atheism — have, since the time of

---

"Aus einem Privatschreiben" was published by Fichte in vol. IV, no. 4 of the *Philosophisches Journal* (which appeared early in January of 1800), pp. 358–90 (in SW, V, pp. 375–96, the pagination of which appears in the margins of the English translation; and GA, I,6: 369–89, the pagination of which appears within parentheses in the margins of the English translation). Through such devices as directly addressing his unnamed correspondent and describing the notes as "remarks added by the author at the time of publication," Fichte plainly suggests that this text is what its title declares it to be, that is, a "private letter," not originally intended for publication. The editors of GA, however, conclude that this is only a rhetorical pretense on Fichte's part and that, its title notwithstanding, this text was originally written solely for publication in the *Philosophisches Journal*.

1. "On the Basis of Our Belief in a Divine Governance of the World." In what follows, Fichte refers frequently to specific pages in this earlier essay. His references to the pagination of the original article, as published in the *Philosophisches Journal*, have been replaced with references to the pagination of the English translation contained in this volume, pp. 142–54. Also, whereas Fichte occasionally abbreviates his citations from "On the Basis of Our Belief," the translation provides the full text of each of the quoted passages.

The "powerful people" who first declared Fichte's essay "atheistic" were various members of the court and administrative council of Friedrich-August, Prince-Elector of Saxony, who officially declared Fichte's essay atheistic in a confiscation decree of November 26, 1798. The "others" whom Fichte describes as subsequently echoing and attempting to justify the charge of atheism include various advisors to Duke Karl Augustus of Saxe-Weimar-Eisenach and, more specifically, the authors of the numerous pamphlets and fugitive pieces directed against Fichte during the Atheism Controversy.

this official declaration, interpreted my words in such a way as to derive from them a noticeable atheism.

"This is an atheistic document" — this was the proposition with which they began, and they did not have the slightest doubt concerning the accuracy of this claim — "consequently, it must be understood and explained in such a way that it will be atheistic." This was the quite natural conclusion they drew. They have succeeded in accomplishing what they wished. I agree that what they have characterized as my theory is certainly an atheism of the most unequivocal sort — as well as being the most superficial, unfounded, and irrational nonsense.

I have, for the moment, no desire to disturb them as they go about their appointed business. Almighty time is on my side. *They* will ultimately discover that they have already accomplished quite enough. At some later time and employing different terms and modes of expression, *I* will once again present the very same thing that I have actually presented [in "On the Basis of Our Belief in a Divine Governance of the World"]. This is how I have proceeded with all of my philosophical theses, and it is how I will continue to proceed in the future. People will eventually become brave enough to look this fearsome apparition in the eye, and when they do they will discover that it is by no means as bad as they had first thought. One mode of expression will allow one person to grasp this theory, while a different mode of expression will permit another person to grasp it, until it gradually obtains the genuine approval of everyone. When this happens some of my literary colleagues will cry, "Is this all there is to it? This is what all the fuss was over! This is something we have known for a long time, though without ever calling the least attention to this fact; nor did we ever understand Kant to be saying anything else but this." At the same time, others will cry out: "Behold! Here we have another example of another man who learns from and is improved by criticism. Note how, thanks to our instructions, he recants his old errors. To be sure, it is wrong of him to try to do this in such a way that no one will notice what he is doing and in a manner designed to deprive us of the honor we are due. But behold, we will honor ourselves! He was previously an atheist, and what we said remains correct. Fortunately, however, we have now succeeded in converting him." — I have not yet decided, my friend, whether or not I will allow these good people to continue to enjoy this pious pleasure and to persevere in their blindness.

You, however, will say that one must not allow such a prophecy to become known in advance, for things may not occur as I have predicted. — Alas, my friend, I am in this case dealing with people whose future behav-

378

(370)

ior can quite easily be predicted, with people who become terribly agitated that one could honestly think so badly of them and who then go on and behave just as one had predicted. Accordingly, in my *Appeal to the Public*,[2] I provided a detailed account of how I would be treated. This was greeted only by a unanimous outcry and by the complaint that I had shrilly exaggerated and overdramatized the situation. Before a year had passed, however, everything I had predicted had been literally fulfilled — and indeed, fulfilled by the very people who had raised this outcry. The worst is now over, and from now on I live in hope of better times.

379   When I wrote my first, and to date only, defenses against the charge of atheism[3] I was in fact sick of the situation, and I was subsequently not in the least surprised that most people affirmed that in these writings I had succeeded only in further incriminating myself, and by no means in defending myself. It is just that it was so baldly shouted at me, "You are an atheist, and you propound atheism in this and this passage!" And yet no one would indicate to me *how* he derived atheism from the passages in question. The charge came from out of the blue, and I could only defend myself from out of the blue, to the extent that I surmised the possible basis of this misunderstanding. I wondered whether the misunderstanding might perhaps lie in the concept of personality, or in the concept of substance, or in the

(371)   concept of existence, or in something similar; and in doing so I only succeeded in raising new points of discussion when I should have held my tongue concerning them. I was far from hitting upon the right course. — Alas, my friend, I am entirely lacking in the talent required for sniffing out the inconsistencies and contradictions that ceaselessly rattle around and patiently tolerate one another's presence within the heads of our half-wits; nor do I always bear in mind the fact that one can accomplish nothing with such people by means of any general remark unless one repeatedly shows how this general remark applies in each individual case and makes such an application explicit before their very eyes. I am entirely lacking in this skill, and I fear that I shall not be able to acquire it through any amount of

---

2. *J. G. Fichtes d. Phil. Doctors und ordentlichen Professors zu Jena Appellation an das Publikum über die durch ein Kurf. Sächs. Confiscationsrescript ihm beigemessenen atheistischen Aeusserungen*, published in January of 1799 (SW, V, pp. 239–333 = GA, I,5: 415–53).

3. The *Appellation* and *J. G. Fichtes als Verfassers des ersten angeklagten Aufsatzes, und Mitherausgebers des phil. Journals Verantwortungsschrift*, written and submitted, along with Niethammer's "Reply" and various other documents, to the Weimar authorities in March of 1799; published in May of 1799 (SW, V, pp. 242–33 = GA, I,6: 25–144).

experience and that I will always continue to speak to the public as if it possessed a certain consistency and was able on its own to draw particular inferences from general principles. After the fact, I always know very well how I might have been able to prevent *this particular* misunderstanding — though the question of which additional misunderstandings might still be raised is one that I must leave to the gods. If anyone could answer this question for me *prior* to the fact and could discover the art of writing in such a way that one could actually say something without opening oneself to any misunderstanding whatsoever, then I would consider that person to be the great Apollo.

Now, of course, I have received the relevant information [concerning possible misunderstandings and misinterpretations of "On the Basis of Our Belief"]. The first *scholarly* criticism of this notorious essay (published in the first number of the current volume of this journal) to come to my attention was that advanced by a reviewer in the *Oberdeutsche allgemeine Litteraturzeitung*.[4] (Despite the fact that one occasionally encounters gross blunders in this scholarly journal, there nevertheless prevails there, on the whole, a tone of honesty, of the love of truth, and of impartiality, which one often finds missing in other scholarly journals.) In any case, this honest reviewer asserts that if the moral world order of which I speak were not only supposed to be *in* and *present to* the finite moral being, but were also supposed to exist *outside of* this finite moral being, then my system could be defended against the charge of atheism; and he calls upon me to explain myself clearly on this point. Honorable man, I thought to myself, perhaps if you were simply to read my essay once again you would no longer require any further explanation of this point, which is, in my view, very clearly expounded. Who knows how difficult they made it for you, in some lonely cell,[5] to penetrate to the light that you have nevertheless actually obtained, and how difficult they made it for you to obtain the use of the most ordinary literary resources, which would have instructed you on this topic. It will not be easy for anyone else to misunderstand me in the manner in

4. This anonymous review appeared in the March 1, 1799 issue of the *Oberdeutsche allgemeine Litteraturzeitung*. The reviewer criticizes Fichte for not explaining how the supersensible world (the moral world order) was created.

5. In the postscript to his *gerichtliche Verantwortungsschrift*, Fichte refers to the *Oberdeutsche allgemeine Litteraturzeitung* as a "journal founded by Catholic authors" and to the anonymous reviewer as "a Catholic reviewer" (GA, I,6: 87). In this same passage he further characterizes the review in question as "genuinely religious, spiritually uplifting, and written in the true language of one heart to another." Hence the allusion in this passage is presumably to a monastic cell.

which *you* have misunderstood me! — These were my thoughts not quite
one year ago. I no longer think in this way, and I now offer a heartfelt
apology to this man. Now almost everyone misunderstands me in the same
way in which he misunderstood me. From the variously confused rubbish
that was written against me I was able to obtain little or nothing that was
clear, until finally, *in oral conversation, through questions and answers* from
honest men — whom one could certainly not presume to have any acquaintance with the more recent forms of speculation — I was able to
gather the following:

    "My theory is — if, out of tolerance, one wishes to spare me from the
hateful term *atheism* — at the very least a form of *pantheism*. According to
me (p. 150), *the moral world order itself is God, and we require no other God.*

381   Indeed, *they* and *I* and *all of us* are the members who constitute this moral
world, and *our relationship to one another* (for the moment, anyway, it may
remain undecided whether this relationship is present without our having
to do anything, or whether it has to be produced through our morality) is
the *order* of this world. We ourselves, therefore, either *are* or daily *make*
God, and nothing similar to a God remains anywhere — nothing except
we ourselves." — Once instructed in this way, it also became easier for me

(373) to read approximately the same thing asserted in the previously mentioned,
confused rubbish, and since then I have no longer been in the least surprised to read, not only in the most insignificant philosophical reviews and
occasional writings, but also in the writings of men who have indisputably
penetrated the innermost speculative depths, that I deny the existence of a
living, powerful, and *active* God (this, despite the fact that my own words
on p. 150 expressly state that "this *living* and *acting* moral order is God")
and that my God is *nothing but a concept*, etc.

    The situation with this misunderstanding is as follows: These writers
take as the most proximate objects of their own philosophizing nothing but
concepts, concepts that are present in finished form and are, taken by themselves, dead. They then hear the word "order," a term they understand
very well. It designates something *already made*, an already completed,
determinate *being*-alongside-one-another and *being*-one-after-another of a
manifold — just as, for example, the household items in your room are
arranged in a certain order (*ordo ordinatus*).[6] It never occurs to them that
this same word might also have another, higher meaning, for they entirely
lack the organ required for grasping this higher meaning. When they hear

    6. "ordered order." (Compare with Spinoza's *natura naturata* and *natura
naturans*.)

it said that "God is the moral world order" they reason in the manner just indicated; and *for them* such reasoning is correct, unavoidable, and irrefutable. Starting with their own premises, they are *unable* to infer in any other way than this.

In contrast, something stable, at rest, and dead can by no means enter the domain of what *I* call philosophy, within which all is act, movement, and life. This philosophy discovers nothing; instead, it allows everything to arise before its eyes. One of the implications of this is that I completely deny the name "philosophy" to the above sort of trafficking in dead con- *382* cepts. In my view, the latter is nothing but reasoning for the purposes of *actual life*, the business of which is precisely the opposite of speculation. In actual life, one proceeds by way of concepts simply in order to shorten one's path and to arrive more quickly at one's destination, which, to be sure, must once again be some type of acting — if, that is, all of our thinking is not to have been an empty game. Accordingly, if I employ the expression "order" in a speech or in a text that I describe as *philosophical*, then it is and should be clear, without any further ado, that by the term "order" [*Ordnung*] I understand nothing but an *active ordering* (*ordo ordinans*).[7] I am so wedded to this way of speaking that I cannot construe *(374)* any word ending in "*-ung*" in any other way. Thus, for example, I always understand the word "effect" [*Wirkung*] to mean the very act of effecting [*Wirken*] and never the mere result or "effect" [*Effect*] thereof (though other philosophers may well understand this word in this way); instead, I render the latter as "what is effected" [*das Bewirkte*].[8] I am so wedded to this way of speaking that when I begin to philosophize in the manner that is natural to me no other meaning comes into my thoughts at all; thus one might have continued for a decade to shout at me "You are an atheist," and I still would not have realized on my own that the basis for this misunderstanding might very well lie precisely here.

Do I then have a right to demand that one be acquainted with the way I use language? I undoubtedly do have this right, because I have loudly and sufficiently indicated — even in the very journal in which "On the Basis of Our Belief" appeared[9] — that one of the distinctive features of my philoso-

---

7. "ordering order."

8. "unter *Wirkung* stets den Act des Wirkens selbst, nie aber, wie es wohl bei andern Philosophen geschieht, den Effect verstehe, für welchen letztern ich *das Bewirkte* sage."

9. See § 5 of the "Second Introduction to the *Wissenschaftslehre*," in this volume, pp. 46–47.

phy is the fact that it deals only with what is living and by no means with what is dead. From this, reasonable readers will undoubtedly draw the small inference that, since this is the case with all of my philosophical theses, it also applies to my assertions concerning the moral world order. Nevertheless, there are those who read, evaluate, pass judgment on, and write about a single essay written by a systematic philosopher without having read a single line by this philosopher beyond what is contained in this one essay, and who even pride themselves in this fact!

383　　　But why do I not confine myself to ordinary linguistic usage? My friend, I wish that you would find the occasion to tell those who ask this question that I consider such a remark to be one of the "formal absurdities" of our age, an absurdity that, it is to be hoped, is merely passed on from one person to another, purely on the authority of the last person who said it, without anyone ever stopping to consider what he is actually saying. To bid a thinker who actually intends to introduce something new to confine himself to ordinary usage is — overlooking the hyperbole — exactly the same as if one were to bid the Pescherais[10] to produce European arts, sciences, and mores, and yet to do so in the words of their previous language and without changing the definitions of these words. If I generate within myself a new concept, then it surely follows that the sign I employ to signify this concept *for you* (since, for myself, no sign at all is required) is, for you, something new; and the word that I employ for this purpose thus obtains a new meaning, since you did not previously possess what is signified thereby. If someone says, "Until now you have had no correct philoso-

(375)　phy; I will construct one for you," then he also asserts at the same time, "You also have had no correct philosophical usage of language; I must also construct this for you as well." Should you seek to quarrel with him, then, in a well-meaning manner, I would advise you simply to attack his philosophy directly, and not his use of language. If you succeed in defeating his philosophy, then, without any further ado, his linguistic usage will perish along with his philosophy. If, on the other hand, you cannot raise objections to his philosophy, then you will have to learn the language of this philosophy simply in order to be able to penetrate this very philosophy. — To claim that one should stick with ordinary linguistic usage is, at bottom, to say that one should stick with the ordinary *manner of thinking* and should introduce no innovations. It is certainly possible that some people who make such a claim actually do understand it in just this way, but if this is

10. The native inhabitants of Tierra del Fuego. The Pescherais are mentioned by Kant in the First Supplement to his 1795 work *On Perpetual Peace* (*Zum ewigen Frieden*, KGS, VIII, p. 365.)

the case, then they could express their true opinion in a much more direct manner.*

I said that *I had the right to demand* that no one pass judgment on me without being acquainted with my way of using language. However, once one has acquired such an acquaintance — and this is far and away the main point — one should then be able to gather from the context what I mean by the concept of a moral world order. You, my friend, have the opportunity to meet with some of my opponents. I would ask that you acquaint them with this context and that you present them with an overview of my argument in the notorious essay in question, and, with this goal in mind, I will now do the same for you.

*384
(376)*

(377)

---

* Another of these formal absurdities of our age is the ridicule and persecution directed against "one-sole-philosophy philosophers,"[11] which one must continue to put up with right up to this very moment. — I would speak as follows to a respectable person with whom I wished to discuss this point: Tell me, when you step forward without having been asked to do so and make a public assertion, in what sense do you do this? Do you mean to say that *you, for your own person* — for example, *you, this person named Caius* — hold this particular non-authoritative opinion? If so, then you might have kept quiet, for, among all uninteresting things, there is nothing less interesting than some individual's non-authoritative opinions, and it is an unparalleled arrogance on your part to suppose that we would have been anxious to learn your opinion, the opinion of this person named Caius. For who are you? Who is this Caius? If you are to have the honor of speaking, then you must intend to put forward a pronouncement of universal reason and not simply your own pronouncement; and you must be able to vouch for this with your entire inner dignity and morality: namely, that when you speak you are most sincerely convinced of the absolute universal validity of what you assert. So long as you cannot do this, nothing forces you to open your mouth. As certainly, however, as you do make this assumption — and there is no escaping this conclusion — you must also assume that everyone who has, since the beginning of the world, ever asserted anything different from what you are asserting; and everyone who, until the end of the world, will ever assert anything different, is simply wrong; and that you and those who agree with you are *alone* right; and that, so long as they have not refuted you, all mortal creatures should and must acquiesce in this. — *In speaking,* you simply must not know any more than this: that you *alone* are right; for otherwise you should not have spoken at all. You are still free to think that *in the future* you may, as a result either of your own more mature reflection or of rebuke from others, become better informed. Should this happen, you will then retract your first assertion and remain as respectable as before.

(377)

Not only philosophy but all science is, in its very essence, "one-sole-science." Every philosopher is necessarily a "one-sole-philosophy philosopher," for if he is

385

not, then he is wrong, and he is *no* philosopher *at all*. *Philosophy* and all science come to an end where the "sole" comes to an end, which is also the point where all conceit, delirium, and babble first arise. — Why do people not make fun of that *most intolerant* of scholars, that is, of the "one-sole-mathematics mathematician"? Just go up to a mathematician and say, "It is surely presumptuous to assert that we might not at some point find a right triangle the sum of whose angles is either more or less than two right angles." You will see how he will turn his back on you and leave you standing there.

I hereby earnestly entreat such critics to tell me what we should do in order to escape their criticism. Should we actually rush to market with our haphazardly ventured bright ideas, without either investigation or conviction concerning their objective validity? Or should we, when we possess actual, inner conviction concerning the universal validity of our assertions, only behave outwardly as if we intended to *offer as an opinion* something that we really think that we *know*[12] — thereby becoming liars and hypocrites in our own eyes and publicly exposing ourselves as ridiculous idiots who believe that their own individual opinions are meaningful? And we should do all this in order to avoid the appearance that we wish to be more right than those who are wrong? If you are unable to provide me with a rational reply to these questions, then I call upon you to refrain completely from repeating this assertion in the future.

There is indeed a great diversity among human beings! Thus, for example, in a flyer directed against me, the book dealer Dyk,[13] who is also a German philosopher and an opponent of the *Wissenschaftslehre*, recently expressed his bafflement as to how any person could say of his own theory, "It is true." I, in contrast, would be surprised if anyone were to teach something of which he himself believed and said, "It is *not* true."

(Remark added by the author at the time of publication.)

11. *AlleinPhilosophen*. The contrast between those philosophers who insist there can be only "one sole philosophy" (the *AlleinPhilosophen*) and those other, superficially more tolerant philosophers who recognize the possibilities of "many different philosophies" (the *VielPhilosophen*) was explicitly proposed by F. H. Jacobi in his published, open letter criticizing Fichte and transcendental idealism, *Jacobi an Fichte* (originally written in the spring of 1799 and published in September of 1799; in GA, III, 3: 224–81; English trans. Diana I. Behler, "Open Letter to Fichte," in *Philosophy of German Idealism*, ed. Ernst Behler, pp. 119–41 [New York: Continuum, 1987]).

12. "als ob wir meinten *zu meinen*, was wir doch meinen zu *wissen*."

13. Johann Gottfried Dyk (1750–1813) was a Leipzig publisher and poet and the author of a pamphlet entitled *Ueber des Herrn Professor Fichte Appellation an das Publicum. Eine Anmerkung aus der deutschen Uebersetzung des Ersten Bandes von Saint-Lamberts Tugendkunst besonders abgedruckt* (1799), in which he did indeed maintain that it would be presumptuous of anyone to assert the truth of his own theory.

First of all, I solemnly affirm the following (and it is in fact remarkable that people do not yet listen to me concerning the chief and most characteristic point of my system): I solemnly affirm that no part of my philosophy, including my philosophy of religion, seeks to produce anything new within the minds of human beings. (On the contrary, my philosophy seeks to liberate the human mind from all the useless enrichment with which other systems have burdened it.) For the non-philosopher — and within life we are necessarily all non-philosophers — something is simply present; it remains present and presses itself upon one irresistibly, and one is unable to remove it by means of any effort. This is sufficient for one's non-philosophical endeavors. The philosopher, however, has the obligation of deriving this same "something" from the entire system of our thinking and connecting it to this system. That is to say, the philosopher has the task of indicating the *locus* of this "something" within this necessary system of human thinking. In the course of his philosophical enterprise, this "something" remains as it is and is not altered thereby. Indeed, if the philosopher had to alter it in order to be able to derive it, this would be a proof that he did not understand his own craft and that his system was false. — I stated this on pp. 143 of my essay, where I wrote, "Until now, almost every view of this topic has been confused, and will perhaps continue to be confused for a long time to come, by treating the so-called moral proof of a divine governance of the world (or indeed, any philosophical proof of the same) as if it constituted a *proof* in the proper sense of the term. The confusion lies in the apparent assumption that belief in God is supposed to be first inculcated in and demonstrated to humanity by means of such a demonstration. Poor philosophy! Were such a belief not already present within human beings, then from where, I would like to know, did philosophy's representatives (who, after all, are also nothing but human beings) themselves obtain what they wish to convey to us through the force of their proofs? Or, if these representatives are, in fact, superior beings of some sort, then how can they expect to obtain a hearing from the rest of us, and how can they expect to be understood by us unless they presuppose that we possess a belief analogous to their own? This is not the actual state of affairs, however. Philosophy can do no more than *explain* facts; by no means can it produce any facts — beyond, that is, the fact of philosophy itself. Just as it would never occur to a philosopher to try to persuade men that from now on they are entitled to think of objects as matter in space and that they may also think of the alterations of these objects as following each other in time, so too would it never occur to him to try to persuade men that they do indeed believe in a divine governance of the world. Both surely occur

385

386

without any help whatsoever from the philosopher, who presupposes this as a fact, and whose sole task is simply to derive such facts, as such, from the necessary manner in which every rational being must operate. Consequently, we by no means wish our argument to be viewed as a means for convincing the unbeliever; instead, we wish it to be considered as a derivation of the believer's conviction. Our sole concern is to answer the causal question, 'How does a human being arrive at this belief?'" Consequently — and I ask you to state this loudly and clearly to my opponents — my philosophy alters nothing concerning *religion*, as it has dwelt within the hearts of all well-meaning people from the beginning of the world and will continue to dwell there until the end of time; and my philosophy would be false just as surely as it did alter anything. I am engaged in an enterprise that no one before me has undertaken (at least not in its full determinacy) and that is, to this extent, something new: I am concerned with the *derivation* (deduction) *of the above-mentioned religion from the very nature of reason*. It is by no means my intention to use this deduction to impart religion to human beings; my purposes are purely and exclusively *scientific*, and no one can engage in a dispute with me over the latter unless he has already penetrated into the interior of my philosophy. This philosophy should, however, alter something within *theology* (insofar as the word "theology" does not designate *the theory of religion*, that is, *the theory of the relationship of God to a finite being*, but instead designates, as it should, *the theory of the nature of God in and for himself, apart from any relationship to a finite being*).*
Such theology should be altered by my philosophy; indeed, tell my opponents straightforwardly that such theology is supposed to be entirely destroyed, as a figment of the brain which transcends all finite power of apprehension.

(378)

387

---

* Herr Eberhard[14] says that in order to recognize the relations of a thing to me I must first possess a concept (presumably a concept of the inner nature of the thing in question). It thus appears that, according to him, these relations are only *inferred*, that is, only *thought of*, and by no means *sensed*. I therefore call upon him to reconsider the example he himself uses against me.

I, on the contrary, contend that it is by means of the cognition of the relations [of things] to me that I first obtain a concept, which is never anything other than these relations themselves as *combined by thinking*, which is something quite different from their being *cognized* by means of an act of sheer thinking. — It may well happen that something or another prompts me to *renew* within my consciousness some concept that was once produced within me (so that, *in this act* of renewing, I encounter this very concept, as something already finished or completed), and that I then *develop* this concept, and that *this time*, through thinking alone and without

The *locus* of religious belief [within the necessary system of human thinking] not only can but well nigh must remain hidden from the ordinary religious person, though the educator of the people should be acquainted with it, so that he can design his plan of religious guidance in accordance therewith. In any case, this locus, this "something" contained within the system of necessary thinking, this "something" to which religious belief is attached and from which it proceeds, is, according to my philosophy, *the necessary goal of man whenever he obeys the command of duty.* *(379)*

On pp. 146–47 the concept of the supersensible is presented as follows: (1) "I discover myself to be free of any influence from the sensible world, absolutely active in and through myself." (2) "This freedom, however, is not undetermined (with respect to its goal); it possesses a goal of its own."

Now ask my opponent (for this is the decisive point, a point that has been completely overlooked in the present misunderstanding) whether this freedom (no. 1, above) and this goal of freedom (no. 2, above) are one and the same or are two separate things. Clarify this for him by means of a sensible example, if, that is, you trust him not to construe the example in such a way that it goes beyond the point of comparison, which in this case concerns nothing more than the distinction between an action and the external goal of that same action. — Say to him, "Suppose that you are engaged in sowing seeds; this will count as your action. You undoubtedly engage in this act of sowing, however, not merely for the sake of sowing seeds, but so that your seeds will germinate and bear fruit. The latter, that *388*

---

any actual, direct perception, I give particular prominence to *one* feature of this concept, etc. Herr Eberhard's philosophy appears to reflect only upon this business of analysis, and I concede everything that he says concerning this act of analysis. My philosophy, however, does not concern itself with this act [of analysis] at all, but raises the higher question, How did this concept itself, which you discover before you, first arise? And how did the particular feature that you now develop from it [via analysis] become part of this concept in the first place? — Herr Eberhard must deal with the *original genesis* of the concept. To say that it is innate (as a concept) is, in my view, a mere *assertion*, made for the purpose of avoiding an inconvenient question, by no means an *explanation*, and still less a *proof*. — In what follows above I hope to have succeeded in making it a bit clearer to him than before how, *according to me*, the concept of God is originally produced. *387*

(Remark added by the author at the time of publication.)

14. In his 1799 pamphlet *Ueber den Gott des Herrn Professor Fichte und den Götzen seiner Gegner*, Eberhard contended, against Fichte, that our ethical feelings are dependent on concepts of the external things to which we are related, concepts constructed by our own reason and understanding.

is, the future harvest, is no longer your action itself but is the goal of the same, and you will undoubtedly recognize that these are two things rather than one."

Now ask him further, "Does your sowing, your act of casting the seeds upon the earth, contain within itself the *ultimate sufficient ground* of germinating and bearing fruit? — This much is certainly clear: If you did not sow this field, and if you did not sow it with precisely this sort of grain, then you would never harvest this sort of grain from this same field. Your act of sowing is thus at least *a necessary condition* for the future harvest. If, however, there were not, in addition to your act of sowing and independent of it, a fructifying force within nature, then your seeds would never bear fruit. Not your own act of sowing, but this fructifying force is the *ultimate sufficient* ground of the harvest. When you sow your seeds you count upon this force, this order of nature, according to which you cannot harvest unless you have first sown, though, in accordance with the orderly course of nature, you may also count on a harvest from your sowing. Only by counting upon the order of nature in this way does your broadcasting of seed corn, which otherwise would be either a pointless game or an inexpe-

(380)   dient throwing away of something very useful, become a purposeful enterprise. Your confidence in this order of nature is so great that you actually stake upon this belief the very grains that you could use, just as they are, for your own nourishment."

If our opponent cannot yet grasp this point, then present it to him in a bit stronger and more comprehensible form. Say to him, for example: "Both of these, the sowing and the harvest, are connected within your concept, and both are intended by you: the second as the *result* of the first, and the first only for the sake of the second. But where is *that which connects* the harvest, as the result, with the sowing, which precedes it? Where is the mediating link? Does it lie in your action of sowing, in *what you are doing*

389   *when you are sowing the seeds*? Or do you posit this connecting link outside the act of sowing? If you have actually made the distinction I indicated [between sowing and harvest], then I certainly think that you will posit this outside of yourself. *That which is outside of you*, however, is set in motion and posited in its active condition only by something *within you*, that is, by your own free deed.

"In your act of sowing, an act from which a harvest is supposed to follow, you therefore anticipate and count upon something *two-fold*: upon one thing that is wholly and solely your own product, and upon a second that is present and efficacious quite independently of you, something with which you are merely *acquainted* — namely, the eternal order of nature —

and you do the same in the case of all your sensible actions. You can move neither your hand nor your foot without presupposing, perhaps unconsciously, both [1] your own pure and bare act of willing that your hand move, an act that depends absolutely upon you, and [2] *the laws of the organization and articulation of your body*, in accordance with which the actual movement of the hand follows from this act of willing and will cease to follow as soon as this articulation is damaged and, for example, your hand becomes paralyzed."

If you can get our opponent to comprehend this last point then we have won, and this will put an end to all the confused talk, which has now been repeated to the point of weariness, concerning the alleged claim *that the moral order is supposed to be sufficiently guaranteed through the mere ethical law.* In what sense is the expression "the ethical law" being employed in this case? Does this refer to a law that determines even God's efficacious power? If so, then this assertion cannot be used against my theory. Or should the expression "the ethical law" be taken as referring to the voice of conscience within a finite being? The moral order that can be grounded (albeit not guaranteed) in such a manner is indeed something to be discussed within a theory of ethics, but it is by no means a topic to be discussed within a theory of religion. I was talking about something else. — I said "If you *can* get our opponent to comprehend this point," but I fear that *(381)* you will be able to make this comprehensible only to a very few; for it is precisely here that so many people encounter a conceptual barrier. I, at any rate, have encountered many people who — even if one were to crush them in a mortar[15] — are unable to know or to grasp this in any other way than this: that *they*, all alone and solely through their own force, without the *390* help of any external order or law, move their own tongue, hand, or foot; and these same people are, presumably, also of the opinion that the maturation and fruition of the seed corn are also sufficiently grounded merely by their own act of scattering seed corn. There is nothing more to be done with people of this sort; all that one can do is to ask them politely to quit talking about something they obviously do not understand, and to ask them not to take this polite request badly. — The reason for this incapacity on their part is that they completely fail to notice what is actually present and is in fact within their own power and constitutes their own true self: namely, their will. For this reason, they are of course unable to enumerate *two things*; that is, they are unable to distinguish an A from a B in this case,

---

15. "Crush a fool in a mortar with a pestle along with crushed grain, yet his folly will not depart from him" (Proverbs 27:22).

since *for them* there is in fact only one thing present, and the other (= A) is completely lacking. To be sure, they are then required to displace *their own personality*, which they surely cannot lose, into B, into that which is for us (at the present standpoint) nature; and they *must* firmly and steadfastly believe and, through their own innermost consciousness, *perceive* — and know nothing whatsoever beyond this —that *they themselves* do that which we others know very well that we ourselves do not do, but is done by nature. There is no arguing with such people. If they are still young enough, one must cultivate them; if not, they must be allowed to die off in their errors.

After this first trial, nine-tenths of our opponents will no longer remain and will be justly sentenced to eternal silence. To the remaining one-tenth, you may then address the following question:

"With respect to morality, what is it that is wholly and solely in your own power, such that it alone is commanded of you and you are responsible only for it?" If they understand your question at all, these remaining opponents must respond as follows: "All that is in my power, all that is required of me and for which I am responsible, is the mere *act of willing*, as an inner determination of my character or disposition, and I am responsible for nothing whatsoever beyond this." This is also true in the case of every sensible action — with the difference that, in the case of sensible action, what one has in view is a material goal, a goal that lies outside of the act of willing, whereas in the case of ethical action, what one has in view is the inner purity and probity of the act of willing itself. — In every sensible endeavor, willing is only the means toward some goal that is willed. Willing is merely what first moves and stimulates that which is then continued by the force of nature, and the [inner] determination of the will would not have been accomplished if this [external] goal had not been willed. In the ethical determination [of the will], however, the will itself is the final goal of the act of willing; it ought to be in a certain state simply in order to be in this state.

391
(382)

After you have requested of them this two-fold attentiveness, ask our opponents this: "Despite the fact that the ethical will itself, as such, must be the final goal of *our* willing, could it nevertheless not also be the case that *something might result* from this willing, though, to be sure, not as a result of our own efficacious power? That is to say, the good will is admittedly all that lies within our power and is all that *we*, for our part, have to worry about, and it must be, *for us*, the final member[16] [of the series]; yet it could

16. "das letzte Glied." Fichte uses the term *Glied* to designate an individual element or member of a linked series, whether of things, events, or thoughts. In the

nevertheless still be the case that the good will *as such* (that is, for some other will) is not the final member, but is followed by another one, though admittedly not as a result of anything that we do. — Similarly, the actual movement of my hand was certainly supposed to result from my act of willing that my hand move — not, to be sure, as a result of the mere force of my will, considered purely on its own, but in consequence of a natural arrangement, *in accordance with which* this movement first follows from this act of willing. But I would by no means have produced this act of willing within myself if I had not counted upon this natural arrangement, in accordance with which my act of willing has this result. In such a case I will only for the sake of the result. In contrast, I will to do my duty not for the sake of any result, but for its own sake; and only insofar as I will in this manner do I actually will to do my duty. Yet it could nevertheless happen that such willing might have results, results that would likewise occur in accordance with some order — though, to be sure, I could not will to do my duty *for the sake of these results*, for were I to do so, then I would not be willing to do my duty at all, and thus the results [of willing to do my duty] could not occur. What results from the mortality of a finite being is necessarily of the type that it can occur only on the condition that it is not actually *willed* (though it is *postulated*), that is, only on the condition that it provides no motive for willing. *392*

Were something like this to be the case — I had asserted this, and I will now discuss the basis for this claim — then how far does *my own* force and that of *all finite* beings extend, and where does the realm of a foreign force, one lying outside of all finite beings, begin? My own force would undoubtedly extend only to the determination of the will (= A); whereas that by means of which some result (= B) of this determination of the will is necessarily attached to this same determination of the will would *not* be my own force, but would lie outside of my force and outside of my own nature. If, therefore, one calls the law according to which B necessarily follows A an "order" and, in order to distinguish this order from the order of nature, calls it a "moral" or "intelligible order," an order by means of which there *(383)* arises a moral or intelligible *interconnectedness*[17] or *system* or *world*: if so, then the person who posits this moral order undoubtedly does not posit it

---

discussion that follows, the question is whether or not the act of willing is simply the final member of a series of mental acts or may also be viewed as constituting the first member of a causal series that includes real events in the external world. See Kant's celebrated account of "freedom" as "the power to initiate, on its own, a series of events" (KRV, A554/B582).

17. *Zusammenhang.*

within the finite, moral being, but posits it outside of the latter. Accordingly, he undoubtedly assumes something else in addition to and outside of this finite being.

For the most part, those who pass this judgment [of atheism on the *Wissenschaftslehre*] are, of course, acquainted with the Kantian theory of religion, and they have not accused Kant of atheism. He teaches that from morality there must result a kind of happiness proportionate thereto, and for him, the ground of this result, that which mediates between happiness and morality, is God.[18] Why were these judges quite able to distinguish in Kant's case between what is ascribed to the finite being and what is ascribed to an alien force, *external to* the finite being, and yet unable to make this same distinction after I had spoken?

My friend, after you have in this manner succeeded in dispelling the timidity of these judges and have thereby provided them with the courage to look this fearsome thing in the eye, you may then proceed to raise to the level of certainty what has hitherto been only presupposed. Say to your *(384)* opponent, "Were you nothing whatsoever but *will* (and were this even imaginable), then all you would need to accomplish would be to will ethi- *393* cally, and with this you would fulfill your nature; and this is also the manner in which you should actually *will* to do your duty. You, however, are [not merely will; you are] at the same time *cognition*; you contemplate and observe yourself, and, in the case we are here considering, what you observe is your own ethical willing. In doing so, you fall under the *laws* of your own objectifying and discursive thinking, and you thereby become, for yourself, something *given* and become part of a *series* — though not in the sense that there was, *before* this [act of willing], a previous member which was either theoretically grounding or practically motivating, for in the first case you would not be free, and in the second your decision would not be morally good. Your will is purely and simply the first, initiating member of this series. Thus, you are given to yourself as part of a series in the sense that this first, initiating member of the series is supposed to be *followed by* a second one, i.e., in the sense that your good will is supposed to have some result. This result, which must necessarily be thought of as well, is here called the "goal," and it is thought of not as what motivates one's decision but rather as what satisfies cognition. Insofar as I posit you as *engaged in willing*, you simply ought to obey [the dictates of conscience], without any reference to any goal whatsoever. When, however, you *con-*

18. See Kant, *Critique of Practical Reason*, bk. II, ch. 2, pt. 5: "The Existence of God as a Postulate of Pure Practical Reason."

template your own willing, it would then appear to you to be contrary to reason if your act of willing were to appear to you to be without a goal and without a result; and, at the same time, what is commanded by such willing would also appear to you to be contrary to reason. Perhaps this is how it really does appear to you, and for this reason you disavow this command and, as a eudaimonist, look for an empirical ground to determine a material act of willing. In that case, however, you will neither have a part in nor be interested in this conversation, and we are talking neither about you nor with you. You are dismissed. As certainly, however, as you believe this command and decide to obey it, then it is equally certain that you do not consider it to be contrary to reason; that is to say, it is certain that you do not consider your obedience to be either pointless or lacking in any result. Without any voluntary decision on your part, simply because the mere laws of thinking require it, you also think of a result of your morality — *and so does every person* who manages to raise himself to a moral disposition, perhaps without ever becoming conscious of this and without rendering an account to himself of the connections within his own thinking. Anyone, however, who does not believe this command, because he has not decided to heed it, also does not believe in what follows therefrom, but thoughtlessly parrots, as it were, the religion of his country, which he has learned by heart. Such a person is unable to understand a rigorous theory of religion, but will instead slander it and denounce it as "atheism." — I carefully discussed this important point on pp. 148–50 of my essay, and I did so in order to oppose a number of currently fashionable false opinions regarding belief, opinions that view belief as no more than an aid to lazy and despairing reason — a view that animates the very essay that my own was written to correct[19] — and I have done nothing either to deserve or to provoke the deceitful distortions of my words provided by, for example, Herr Heusinger.[20]*

394

(385)

19. Viz., Forberg's "Entwicklung des Begriffs der Religion," the essay that provoked Fichte to write "On the Basis of Our Belief in a Divine Governance of the World."

20. Johann Heinrich Gottlieb Heusinger (1766–1837), who had been a colleague of Fichte's at Jena from 1795 until 1797, was the author of *Ueber das idealistisch-atheistische System des Herrn Profeßor Fichte in Jena* (1799), one of the more scurrilous of the many pamphlets directed against Fichte during the Atheism Controversy.

* In order to express the necessary consequences of both ways of thinking, I say (on p. 148) that "*unless I want to disown my own essence, I must* propose for myself the

145

(386)   This then is, in my view, the *locus* of religious belief [within the system of human thinking]: this necessary way of thinking and demanding an intelligible order, law, or arrangement — call it what one will — an order *(387)* according to which true morality, the inner purity of the heart, necessarily has results. I maintain that all belief in God and in something divine develops and has always developed in the minds of all good human beings from this necessary way of thinking (necessary, that is, on the presupposition of the freely produced moral disposition) and that their belief is never any-

---

accomplishment of this goal (of morality)." Since I have to analyze this proposition, I repeat it on the next page, *in an abbreviated form*, leaving out those features that require no analysis, as follows: "I simply must propose for myself the goal of morality. This means, etc." — This is thus just like saying, "In a *right* triangle the square of the hypotenuse equals the square of the two legs." [And then repeating this as,] "In *a triangle* the square of the hypotenuse means, etc." — Herr Heusinger, however, confines himself to the latter expression of this proposition and treats it as if it were the *direct* expression; then he explains my entire theory from this immediately posited "must," in order to accuse me of fatalism (despite the fact that anyone who has read even a syllable of mine must realize that all of my thinking is constructed upon the freedom of the will) and in order to show clearly how, accord-
(386)   ing to me, the moral order "makes itself" and how I am, with full knowledge of the fact, a manifest atheist. — In ordinary life everyone who cherishes honesty calls such behavior villainy, knavery, or lying. What should one call it when it occurs within the domain of literature?

There now steps forward, in the Erlangen *Literatur-Zeitung*, a reviewer[21] who has, with disdain for all possible morals, long preached good morals to me, and who now extols Heusinger's miserable concoction as an extremely important work and
(387)   solemnly entreats me to provide a thorough refutation of the same. This reviewer, however, is not the least bit upset by this falsification; instead, he quite confidently reports it to the reader. — In addition, this same Heusinger imagines nothing less than that he can destroy the entire system of the *Wissenschaftslehre* in a single stroke simply by asserting that this "I" upon which this system is erected is not be found within his own consciousness at all, but is a psychological delusion. The point, however, is that whereas psychology teaches us about facts of consciousness, what the *Wissenschaftslehre* is talking about is what one finds to be the case only when one discovers oneself! — I assure Herr Heusinger, as well as his immature reviewer, that they would do well to trade their actual and imagined wisdom for some knowledge of *what this system is actually about.*

(Remark added by the author at the time of publication.)[22]

21. The anonymous review to which Fichte refers appeared in the December 2, 1799 issue of the Erlangen *Literatur-Zeitung*.

22. This note is not reprinted in SW.

thing other than belief in this order, the concept of which they have merely *further developed and determined*, albeit unconsciously and guided by the instructions they have received within society. Only after this further development have they then discovered the concept of this moral order to be present within their own consciousness, and since making this discovery they have never again traced it back to its original, unitary simplicity, which, in the end, is something that only the philosopher and the educator of the people need to do. — In short, in all human action we count upon something *two-fold*: upon something that is dependent upon man himself, *(388)* upon the determination of his will, as well as upon something that is not dependent upon man himself. In the case of sensible acting, the latter is the *order of nature*, and anyone who acts only in a sensible fashion needs to rely upon no more than this; and if he is consistent, he *has* nothing more to rely upon. In the case of ethical acting, that is, in the case of the pure, good will, what is not dependent upon man himself is *an intelligible order*.

Every belief in the divine which *contains more* than this concept of the moral order is, to that extent, fiction and superstition. Though such a belief may be *harmless*, it is nevertheless always *unworthy* of a rational being *395* and is highly *suspicious*. Every belief that *contradicts* this concept of a moral order (every belief that wishes to introduce an *amoral chaos*,[23] a lawless arbitrariness on the part of a superpowerful being, mediated through senseless, magical means) is a *reprehensible* superstition and is *aimed at the total destruction of human beings*.

Regarding this point, which concerns only the *deduction* [of such belief], I am dealing only with philosophers, and indeed, only with those whom I myself consider to be "transcendental" philosophers. I wish to heaven that I had to deal only with such philosophers, and that others might finally understand what the word "deduction" means for me and see that the essence of *my* philosophy, and in my view of *all* genuine philosophy, consists exclusively in deducing! On this point I do not have anything whatsoever to say to an adherent of the popular religion or to the guardians of the same, the church and the state. An adherent of the popular religion *possesses* belief, without particularly inquiring concerning the deduction of the same. Nor is the concept of *an intelligible moral order*, in its philosophical purity, simplicity, and precision, by any means to be attributed to such a person — though one can expect that everything he believes *can be* traced back to this concept (perhaps by his religious instructor or by some other philosopher). Only after the basic principles of our philosophy have un-

---

23. "eine *unmoralische Unordnung*."

dergone *further determination* and *development* will the adherent of the popular religion be able to perceive his own interest in these principles and be able to relate them to his own convictions. I did not attempt to determine and to develop these principles in my essay, nor was it my intention to make this my next goal. Consequently, the only people who should have engaged in this discussion should have been those who could, with some justification, consider themselves to be transcendental philosophers, whose number in Germany is, as is well known, not yet so large as is the number of those who have actually engaged in this discussion and have joined in the *hue and cry*. As previous experience has shown, such development and derivation [of the principles of the *Wissenschaftslehre*], even within my own soul, is a difficult enterprise, one which my opponents have never wished to succeed and which will not be accomplished soon. Even if these opponents were to understand my premises, which, on this occasion at least, they did not understand, they would still have much more to do before they would have succeeded in mastering my synthetic method. They may well be able to go on making straightforward inferences, but this is not what is needed here.

(389)
396

To date, I have advanced this development furthermost in my *Vocation of Man*, which you should probably receive shortly after this letter.[24] But I would almost prefer to speak with you, where I can speak freely from my heart, than with the vast public at large. Be prepared, therefore, to receive in the mail in the near future a manuscript, written in the manner that I use when writing letters, further developing this fundamental concept and examining the questions: *What* is the result of morality, and *how* is this supposed to be produced?

24. Fichte conceived the plan of writing a popular presentation of some of the results of his philosophy in the spring of 1799, immediately after losing his position at the University of Jena. He worked on this text, *The Vocation of Man*, in Berlin throughout the summer and fall of 1799. It was finally published in mid-January of 1800, shortly after the appearance of the above article in the *Philosophisches Journal*.

Concluding Remark by the Editor

Published in the *Philosophisches Journal* 1800.

Concluding Remark by the Editor

(411) We have allowed the author of the preceding article to exercise his own judgment concerning the allegedly new proof of the existence of God propounded by Dr. Vogel,[1] a proof that first came to the editor's attention through this very article. Moreover, we find this judgment to be perfectly adequate for a proof of this type. Nevertheless, in order not to leave our readers with the impression that this represents the strongest case that can be made against such a strategy for proving the existence of God and with the impression that it might perhaps be possible to come to the aid of this proof by introducing a few minor improvements, we think it will be beneficial to add the following comment.

First of all, we need to ask what the word "proof" means in this context. Why does Herr Vogel seek a proof of the objective existence of God? What is the real aim of his proof? Does he really intend (as, judging from the content of his essay, it would appear that he well may intend) to demonstrate belief in God to human beings, and does he think that by means of his proof he will, for the first time, succeed in placing the concept of a God within their understanding? If so, then the editor believes that it has long been shown that any such proof is superfluous, impossible, too late, and (in those areas where argumentation is appropriate) certain to fall far short of its goal. Suppose that some sophist[2] were to come forward and attempt to convince us that we are justified in positing bodies in space or in assuming

---

The remark that follows was appended by Fichte, acting in his capacity as co-editor of the *Philosophisches Journal*, to an article published in vol. X, no. 3 of the *Philosophisches Journal* by an obscure — his first name is not even known — doctoral candidate by the name of Ritter and titled "Streit des Idealismus und Realismus in der Theologie" ("The Struggle between Idealism and Realism in Theology"). Fichte's "Concluding Remark" appears in vol. X, no. 3 of the *Philosophisches Journal*, pp. 215–45, dated "1798" but actually published in September of 1800 (in GA, I,6: 411–16, the pagination of which appears within parentheses in the margins of the English translation; not in SW).

1. Paul Joachim Siegmund Vogel (1753–1834) was a professor of philosophy at Altdorf and author of an essay titled "Theoretisch-praktischer Beweis des objectiven Daseyns Gottes" ("Theoretical-Practical Proof of the Objective Existence of God") and published in the *Neuest theologisches Journal*, I,1 (1799), pp. 19–34. Ritter's essay is primarily a polemical reply to Vogel's.

2. *irgend ein BegriffKünstler*: literally, "some artist with concepts."

the existence of things outside of us, etc. Anyone who needs a proof of the former (that is, of the existence of God) more than of the latter will obtain no assistance from such a sophist. Belief in God is a living and animating principle within human beings, and it springs from life itself and not from dead concepts.

Or does the word "proof" mean here what it must mean in every correct *(412)* philosophy, namely, a deduction, a genetic explanation (that is to say, an explanation based upon the nature of the system of reason as such) of some specific consciousness that is presupposed to be already present? If this is the sort of proof that is here in question, then it is a simple matter to show that Herr Vogel's proposed deduction is full of sophisms, question-begging, and leaps. I will limit my examination to the first step of the argument, which will permit me to ignore all of the extraneous elements inappropriately incorporated within this proof. In addition, I will examine another obvious error in the premises, and my censure will lead me further than Herr Vogel may wish to follow.

"It is simply necessary for human reason to think of *the earth* in its entirety as an effect and to derive it from a cause," says Herr Vogel (according to the foregoing account). — Let us overlook the error that is concealed in this assertion and agree to take Herr Vogel's words in the way in which they are undoubtedly meant to be understood. What does my reader think follows from this premise? Must I also assume the existence, *outside of the world*, of forces — *homogeneous* forces, to be sure — which have produced and determined the world? In short, am I forced to assume that the world itself cannot be the universe, but is only a part of the same — which is also the only way it has ever appeared to my sensory perception? Is this how I should think of it? "No," says Dr. Vogel, "what follows is that I must assume a *creator* of the earth." Thus, via a most remarkable transformation, the "cause" that appears in the major premise of the argument becomes a "creator" in the conclusion.

To be sure, Herr Vogel subsequently ascends to the level of the universe and offers another special demonstration that the creator [of the earth] is the creator of the universe too. Yet I fail to grasp why he does not content himself with the first successful Q.E.D.[3] or to see why, if he himself does not completely trust the first proof, he does not simply start with the second, decisive step [viz., with the proof that the universe as a whole, and not merely our own earth, requires a creator].

---

3. *Quod erat demonstrandum*: "which was to be demonstrated" ("thus it is proven").

Let Herr Vogel simply show us in either case — be it that of the earth or that of the universe — that it is possible for original reason (that is, for reason that systematically constructs its own consciousness) to make this μεταβασιν ἐις ἀλλο γενος[4] and to ascend from the sensible and material effects to an utterly opposed, intelligent cause of the same! Let him simply

(413) indicate the precise point where reason unites these absolute and contradictory opposites! Everything depends upon this, and upon this alone. Everything else is irrelevant. Yet one will surely not expect me to go into any further detail on this point. What Herr Vogel has here overlooked pertains to the very rudiments of the Critical philosophy and can be read in some thirty volumes. Herr Vogel announces his departure from the Critical philosophy with great fanfare. If only he were to take advantage of this occasion in order to become acquainted with this same philosophy, he would discover that reason, when it thinks about the cause of the world, arrives only at [the thought of] a universal force of nature, a force that continues to organize itself in the universe, that is, a *world-soul*.[5] By no means, however, could reason ever arrive in this way at what the theory of religion calls *God*. Furthermore, he would also discover that, if (to assume for the moment something that is impossible, though it is precisely what is assumed by all proofs of the sort examined here) man were nothing but a creature aware of nature and were not also an ethical being, then the concept of a God would simply never arise within his soul. The Critical philosophy would also teach Dr. Vogel that the *purposefulness* of the sensible world (which plays a role later on in his so wonderfully constructed proof) is present for man only insofar as and only because he is able to set *goals* for himself, and that he is able to do this only because his own reason provides him with an absolutely *final goal* (viz., morality). In addition, Dr. Vogel would discover that, in consequence of positing such a goal, one is also required to postulate an intelligible order within which the mere pure will can be a cause, as well as an intelligent, holy, and omnipotent principle of such an order. Here and here alone — and by no means in the concept of a sensible world — is the *original locus* of belief in a God.

No continuous advance from the sensible to the supersensible realm is possible. The latter must be innate within us and can by no means be acquired through argument and inference. It is, however, quite possible to descend from the supersensible to the sensible world and to view the latter

4. "transference to another domain."

5. *Welt-Seele* is a term from Schelling's *Naturphilosophie*. See especially his *Von der Weltseele, eine Hypothese der höheren Physik* (1798).

in the light of and for the sake of the former.[6] Consequently, to view the
sensible world as purposively arranged already presupposes a belief in a
rational creator of the same, even if one is not clearly conscious of this; and
hence it is far from being the case that the latter is based upon the former.
The philosopher concerns himself with this systematic order of concepts
within reason. The whole aim of his endeavor is to ascertain this order, and
he cannot permit other academic disciplines to confuse this order and allow what is lowest to usurp the place of what is highest.

If, however, what one is trying to do is to raise to clear consciousness, to
develop, and to animate certain concepts that one already assumes to be
present, then one must pursue a different path, *one which, for the most part,
follows a direction directly opposite to the path of transcendental deduction.*
Thus it is both true and philosophically demonstrable that the assumption   *(414)*
of a purposefulness (which is not at all the same as a mere *regularity*) within
nature presupposes the assumption that there is a rational creator of nature. It is, however, not merely possible but even probable that any actual
individual will become aware of and will apprehend the former earlier than
the latter. This individual's educator or public-school teacher will then
step forward and, on the basis of this individual's belief in the purposefulness of the world, demonstrate to him — what? That there is a rational
creator of the world? Is it by means of the concept of purposefulness that
the teacher introduces the latter concept into this individual's understanding? Surely not. He merely convinces him that, in admitting the former, he
himself has already admitted and assumed the latter. — As far as we are
concerned, one can also, in popular dogmatics and in instructing educators
and public-school teachers, continue to employ the term "proof" to designate this process of developing finished concepts and tracing the elements
of the same forward and backward. One should, however, never employ
such "proofs" to contest a genuine proof (that is, a transcendental deduction), for they are poorly suited to this purpose.

Incidentally, the editor of the *Theological Journal*, Dr. Gabler,[7] is quite
correct when he forbids (transcendental?) idealism any entry into his journal; for, to the extent that this journal remains a purely theological one and
thus concerns itself only with the purely historical and *scholarly* question
concerning the origins of the religious documents we now possess and the

6. "Wohl aber giebt es ein Herabsteigen vom Uebersinnlichen zum Sinnlichen;
und eine gewisse Ansicht des letztern um des erstern willen."

7. Johann Phillipp Gabler (1753–1826), editor of the *Neuest theologisches Journal*,
was, like Vogel, a professor of theology at Altdorf.

actual intentions of the authors of the same, or with the *practical* question of what is useful therein for the teaching, punishment, improvement, and discipline of righteousness, to this extent it confines itself completely to the standpoint of actual life, a standpoint that is realistic and by no means idealistic. In all fairness, this also presupposes that an educated theologian will first have come to terms, not with the philosophical *components* of his field, but rather with those philosophical *exercises* that constitute the *preliminary portions* of the same. The lower branch of the philosophical faculty may not presume to examine one of the higher ones, and it betrays a by no means compulsory lack of prudence when a theologian, acting as such and within his own field, nevertheless produces a specimen of philosophy and, as can well happen, exposes his errors.

One and the same person can undoubtedly be both a theologian and a philosopher. But a theologian, as such, is simply not a philosopher — no more than a philosopher can be a theologian. For its part, theology begins precisely where philosophy[8] ends, and it encounters the human being precisely where the philosopher leaves him. The theologian is no more of a philosopher than is any other human; he discovers human beings and places himself alongside the latter, within the standpoint of life. The philosopher occupies the transcendental standpoint above life and looks down from there upon life and upon every science that is concerned with life. The domains of the two sciences [of philosophy and theology] are thereby eternally separated.

(415)

The theologian's science comes into being precisely as the philosopher's deduction comes to an end. Yet the theologian has no knowledge of the philosopher's deduction, and hence he treats as a *fact* what for the former is the *result of a deduction*. If these two academic disciplines fail to agree in their view of the content of the matter at hand, then the fault is either that of the philosopher, who has philosophized incorrectly, or of the theologian, who wanted to be a philosopher but could not; or else it is the fault of both. When, for example, a *philosopher* says, "God is the moral order of the world itself, and beyond this there is no God, etc.," his remarks are by no means intended for the theologian. The theologian, for his part, will think, "Whether the philosopher is correct or incorrect, what he says is of no concern to me. What God may or may not be, considered purely philosophically, is something for those who belong to this discipline [of philosophy] to settle among themselves. For me, God is an omnipotent, omniscient, and holy being, along with whatever else this word may mean

8. Reading "die Philosophie" for "der Philosoph."

in every catechism." The theologian is correct, even according to the philosopher, who, as part of his professional duties, has to be thoroughly familiar with the theologian and must take note of his work. The theologian is correct even in what he says about the contents of his confession of faith; and if people would only allow the philosopher who begins his remarks in the manner we have noted above to finish speaking and did not immediately drive him from his lectern the moment he opened his mouth, then he would undoubtedly conclude with the theologian's confession of faith, which, moreover, would have thereby gained a great deal in both clarity and precision.

But suppose a *preacher* were to mount his pulpit and say, "Ladies and gentlemen, God is the moral order of the world, and beyond this there is no God. Furthermore, the concept of being, which philosophical language has its own reasons for keeping as a term for designating mere material endurance, must, strictly speaking, not be applied to God." That a preacher should speak from his pulpit in this manner is something that does matter to the theologian and to all consistories; and the philosopher would be the first to sign the decree removing such a preacher from office — not, to be sure, on grounds of *atheism*, but rather on grounds of *official incompetence* — and he would be the first to advise such a preacher to return to a good university and to pursue a more thorough course of study.

"A pastor is one thing; a librarian, something else again."[9] Allow me to *(416)* repeat these words of Lessing — which have already been quoted by a contributor to this journal — since I consider the vocation of the pastor to be a very important one, and I sincerely admire any member of this class, so long as he knows what he intends to accomplish and what he should intend to accomplish.

I would hope that the theologians would approve of this boundary settlement, and that henceforth everyone would tend to his own house, where there will undoubtedly always continue to be enough work to occupy everyone. Surely, for example, a theologian as careful and as sober as Dr. Gabler would not condone it if young authors in his own discipline who had attended various lectures but understood nothing were to appeal to their philosophy whenever a theologian found their knowledge of his-

9. A well-known quotation from Lessing's *Eine Parabel. Nebst einer kleinen Bitte, und einem eventualen Absagungsschreiben an den Herrn Pastor Goeze, in Hamburg* (1778). Lessing's point on this occasion was to emphasize that the mere difference in *names* of the two professions corresponds to and indicates a more fundamental difference in the *duties* and *obligations* of each.

tory and their concepts of public leadership to be shallow, and then were to appeal to their historical knowledge whenever a philosopher found their philosophy to be shallow. In doing this they would be proceeding in a manner that could hardly be more confusing and that, in any case, must prove to be a great detriment to the study — not, to be sure, of philosophy, but of theology. Let us reject such a hybrid, and let everyone protect his own boundary without concerning himself with any alien field.

The above remarks are predicated on the assumption that Herr Gabler will confine himself to publishing a purely theological journal. If, however, he also decides to deal with the philosophy of religion in his journal (as is obviously the case with the proof by Herr Vogel which is here under scrutiny), then he undoubtedly submits himself to the judgment of philosophy. Supposing he were to do this, that is, supposing he were to achieve the goal of his journal, which is the establishment of an exclusively *theological* philosophy, a philosophy from which his own theology would have nothing to fear. Under such circumstances, our thoughts about his decision to forbid transcendental idealism any admission to his journal would amount to a repetition of what has already been said quite often, though it has seldom been taken to heart and has never been refuted — even though such protracted repetition eventually becomes tiresome. We doubt, however, whether even other theologians would really welcome such a timorous measure.

[*Public Announcement of a New Presentation of the* Wissenschaftslehre]

Published January 24, 1801 in the *Allgemeine Zeitung 1801* and the
Oberdeutsche allgemeine Litteraturzeitung.

[*Public Announcement of a New Presentation of the* Wissenschaftslehre]

(153) The *Wissenschaftslehre* has been available to the German public for six years now. It has received a very mixed reception: For the most part, it has met with vehement and passionate opposition, though it has also attracted some praise from inadequately trained people and has even found a few gifted followers and co-workers. — For the past five years, I have had in my desk a new version of the *Wissenschaftslehre*[1] which I have been employing in my classroom lectures on this science. This winter I am busy revising this new presentation, which I hope to be able to publish this coming spring.

I strongly wish that the public would *provisionally* (that is, until such time as it becomes possible for them to convince themselves on this point) accept the following two assurances from me, and I hope that people will keep both of these points in mind while reading the new presentation: First of all, *hardly any* information *whatsoever* concerning the *Wissenschaftslehre* is currently to be found among the educated public, with the exception of a few individuals (not counting my own students and immediate listeners, to whom the present remarks are not directed). Secondly, this science represents a thoroughly *new discovery*, the very Idea of which did not exist previously and can be obtained only from the *Wissenschaftslehre* itself. This new science can be judged only on its own terms.

Concerning the first point: The text that appeared six years ago and was published as a manuscript for the use of my listeners, viz., the *Foundations of the Entire Wissenschaftslehre*,[2] has, to the best of my knowledge, been

This lengthy announcement, dated November 4, 1800, was published by Fichte and his publisher, J. G. Cotta, without any title, in Beilage no. 1 of the *Allgemeine Zeitung 1801*, Jan. 24, 1801 and, under the title "Fichte's *Wissenschaftslehre*," in Stück XI of the *Oberdeutsche allgemeine Litteraturzeitung*, Jan. 24, 1801 (reprinted, under the title "[Ankündigung:] Seit sechs Jahren," in GA, I,7: 153–64, the pagination of which appears within parentheses in the margins of the English translation; not in SW).

1. Viz., the so-called *Wissenschaftslehre nova methodo* (see above, Editor's Introduction, p. xii).

2. The title page of the first published edition of Fichte's GWL identified the text in question as *Grundlage der gesammten Wissenschaftslehre als Handschrift*

understood by almost no one and has been made use of by hardly anyone at all, apart from my own students. This is a text that does not appear to be readily able to dispense with oral assistance. It seems to me, however, that in my books on *Natural Right* and *Ethical Theory* I have been somewhat more successful in presenting my thoughts concerning philosophy in general as well.[3] Nevertheless, to judge by all of the comments I have heard on this topic since the publication of these two works (including those comments which concern these very works), it would appear that even these latter books have not helped the public to advance much further in its understanding of the main point at issue. I am not sure why this is so — whether it is because people have usually *skipped* the introductions and the first sections of these two books, or whether it is because it is simply not really possible to provide the remote conclusions of my system (taken in isolation from the premises from which they are derived) with the same *(154)* degree of evidence one can easily give to the first premises themselves. The only texts that seem to have been better understood and that appear to have succeeded in raising high expectations concerning the *Wissenschaftslehre* on the part of many open-minded people are the two "Introductions to the *Wissenschaftslehre*," as well as the first chapter of a *New Presentation* of this system, which appeared in the *Philosophical Journal*.[4] At best, however, these essays can do no more than convey a preliminary conception of my project; the project itself is by no means actually implemented and brought to completion in these essays.

I do not intend to investigate here the extent to which my talented co-worker, Professor Schelling, both in his writings on the natural sciences and in his recently published *System of Transcendental Idealism*,[5] may have had greater success in introducing readers to the transcendental point of view.

---

für seine Zuhörer. However, Fichte himself subsequently authorized the publication of a second edition (in 1802), which dropped the subtitle "a manuscript for the use of his listeners."

3. Each of the works to which Fichte here makes reference, that is, the *Grundlage des Naturrechts* (1796/97) and *Das System der Sittenlehre* (1798), opens with a succinct recapitulation of the first principles and most important conclusions of the *Wissenschaftslehre*.

4. *An Attempt at a New Presentation of the Wissenschaftslehre* (1797/98), translated in this volume (above, pp. 2–117).

5. Schelling's *System des transcendentalen Idealismus* was published in the spring of 1800. (In *Werke*, III, pp. 327–634. English translation by Peter Heath [Charlottesville: University Press of Virginia, 1978].)

I have previously stated elsewhere[6] that, for my own part, I would be willing to shoulder all of the blame for the nearly universal lack of understanding [concerning the *Wissenschaftslehre*] that has prevailed in the past if by doing so I could only move the public to grapple anew with the issues in dispute. In the case of a completely new system, one not discovered by *(155)* further development of the previously existing science, but discovered instead in a completely different way, it is only by dint of long practice undertaken with the most varied types of individuals that the discoverer of the same will acquire the facility for communicating this system from his own mind to the minds of others.

Consequently, in order to ensure greater success for the study of the new presentation I am here announcing, I would hope that one would embark upon the study of the same by putting aside completely not only (as goes without saying) *any philosophical concepts one may have obtained from other systems of philosophy*, but also *any concepts concerning the Wissenschaftslehre itself one may have obtained from my previous writings on this subject* and will, for the time being, pretend that these other writings do not exist, and thus will consider oneself to be invited to participate in an entirely new inquiry. *For the time being*, I say: i.e., until such time as one is able to re-adopt these same concepts, but with better justification and with a higher degree of clarity, and will thus be in a position to view these earlier writings in a different light — which will reveal that they are by no means unserviceable. For no one should think that what I have just said in any way fulfills the fear that has been frequently expressed by certain cautious people who do not like to plunge into thinking in a merely haphazard manner: the fear that, after having tormented the public and after having persuaded people to embark upon a most strenuous study of an abstract theory, I may very well turn around — sooner or later — and retract my own philosophy, in which case all the effort that one might already have applied to its study would simply have been wasted. One can retract only an *opinion*; once one has really *known* something, one cannot take it back. One *can know* only what is completely certain and always remains so. If such certainty has ever been vouchsafed to a person, then it will remain with him for as long as he himself remains. If, therefore, through the discovery of the *Wissenschaftslehre*, I have managed to generate within myself any actual knowledge (which is precisely what I claim), then, though it is certainly possible for this knowledge to be presented more clearly *to others* (though not *to me*), it can never be retracted; and if, through the study of my writings, one of my readers should succeed in generating any knowl-

6. Namely, in the preface to *An Attempt at a New Presentation of the Wissenschaftslehre* (above, p. 4).

edge within himself, then this knowledge can never be taken away from him — even if I myself, as a result of sickness or old age, should someday become so feeble-minded that I cease to understand what I understand quite well today and should no longer be able to understand my own writings and should, in consequence of this misunderstanding, retract them.

I now come to my second point: I said that the *Wissenschaftslehre* is a completely new science and that, prior to it, nothing even similar to it existed.

Right up to the time of Kant, philosophy has been considered to be a form of rational cognition *based on concepts*,[7] and for this reason it is contrasted with mathematics, which is considered to be a form of rational cognition *based on intuitions*. (I say "up to the time of Kant," for Kant certainly raised philosophy to a height it had never attained before, though it is equally certain that the Kantian school has gone no further than Kant himself.)*   *(156)*

Such a view of the nature of philosophy fails to take into consideration several things.

First of all, since there is certainly supposed to be a kind of rational cognition *based on intuitions* (for this is what one claims mathematics is), then — so long as all cognizing and thinking is not supposed to come to an end with this sort of cognition, and indeed, so long as it is supposed to be possible for us even to assert *that* there is such cognition — there must, in addition, be some *cognition of this cognition*. And since an intuition, as such, can only be intuited, this latter sort of cognition must itself be based on *intuition*. Where then is this *mathesis* of *mathesis*[8] made real?

---

7. "eine VernunftErkenntniß *aus Begriffen*." Kant defines philosophy in precisely these terms at the conclusion of the *Critique of Pure Reason* (in the "Transcendental Doctrine of Method," A837/B865) and draws an explicit contrast between philosophical and mathematical cognition on precisely these grounds: viz., that the former is based on concepts, whereas the latter is based on intuitions.

* I do not include Prof. Beck, author of the "Standpoint Theory," among the members of the Kantian school, just as Kant too distinguishes himself from this author. Prof. Beck was on the path to the *Wissenschaftslehre*, and if he had only clearly grasped the nature of his own project, then he would have discovered the *Wissenschaftslehre*.

8. "*mathesis*" is a Greek word that means "study of," "science," or "knowledge" and is one of the roots of the word "mathematics." Leibniz frequently employed the term *mathesis* in the sense in which Fichte employs it here, and often wrote about the need to discover or to invent a "universal science" or *mathesis universalis*, a project Fichte believed had finally been accomplished by his own "science of science": the *Wissenschaftslehre*. (See Fichte's discussion of this in § 1 of BWL.)

Thus I would reply as follows to those who deny that philosophy can be anything more than rational cognition based on concepts: You wish to generate *rational cognition* purely *from concepts*. (Here, as in mathematics, "rational cognition" undoubtedly signifies a cognition *by means of* reason, as *engaged in the act of cognizing*, and indeed, as pure reason, apart from any reference to perception.) As for these concepts from which you wish to generate cognition: You undoubtedly *possess* these concepts prior to this cognition you generate from them by dissecting them and separating what is combined within them. I can understand quite well how, by such means, you will correctly be able to rediscover within these concepts whatever was already contained within them, and I can see how you are able to make your

(157)   cognition *clearer* by developing your concepts in this manner. What I cannot understand at all, however, is how you can thereby succeed in *expanding* your cognition, or in *criticizing* it and providing it with a *foundation*, or (in case it is incorrect) in *purifying* it.

You possess a concept, and your development of some cognition from this concept presupposes the concept in question. But how did you arrive at this concept in the first place? *What* did you grasp or comprehend within this concept? And what sort of access did you have to it *before* you comprehended it and *while* you were engaged in grasping it conceptually? In order, therefore, for the concepts that your science presupposes and treats as what is highest to be possible at all, you have to assume that there is something higher than any concept.

On the other hand, the very nature of reason itself undoubtedly assures that you will be unable to comprehend and to present us with concepts of what is incomprehensible, i.e., of anything that is simply not to be found within this higher "something" that contains within itself the content of all concepts,[9] and we admittedly do not fear that you will attempt to do anything of this sort. But since you intend to establish a necessary and universally valid science, you will undoubtedly begin with concepts whose necessity *as concepts* you affirm; i.e., you must begin with concepts that (so you claim) contain a manifold that is combined with absolute necessity and whose elements are inseparable from one another. But how do you propose to demonstrate the basis of the necessity of this combining? Where does its basis or foundation lie?[10] This foundation is undoubtedly not to be sought

9. "Dagegen, daß ihr das nicht begreifbare, das in jenem höhern den Stoff für alle Begriffe enthaltendem durchaus nicht liegende, begreifen, und Begriffe von dieser Art uns aufstellen solltet, ist ohne Zweifel durch das Wesen der Vernunft schon gesorgt."

10. "Wie, und worin denkt ihr denn nun den Grund dieser Nothwendigkeit des Zusammenfassens nachzuweisen?"

within the act of combining itself; for in that case this act of combining would be its own foundation, and hence the combination in question would be a freely achieved and not a necessary one. Do you then place the foundation in something outside of the combination itself? If so, then you will constantly be driven beyond the concept itself.

A "critique of reason" involves a cognition *of* reason, which is here the *object of cognition*; and thus reason has been assigned the task, prior to anything else, of cognizing itself. Only after it has done this can it then go on to examine how it may be able to cognize anything beyond itself. Consequently, from the moment that a "critique of reason" became a topic of discussion, it should have been obvious that reason does not grasp itself and cannot apprehend itself by means of anything (such as a concept) that has to be derived from something else and that does not possess its foundation or ground within itself; instead, reason can grasp and apprehend itself only immediately — and there is nothing immediate but *intuition*. Hence,   (158) if philosophy is from now on to be synonymous with *reason's own self-produced cognition of itself*, then philosophy can by no means be considered to be cognition based upon concepts, but must instead be cognition based upon intuition.

Moreover, since mathematics already existed and was something with which we were already acquainted, everyone should have realized and been familiar with the fact that the foundation of immediate self-evidence, necessity, and universal validity is never to be found within any concept, but lies in the intuition of the very act of comprehending. To be sure, such an intuition itself is never either necessary or contingent, nor does it inform us that something exists; instead, it just is, and it is what it is.[11] Such an intuition is "universally valid," not because it itself always remains one and the same, but precisely because it communicates its own unalterability to every concept that comprehends it — precisely because and precisely *inso-*

---

11. "daß der Grund der unmittelbaren Evidenz, Nothwendigkeit und Allgemeingültigkeit nie im Begriffe, sondern in der Anschauung des Begreifens selbst liege: welche Anschauung zwar nie nothwendig, oder zufällig, oder daß etwas ist, sondern die nur schlechtweg ist, und so ist, wie sie ist." Like many other German philosophers, Fichte employs the term *Evidenz* in a narrower and more limited sense than the English term "evidence." Specifically, it carries the connotation of "obviousness" or "self-evidence," as conveyed in the phrase: "It is evident that . . ." In other words, the operative notion here is that genuine "evidence" is always "sufficient" evidence. This is a point emphasized by Fichte's use of the terms "evidence," "necessity," and "universal validity" in mutual apposition with one another. For these reasons, the term *Evidenz* is often translated in the following discussion as "self-evidence."

far as this concept grasps *it.* If people had only recognized this, they would also have discovered that everything really evident and universally valid within both pre-Kantian and Kantian philosophy has its foundation, not in any concept, but only in intuition — even though the philosophers involved may not have had any clear knowledge of this fact.

In our own day it has become obvious on every side that language is no longer adequate for producing agreement concerning philosophical concepts, and it has even been ironically proposed that *the critique of reason should be preceded* — *in advance!* — *by a metacritique of language*; and this proposal has subsequently been taken seriously by Herder[12] and his spiritual ally Jean Paul.* Yet we actually do succeed in understanding one an-

---

12. Johann Gottfried von Herder (1744–1803) was a celebrated and profoundly influential critic and philosopher, best known today for his writings on the origins of language and the philosophy of history. Though he had once been a student of Kant's, Herder was more influenced by J. G. Hamann's philosophy of feeling and belief. In 1776 Herder moved to Weimar, where he was court chaplain and General Superintendent of churches and schools for the duchy of Saxe-Weimar-Eisenach. Herder was also an outspoken critic of Fichte and, as an advisor to the court, was heavily involved in the intrigues and events that ultimately led to Fichte's departure from Jena. During the final years of his life, Herder devoted much of his energy to an attempted "refutation" of the Kantian philosophy (for which, in his view, Fichte was no more than a particularly visible spokesman). With this end in mind, he published in 1799 a very lengthy critique of Kant's first *Critique*, entitled *Verstand und Erfahrung. Eine Metakritik zur Kritik der reinen Vernunft*, which is undoubtedly the work to which Fichte is here alluding. (In Herder's *Sämtliche Werke*, ed. Heinrich Düntzer and Wollheim da Fonseca [Berlin: Hempel, 1869–79], vol. XXI, pp. 1–339. A detailed account of Herder's critique of Kant may be found in ch. XII of Robert J. Clark, *Herder: His Life and Thought* [Berkeley: University of California Press, 1969].)

* The latter in his work entitled *Clavis Fichteana*. This key may very well fail to unlock anything, since the man who fabricated it has failed to gain any entrance with it.[13]

13. Jean Paul Richter (1763–1825), usually known simply as "Jean Paul," was a well-known novelist and humorist. During Fichte's last years at Jena, Jean Paul resided in nearby Weimar, where he and Herder became friends and literary allies. Jean Paul also become personally acquainted with Fichte (of whose philosophy he had been an early admirer) during this period. In the spring of 1800 Jean Paul published, as an appendix to his multi-part novel *Titan*, a short satirical work entitled *Clavis Fichteana* ("The Key to Fichte") in which the *Wissenschaftslehre* is subjected to sometimes witty and sometimes rather heavy-handed ridicule as a mere "game of words" (in *Jean Pauls Sämtliche Werke*, vol. 9, ed. Eduard Berend [Weimar: H. Böhlaus Nachfolger, 1933], pp. 457–501). Jean Paul himself was made

other within the course of life, and hence it should have been apparent that reason must contain within itself some unifying medium[14] that is higher than any *concept* or *word* (for words are nothing but the frequently adulter-   (159) ated, second-hand copies of concepts), for otherwise we could not explain the agreement we encounter *within life*, as well as the agreement — or eternal disagreement — we encounter *concerning philosophy*. It should have been apparent as well that this higher means of unification might well be intuition, in terms of which both concepts themselves and their represen- tatives, words, must be judged; and thus it should have been clear that philosophical language from now on will stand in no need of any sort of "metacritique" — any more than do mathematical expressions such as "point," "line," etc.

   Philosophy, accordingly, would be the cognition of reason itself by means of reason itself — through intuition. The first point [namely, that philosophy is a cognition of reason through reason] was Kant's important discovery, even though he himself failed to carry it through to completion. The sec- ond point [namely, that such cognition is based upon intuition], which expresses the condition for carrying out such a project, was added by the *Wissenschaftslehre*, which, for just this reason, is a completely new science.

   One should not dismiss this Idea immediately and without any exami- nation just as soon as one hears the words "*Wissenschaftslehre*," "*intuition*," and "*intellectual* intuition" (for this is the sort of intuition with which the *Wissenschaftslehre* commences). In other words, one should not follow the example of Kant, who has recently rejected both certain people and their terminology by explaining them in such a way that they must be consid- ered to be false, no matter how they may present themselves. Thus he declares: "*Wissenschaftslehre* is *pure logic*, and for this reason it is a waste of effort to try to cull a real object from it."* "An intellectual intuition would

---

rather uncomfortable by the public ridicule of Fichte that his *Clavis Fichteana* encouraged; accordingly, he made a point of visiting Fichte in Berlin in January of 1801 and went out of his way on several subsequent occasions to express his public respect and admiration for the author of the *Wissenschaftslehre*.

14. *Vereinigungsmittel*: "unifying medium" or "means of unification."

* See Kant's Declaration concerning the *Wissenschaftslehre* in the Jena *Allgemeine Literatur-Zeitung*.[15]

15. In the "Public Declaration" he published in the August 7, 1799 issue of the *Allgemeine Literatur-Zeitung*, Kant stated that: "I hereby declare that I regard Fichte's *Wissenschaftslehre* as a totally indefensible system. For the pure *Wissen- schaftslehre* is nothing more nor less than mere logic, and the principles of logic cannot lead to any material knowledge. Since logic, that is to say, *pure logic*,

be *a non-sensible intuition of something that continues to exist in a state of repose* — which is nonsense."* I, however, do not consider *Wissenschaftsle-hre* to be logic in any sense whatsoever, and I would even go so far as to

---

abstracts from the content of knowledge, the attempt to cull a real object out of logic is a vain effort and therefore a thing that no one has ever done. If the transcendental philosophy is correct, such a task would involve metaphysics rather than logic. But I am so opposed to metaphysics, as defined according to Fichtean principles, that I have advised him, in a letter, to turn his fine literary gifts to the problem of applying the *Critique of Pure Reason* rather than squander them in cultivating fruitless sophistries. He, however, has replied politely by explaining that 'he would not make light of scholasticism after all.' Thus the question whether I take the Fichtean philosophy to be a genuinely critical philosophy is already answered by Fichte himself, and it is unnecessary for me to express my opinion of its value or lack of value. For the issue here does not concern an object that is being appraised but concerns rather the appraiser or subject, and so it is enough that I renounce any connection with that philosophy" (trans. Arnulf Zweig, in *Kant: Philosophical Correspondence*, pp. 253–54). For further information concerning Kant's "Declaration," see above, footnote 18 to the "Second Introduction" to *An Attempt at a New Presentation of the Wissenschaftslehre*.)

* This is the meaning of what Kant says (though he does not use these precise words) in his treatise against Schlosser, "On a Newly Arisen Superior Tone in Philosophy."[16]

16. Cf. "Von einem neuerdings erhobenen Ton in der Philosophie" (in KGS, VIII, pp. 387–406; English trans. by Peter Fenves in *Raising the Tone of Philosophy, Late Essays by Immanuel Kant, Transformative Critique by Jacques Derrida*, ed. Peter Fenves, pp. 51–81 [Baltimore, Md. and London: Johns Hopkins University Press, 1993]). Kant's entire essay (which originally appeared in the May 1796 issue of the *Berlinische Monatsschrift*) is devoted to a critical attack on the use of the term "intellectual intuition" by J. G. Schlosser in his treatise *Platos Briefe über die syrakusanische Staatsrevolution* (1795). The main objection that Kant advances in this essay is that Schlosser's "intellectual intuition" is nothing more than an instance of wishful thinking, a shortcut appealing to those who are too lazy to engage in what Kant describes as "the Herculean labor of self-knowledge." Fichte does not disagree with Kant on this point; however, he insists that the term "intellectual intuition" means something quite *different* within the *Wissenschaftslehre* and thus is unaffected by Kant's criticism, however applicable this criticism may be to the use of this term by other thinkers (e.g., Schelling). One of the major themes of Kant's essay is a reiteration of his claim that philosophical cognition, unlike mathematical cognition, must always be based on concepts. Fichte's criticism of this claim in the present "Announcement" may therefore be considered as a tacit rejoinder to Kant's public criticism of the *Wissenschaftslehre*.

banish pure logic from the entire domain of philosophy.[17] Nor do I consider intellectual intuition to be an intuition of some enduring "some-   *(160)*
thing." Precisely because all intuition lies higher than any concept, one
cannot employ concepts to explain what intellectual intuition is;[18] the only
way one can become acquainted with it is by posssessing it. Anyone who is
not already familiar with intellectual intuition will have to await our [new]
presentation. In the meantime, let such a person think about his own consciousness of *the act of drawing a line* (not his consciousness of the line
itself, as something *already drawn*), for such an act of drawing is also not,
one would hope, something that continues to exist on its own. *The Wissenschaftslehre is mathesis* — not only with regard to its *external form*, but also
with regard to its *content*. It describes a continuous series of intuitions, and
it establishes all of its propositions within intuition. It is the *mathesis* of
reason itself. Just as geometry comprises the entire system of our ways of
limiting space, so this system comprises within itself the system of reason
as a whole. — I would hope that no one would wish to begin a study of the
Wissenschaftslehre without some prior familiarity with mathematics, which,
with respect to its contents, is the only completely scientific undertaking
with which we are presently acquainted.[19] In other words, I would hope

17. In discussing the various "divisions" of the science of philosophy at the conclusion of his course of lectures on *Wissenschaftslehre nova methodo*, Fichte comments: "Logic cannot be considered to be a part of philosophy. It is merely an
instrument of philosophy — and not merely of philosophy, but of every part of
knowledge, and hence of reason as such" (GA, IV,2: 265). See too the more detailed discussion of the relationship between philosophy and formal logic in § 6 of
BWL.

18. "Was [Anschauung] sey, läßt sich [. . .] nicht begreiflich machen."

19. "des einigen materialiter durchaus wissenschaftlichen Verfahrens, das unter
uns vorhanden ist." In contrast with a purely "formal" science such as logic, mathematics possesses a specific content of its own, and is thus a "material" science.
One can, of course, adopt a purely formal attitude toward mathematics as well, but
it is important to recall that Fichte, following Kant, rejected such a view of mathematics and insisted that mathematics is a "material" science, precisely because it
is based upon intuitions. The natural sciences are also "material" sciences, of
course; but, in contrast with mathematics, they lack universality and necessity and
are thus, according to Fichte, only "incompletely scientific." Unlike logic, mathematics possesses a content of its own; unlike the natural sciences, it is truly and
completely "scientific." (For further discussion of this point, see BWL and the
conclusion of the *Wissenschaftslehre nova methodo*, as well as Reinhard Lauth's
monograph, *Die transzendentale Naturlehre Fichtes nach den Prinzipien der Wissenschaftslehre* [Hamburg: Felix Meiner, 1984].)

that no one would begin a study of the *Wissenschaftslehre* without first obtaining a clear insight into the foundation of the *immediate self-evidence* and *universal validity* of mathematical postulates and theorems. If a person possesses a mathematical understanding of why, for example, only one straight line is possible between any two points; if he combines into one the infinite number of possible cases and visualizes them as such, so that he thereby sees the origin of his immediate certainty that — so long as reason remains reason — he will never encounter a case that conflicts with this: if a person can grasp this, then I can confidently assure him that he will find the *Wissenschaftslehre*, in its new presentation, to be just as easy to understand as geometry. If, however, a person lacks such an understanding of mathematics — and I have reason to believe that many people lack even the sense for this sort of self-evidence and universal validity and refrain from contradicting geometry solely because it is already established as a self-evident science — then I would advise him to abstain from a study of the *Wissenschaftslehre*. It lies in a world that simply does not exist for such a person.

Since the *Wissenschaftslehre* is a kind of mathematics,[20] it also possesses the advantages of mathematics.

First of all, it possesses the same sort of *immediate self-evidence*. Whether one will credit this assertion or not, there is no room in the *Wissenschaftslehre* for any wavering, deliberating, and weighing of pros and cons. If one does not hit upon the right point, then one will not be able to understand the *Wissenschaftslehre* at all; but if one does, then the *Wissenschaftslehre* will surprise him with its immediate clarity and necessity. He will be *unable* to see things in any way other than the way in which he does see them. — [Secondly,] the *Wissenschaftslehre* has the same sort of thoroughgoing *determinacy* as mathematics. It does not matter what sign it attaches to its object — whether it calls it "I" or "Not-I," X or Y. The sign itself is nothing; the *Wissenschaftslehre* is concerned only with what occurs within the immediate intuition of everyone. This is not something that can vacillate

(161)   and change surreptitiously, like a shaky grasp produced from a shaky language in which different people associate in their imagination different things — some more, some less — with one and the same sign, with the result that they construe the same subject with different degrees of precision. Instead, what is encountered within intellectual intuition is the same for all reason, and it remains unalterably the same for every rational being,

20. "weil die Wissenschaftslehre Mathematik ist." Fichte, of course, is here using the term "mathematics" in the sense of *mathesis* or "science."

just as long as he remains rational. — [Thirdly,] the *Wissenschaftslehre* also possesses the same *irrefutability* as mathematics. There can be no dispute whatsoever concerning the *Wissenschaftslehre* and no argument against it. Either one understands its [first] principle, in which case one will immediately accept it; or else one does not understand it, in which case it is not present for one at all. If, under such circumstances, one nevertheless continues to contradict the *Wissenschaftslehre*, then what one is contradicting is not anything that *it* asserts, but rather something that one has invented on one's own. — How then and from what premises could anyone engage in a dispute with this science? Could one perhaps do this (as has been done until now) on the basis of certain *concepts* and certain *principles* derived from these concepts? But, according to the rules governing any dispute, one's opponent also has to accept whatever it is one wishes to use as the basis of one's arguments against him. The *Wissenschaftslehre*, however, simply does not admit the validity of any concept whatsoever that it has not produced within its own boundaries from intuition; and none of its concepts count for it as anything more or other than what is contained within intuition. — Yet what if someone wishes to deny this intuition to which the *Wissenschaftslehre* appeals, along with whatever may be contained therein? One may well do this, but if one does, then one will simply be *denying* the *Wissenschaftslehre*; one will not be *refuting* it. If someone denies the geometer's claim that no more than one straight line is possible between any two points, then of course he cannot be convinced, and he has nullified the possibility of all geometry. I think, however, that anyone in possession of healthy common sense would simply leave such a person to himself.

Philosophy, however, does not yet possess the same authority as geometry. (One wonders whether precisely the same sort of objections that are now being raised against philosophy may not also have been raised against mathematics when it first began to be treated in a scientific manner, and one wonders too whether it is anything but the authority now enjoyed by mathematics that prevents the pseudo-thinkers of our own era from raising such objections against mathematics even now.)* — Philosophy is not

---

* Indeed, the founder of an allegedly new system of dogmatism (viz., Herr Werner) has stated, for all his contemporaries to hear, that "the claim that space is infinitely divisible is an absurdity uttered by the geometers, one which brings dishonor upon their otherwise *useful* science."[21]

21. See the discussion of Werner's "new system of dogmatism" contained in Fichte's review of the *Journal for Truth* (translated in the present volume, above, pp. 119–26).

yet allowed to deal with such objections in the same way as mathematics, and it is not yet permissible within philosophy simply to leave to himself, *(162)* without any further ado, anyone who, within the realm of philosophy, asserts things that are comparable to asserting, within the realm of geometry, that an infinite number of straight lines are possible between any two points. Philosophy must, consequently, resort to an alternative that is unavailable to the mathematician *within* his domain — though philosophy can employ such a means *on behalf of* mathematics: Philosophy can deal with anyone who contradicts it by driving such a person backwards from his original claim and forcing him to fall back upon some other claim, one which he himself does not understand and in explanation of which he cannot utter a single intelligible word. This can make it evident to everyone — including the person in question — that his understanding and his reason actually proceed from something that is absolutely neither understanding nor reason.[22]

By means of this new presentation, which I guarantee will be intelligible to anyone who possesses the capacity for understanding science, I would hope that the philosophical public will finally have an occasion *to come to terms in all seriousness* with the *Wissenschaftslehre*. Since Kant, with only a few exceptions, each of the few outstanding thinkers working within this field has continued to carry on his discourse all by himself, without even listening to what any of his colleagues have to say. In this way there has arisen, not a scientific conversation, but a wild and confused hullabaloo in which everyone speaks at once and all of these voices become jumbled. Some independent thinkers have emerged, but the ability to understand what someone else is saying seems to have vanished completely. For the good of science, it is time to embark upon another path.

No matter how sincerely I myself may be convinced of the self-evidence and irrefutability of the *Wissenschaftslehre*, I still owe it *to others*, in recognition of the independence of *their* reason and simply in order to make it possible for every person *to examine this for himself*, to assume that it remains possible that I may have made a mistake. (I am willing to assume this only *provisionally*, however, i.e., until such time as these others have studied the new presentation of the *Wissenschaftslehre*.) The mathematician

22. "daß sein Verstand und seine Vernunft von einem absoluten Unverstande und Unvernunft eigentlich ausgehe."

must also make a similar assumption when he commences his instruction, inasmuch as he first appears to be seeking [to construct or to discover] his science before the eyes of his pupils. Therefore, I hereby make this assumption explicit; *but in return, as I am fully entitled to do, I also demand of all rational beings that they provisionally — i.e., until such time as they have refuted me — assume just the opposite: namely, that it is equally possible that I might be right.*

Promises like the one above, which arise out of reflections that must give pause to anyone who knows anything about science, have been made in public for all the world to hear, and, as has frequently occurred in the past, a promise has also been made to use this philosophy in order to explain and to clarify the nature of every other science. For these reasons it would be unpardonable for anyone simply to continue to carry on his own discourse without even listening to what was said, or, at most (as has happened until now), hastily hurling an asinine witticism or invective in the direction of the speaker.   *(163)*

One is therefore urged to read [this new presentation] and to continue reading until one has understood it. One can then either accept it or — if one is able to do so — refute it. If, however, one does not wish to go to so much trouble, then let him henceforth remain silent concerning everything that has anything to do with philosophy. Under such circumstances, this is the only rational course one can adopt. It is time, for God's sake, to take seriously and once and for all to come to terms with the philosophical revolution that people have been talking about for more than a decade now. Anyone who wishes to do so may, of course, remain behind; but he must realize that he is lagging behind, and he must also maintain his silence, so that he will not cause others who wish to go forward to fall into error.

I will not, on this occasion, discuss the many false paths that have been staked out within the realm of philosophy since the first appearance of the *Wissenschaftslehre* — errors into which people have been led either though opposition to the *Wissenschaftslehre* or without taking the latter into account. Let bygones be bygones. But following the publication of the new presentation, which I quite legitimately expect everyone to understand and to the principles of which I will therefore be able to refer, I intend to establish a separate periodical for the express purpose of observing the progress of philosophy.[23]

23. This promise, which harks back to Fichte's earlier plan to publish a series of articles reviewing the "tone" of current philosophical debates, remained unfulfilled. See the Editor's Preface to "Annals of Philosophical Tone" (in EPW, pp.

I would hope that, until they have understood the announced presentation, people will overcome any offense that they may once again take at this announcement itself or at the tone in which it is written. For even this tone arises from the subject matter itself and can be judged only on this basis.

The charge of arrogance, which has so frequently been brought against me and other defenders of the *Wissenschaftslehre*, overlooks precisely the most terrible aspect of our presumption: namely, that we, with complete seriousness, claim to be in possession of a science — a science! — and we claim to be teaching this same science. People who take delight in exchanging opinions with one another must display mutual tolerance and courtesy toward each other and must modestly grant that the opinions of others might very well have as much worth as their own. Their motto is: "Live and let live; think what you want and let others do the same." They must appear outwardly modest, because they are, in their essence, arrogant through and through: for it is the most enormous arrogance to believe that others have any interest in knowing what our opinions are. But why should (164) science, which is never a purely individual matter but is instead the property of all rational beings, behave modestly and diffidently toward ignorance? This is something I have never been able to grasp. Everything depends therefore upon whether we are correct in our assumption that we are in possession of a science. Let us settle this question first, and this will also settle the question concerning our alleged arrogance.

The zeal of the exponents of "many philosophies" against the defenders of "one sole philosophy" is remarkable indeed.[24] The only way I can comprehend this is to think that one is either a *"one-sole-philosophy philosopher"* or else one is *no philosopher at all*; and so long as no one has succeeded in showing that we belong to the latter class, we will, as before, continue to consider ourselves members of the former.

337–40.) See too the very interesting unpublished fragment from the fall of 1800, "Alle Verhandlungen der Gelehrten unter einander lassen sich betrachten als eine Unterredung" (GA, II,5: 437–42).

24. For a discussion of the contrast between "one-sole-philosophy philosophers" (*Alleinphilosophen*) and "many-philosophy philosophers" (*Vielphilosophen*), terms adapted by Fichte from Jacobi's famous "open letter" to Fichte, see the footnote on the subject to "From a Private Letter" (above, pp. 160–61).

In conclusion, I hope to make this new presentation so clear and so intelligible that it will require no further assistance on this score and that no newer and even clearer presentation will be needed. I will concern myself later with such matters as scientific elegance, the strictly systematic arrangement of the parts, the exclusion of any foreign elements, the adoption of a precise terminology, and the creation of a symbolic system of pure concepts (such as that "universal characteristic" which was already sought by Leibniz and which first becomes possible only subsequent to the *Wissenschaftslehre*).[25] That is to say, I will attend to these matters only after I have found that the age is making some use of this new presentation of the *Wissenschaftslehre* and has thereby made itself receptive to a purely scientific presentation of the same.

Berlin, November 4, 1800

Fichte

The work announced above will be published by our firm around the middle of this year.[26] Anyone obliging enough to enlist subscribers for this work will receive one free copy for every 6 subscriptions.

J. G. Cotta, bookseller

25. Leibniz envisioned the construction of a non-natural symbolic language (*characteristica universalis*) in which all truths could be unambiguously expressed and from which new truths could be developed by deductive, logical analysis. The creation of such a system of symbolic notation was an essential part of Leibniz's project for constructing a "universal science" or "universal mathematics" (*mathesis universalis*). For a discussion of Fichte's pursuit of this goal, see Joachim Widmann, "Exact Concepts: Fichte's Contribution on a Problem of Tomorrow," trans. Joseph G. Naylor, *Idealistic Studies* 11 (1981): 41–48.

26. The announced "New Presentation" was never published. Fichte's literary remains include the manuscript of a rough, working draft of a "Neue Bearbeitung der Wissenschaftslehre," which he prepared during the closing months of 1800 and which was unquestionably intended to be part of the "New Presentation" (GA, II,5: 331–402). This manuscript, however, breaks off at an early stage of the exposition (viz., with the deduction of "feeling"). To be sure, Fichte continued to work on various new versions of the *Wissenschaftslehre* for the rest of his life, but none of these subsequent presentations were published during his own lifetime; furthermore, all of these subsequent versions, beginning with the *Wissenschaftslehre* of 1801/2, differ in fundamental ways from the "New Presentation" envisioned by Fichte in the fall of 1800.

INDEX